THE DURABLE SLUM

Globalization and Community

Susan E. Clarke, Series Editor
Dennis R. Judd, Founding Editor

(continued on page 217)

The Durable Slum

DHARAVI AND THE RIGHT TO STAY PUT
IN GLOBALIZING MUMBAI

Liza Weinstein

Globalization and Community, Volume 23

University of Minnesota Press
Minneapolis
London

Published by the University of Minnesota Press
111 Third Avenue South, Suite 290
Minneapolis, MN 55401–2520
http://www.upress.umn.edu

Library of Congress Cataloging-in-Publication Data

Weinstein, Liza.
  The durable slum : Dharavi and the right to stay put in globalizing Mumbai / Liza Weinstein. (Globalization and community ; volume 23) Includes bibliographical references and index.
  ISBN 978-0-8166-8309-3 (hardback) — ISBN 978-0-8166-8310-9 (pb)
  1. Dharavi (Mumbai, India)—Social conditions. 2. Dharavi (Mumbai, India)—Economic conditions. 3. Slums—India—Mumbai. I. Title.
  HN690.D454W45   2014
  307.3'3640954792—dc23
                                                                    2014001741

Printed in the United States of America on acid-free paper

The University of Minnesota is an equal-opportunity educator and employer.

20   19   18   17   16   15   14   10   9   8   7   6   5   4   3   2   1

For my mother

CONTENTS

PREFACE

I came to Mumbai expecting to document a great transformation, but I ended up writing about the contentious politics of stability.[1] When I began conducting the research that became this book, almost a decade ago, I was basically convinced of the overwhelming power of global capital—and the neoliberal policies that direct it—to destroy communities and oversee mass displacements. With markets having largely recovered from the Asian financial crisis of the late 1990s, global investors were clamoring for the next big opportunity and looking for the newest emerging markets. The Indian government seemed eager to give them a map. In early 2005, as I was preparing for fieldwork in Mumbai, India was further relaxing its restrictions on foreign direct investment (FDI) in property development. Two of the slowest sectors of the Indian economy to liberalize, the real estate and construction industries, were tenuously opened first to nonresident Indians (NRIs) and persons of Indian origin (PIOs) before they were thrown open to global developers and real estate investors at large. Residuals of a nationalist spirit of self-rule, or *swadeshi*, the globalization of property and land—literally, of Indian soil—seemed, for many, to veer too closely back to colonialism. But the nationalist dams could hold back what was certain to be a flood of global capital for only so long: in March 2005 India's Ministry of Commerce and Industry took steps to allow non-NRI foreign investors access to India's increasingly lucrative real estate markets, particularly in the country's newly created Special Economic Zones. Maharashtra's government—ruled by an outwardly looking Congress-led coalition bent on (in their words) "transforming Mumbai into Shanghai"—was eager to capture its share of the spoils.[2]

Land markets in Mumbai were booming, and real estate prices were soaring. After a more than decade-long conflict over the fate of central Mumbai's hundreds of acres of now defunct textile mill lands, the developers had prevailed over the tenuously assembled coalition of labor unions, environmental groups, and affordable housing activists. Mumbai's iconic industrial landscape of imposing brick factories and smokestacks was being converted into a postindustrial playground of shopping malls, television studios, and luxury high-rise buildings. With the contentious land struggles fading into memory, industrial conversions were now as easy as changing one letter on the signs outside the century-old manufacturing estates. Overnight, it seemed, the mills had become malls.

Another visible demonstration that Mumbai was now open for business could be seen in the Bandra-Kurla Complex, a glass and steel office complex built on the north shore of the Mahim Creek. That the complex had taken almost three decades to construct, having been first proposed in 1965, no longer seemed to matter now that most of the buildings were complete and each round of auctions to lease the space was yielding higher and higher prices and was rivaling some of the most expensive commercial real estate in London, Tokyo, and New York. Company names like Citigroup, Sofitel, and Boston-based Bain Capital hung now on buildings that were beginning to look at ease on Mumbai's north suburban landscape.

But one need only look at the Bandra-Kurla Complex from the south—from the Bandra-Sion Link causeway that crosses the Mahim Creek and connects the northern suburbs to Mumbai's island city—to see how precariously assembled this landscape actually is. From this vantage point, the glass and steel offices can be seen on one side of the causeway and a seemingly endless expanse of squat, aluminum-sided, blue tarp–roofed shanties appear on the other. Directly adjacent to the Bandra-Kurla Complex, the showpiece of the new global Mumbai, sits Dharavi, referred to both pejoratively and affectionately as "Asia's Largest Slum." Given the wave of global capital and real estate investment that had begun to subsume the city, Dharavi would clearly soon be taking on water.

At least this was how it looked when I visited Dharavi for the first time during the monsoon season of 2004. I had been sitting in the sociology department at the University of Mumbai's Kalina campus with Professor Sharit Bhowmik and his doctoral student Varsha Ayyar. We were discussing the government's newly announced plans to redevelop the iconic slum settlement, when Bhowmik-sir suggested that Varsha and I head over to Dharavi to take a look. Without other plans for the afternoon, Varsha agreed to play tour guide and led me to the main road to hail a taxi. She told the driver to take us to Dharavi, keeping our destination within the one-square-mile settlement as vague as it was in our minds. But because most foreigners like myself visit the slum only to purchase leather hand-bags and jackets from the air-conditioned showrooms on the settlement's northern perimeter, the driver headed for Dharavi's leather district. It was on this taxi ride that I first saw the adjacency of Dharavi and the then still-under-construction Bandra-Kurla Complex. With Mumbai University located in the northern suburb of Santa Cruz, our route to Dharavi passed right by the new office complex before crossing the Bandra-Sion Link causeway toward Dharavi's leather showrooms.

As we crossed the bridge, the contrast was stark. Immediately, the sanitized vertical spaces on the north bank gave way to the ground level density of Dharavi on the south. From inside the taxi, Dharavi and the throngs of workers and residents we passed looked vulnerable, exposed to the bulldozers and cranes busily working across the river. That afternoon that Varsha and I spent in Dharavi—most of it inside a leatherwork sweat-shop chatting with workers at sewing machines until the shop's manager asked us to leave—began a decade-long journey I have taken inside the iconic settlement. And while I still see that vulnerability I noted on that first trip, I now also see Dharavi's resilience. The cranes and bulldozers are still waiting just outside, along with the global capital that propels them, but I now understand that a powerful set of interests, actors, and institu-tions are working hard to keep them at bay. While this book examines both sets of forces, it is not a simple David-and-Goliath story of the in-nocent grassroots struggling against malevolent globality. The megaslum is a much messier space than those lines would suggest.

Empirical Insertions

My examination of these forces, comprising interviews, ethnography, and historical research, began with that first trip to Dharavi in August 2004. After this brief preliminary visit to Mumbai, most of which I spent walking around the city with my mouth wide open, I returned in September 2005 for a stay of sixteen months. Anyone who has spent time in the field knows that it can be a dizzying loop of orientations and disorientations, with each insight countered by a dozen more questions. I spent most of my time dur-ing the fall and winter of 2005 and 2006 in conversations—I can't really call them interviews—learning as much as I could about the city's labyrinth of institutions, agencies, and political interests, and committing to memory the innumerable acronyms and abbreviations in constant use. A fair bit of this time was spent in the South Mumbai offices of PUKAR, the participatory research collaborative founded by anthropologist Arjun Appadurai and the wonderful, late, Carol Breckenridge. PUKAR's director, Anita Patil-Desmukh, kindly let me hang around in their air-conditioned offices, and many of my early insights came during the buzzing lunchtime conversations around PUKAR's conference table. During those early months, I cornered as many academics, activists, and retired bureaucrats as possible, soaking up (and writing down) everything they told me.

Eventually I found myself spending more and more time in Dharavi. Hesitant strolls through the settlement's crowded *nagars, chawls,* and alleyways gave way to familiar laughter and shared meals (so many *dosas!*) graciously offered in family homes. My first insertions into Dharavi were through some of the area's social service organizations, including Nirman, a group working to raise awareness of HIV and AIDS among Dharavi's mostly male Tamilian migrants. Nirman's committed activists and social workers (especially Suresh Patil) were among my first hosts in Dharavi and they made many valuable introductions for me. Among my early gatekeepers, PROUD—a housing rights organization discussed at length in later chapters—and its administrative director Prashanth Anthony were exceedingly helpful in these first few months, introducing me to residents, workshop owners, politicians, small scale builders, and, most important, to my research assistant, translator, and now friend, Subramani Shankar.

Recognizing early on that my three years of Marathi study and basic knowledge of street Hindi could get me only so far in Dharavi's linguistically complex environs, I asked the help of PROUD's community organizers to identify someone who could provide me translation assistance. One of these men introduced me to his young neighbor at the Jai Bajarang Bali housing society. For the next eight months, Subramani, a bachelor's of commerce (B-com) student at a nearby college and a lifelong Dharavi resident, was my near constant companion. He whispered translations to me during meetings and social gatherings, conducted interviews alongside me, and helped me try to make sense of it all on our walks home. He also introduced me to his friends and family and made people feel more comfortable with my presence. His help was invaluable, and I remain indebted to him—although I never quite got used to being called "ma'am."

After I'd been living in Mumbai for almost a year, I realized that while I had begun to develop a working knowledge of Mumbai's contemporary development context, I had a much more limited sense of the city's history. Recognizing the need to situate historically the knowledge I was acquiring,

I began to ask more questions about the past. I also began spending more of my time reading and collecting papers in document centers and libraries, most notably at the Centre for Education and Documentation in South Mumbai. I was beginning to view the ongoing Dharavi Redevelopment Project as the third in a line of transformative schemes attempted in the settlement (discussed in later chapters as "Developing Dharavi: Parts One, Two, and Three"). This historical research began informing my ethnography as my ethnographic inquiries were shaping the questions I asked of history. My focus sharpened around an effort to explain what was new (and, perhaps more important, what was not) about the current globalizing moment. Meanwhile, I had the good fortune to continue my historical research even after I left Mumbai, as the library at my then home institution, the University of Chicago, happens to have in its archives a wealth of historical planning documents on Indian cities.

The politicians, planning administrators, and property developers who allowed me to interview them (numbering around forty-five) were invaluable to my research. Among these was Mukesh Mehta, the affable and surprisingly open chief architect of the Dharavi Redevelopment Project. Welcoming me into his office and even allowing me to shadow him at the project's planning meetings, his openness and candor helped me learn as much as I did. While I often found administrators and politicians less than forthcoming, usually trying to shine the best possible light on what I was seeing, I rarely questioned Mehta's honesty in our conversations. Apparently operating on the belief that no publicity is bad publicity, he was remarkably willing to divulge the seemingly dirtiest details of his interactions with state politicians and planning bureaucrats. While I have been careful not to abandon my critical perspective, I have tried to show Mehta the same respect in this book that he showed me when I was conducting the research.

Beyond the interviews, archival research, and ethnographic inquiries, this project has been shaped by the flood of scholarly writings on urban India that has appeared since I entered the field almost a decade ago. While I encountered a few other doctoral students traversing Mumbai's crowded streets in late 2005 and 2006, I passed many more, it seemed, at the airport, arriving as I departed with my suitcase full of field notes. Their research is now being published in urban studies and international development journals, offering important insights on spatial configurations, planning coalitions, and innumerable instantiations of politics. Through their writings I have been able to compare what I learned in Dharavi with descriptions of similar developments under way in Ahmadabad,

Bangalaru, Delhi, Kolkata, and elsewhere in Mumbai. Their insights are reflected in this book, intertwined with and inseparable from my own data.

As the development project I studied has gone on longer than my time in the field allowed, I have attempted to continue this research remotely with updates from Mumbai-based friends and colleagues, ever-helpful Google news alerts, and the occasional return visit when my schedule, as a junior faculty member and new mother, allowed. And as the story I present here has not reached a conclusion, I will be continuing to watch what happens next. In the decade I spent in Dharavi, the proposed project brought a significant amount of media attention to the area, and the slum has been profiled in magazines and news programs around the world. *Slumdog Millionaire* brought Dharavi into movie theaters, and tourists can now even take professionally guided tours of the area. But the bulldozers and cranes have not yet crossed the causeway, and the contrasts with the now basically completed Bandra-Kurla Complex remain stark. Yet despite this resilience, Dharavi is not a static place and whether incrementally or more dramatically it will continue to change, even as much as it remains the same.

ABBREVIATIONS

ALIS	Affordable Low Income Shelter
BCCI	Bombay Chamber of Commerce and Industry
BDD	Bombay Development Department
BJP	Bharatiya Janata Party
BKC	Bandra-Kurla Complex
BMC	Bombay Municipal Corporation (became MCGM)
BSP	Bahujan Samaj Party
BUDP	Bombay Urban Development Project
CIDCO	City and Industrial Development Corporation
CISRS	Christian Institute for the Study of Religion and Society
CRH	Committee for the Right to Housing
DBS	Dharavi Bachao Samiti
DCR	Development Control Regulations
DRP	Dharavi Redevelopment Project
EOI	Expression of Interest
FDI	foreign direct investment
GOM	government of Maharashtra
IAS	Indian Administrative Service
IMP	International Monetary Fund
INC	Indian National Congress
LISP	Land Infrastructure Servicing Program
MCGM	Municipal Corporation of Greater Mumbai (formerly BMC)
MEDC	Maharashtra Economic Development Council
MHADA	Maharashtra Housing and Area Development Authority
MISA	Maintenance of Internal Security Act

MLA	Member of the Legislative Assembly
MMR	Mumbai Metropolitan Region
MMRDA	Mumbai Metropolitan Regional Development Authority
MP	Member of Parliament
MUTP	Mumbai Urban Transport Project
NCP	National Congress Party
NGO	nongovernmental organization
NHSS	Nivara Hakk Suraksha Samiti
NRI	nonresident Indian
NSDF	National Slum Dwellers Federation
PIL	public interest litigation
PIO	person of Indian origin
PMC	project management consultant
PMGP	Prime Minister's Grant Project
PROUD	People's Responsible Organisation for United Dharavi
RPI	Republican Party of India
SIP	Slum Improvement Program
SPARC	Society for the Preservation of Area Resource Centres
SRA	Slum Rehabilitation Authority
SRD	Slum Re-Development program
SRS	Slum Rehabilitation Scheme
SUP	Slum Upgradation Program
TDR	Transferable of Development Rights
YUVA	Youth for Unity and Voluntary Action

INTRODUCTION

A Mansion in the Slum

The narrow lanes and pathways through Dharavi's densely packed central neighborhoods open up in front of Aneesh Shankar's house. A flower garden and a courtyard—seemingly out of place in a part of the city where nearly every bit of space is used to either house someone, make something, or sell something—give way to a freshly painted two-story bungalow with a brick-shingled roof. The door to the house, an almost three-inch-thick piece of intricately carved teak, is the building's most striking feature and its most conspicuous display of the owner's wealth. On the other side of the door, the home's interior is equally striking, but more for its sparseness than for any of its particular features or furnishings. One rarely finds this much open space in Dharavi.

Iconic image of Dharavi's seemingly endless expanse of aluminum rooftops. Photograph by Benji Holzman.

1

Aneesh Shankar ushered me inside and into his formal living room. He wore a plain gray T-shirt and a brightly colored *lungi*, a sarong-like skirt worn by South Indian men. Looking as if he had just woken from a nap, he was visibly relieved when his wife entered with a tray of South Indian coffee and sweet biscuits. After just one sip of coffee he looked refreshed, and he launched, practically unprompted, into a story he appeared to have told a hundred times: Dharavi's early history and the role played by his community, the Adi Dravidas, in its economic and social life. A lifelong Dharavi resident and president of the Bombay South Indian Adi Dravida Mahajan Sangh (ADMS), one of the settlement's oldest social organizations, Shankar is both de facto historian and official spokesperson for Dharavi's long-established South Indian *dalit*, or untouchable, communities.

As we sipped coffee in his comfortable living room, Shankar relayed the history of migration to Dharavi from his native place of Tirunelveli, in the southern part of Tamil Nadu. Since the 1930s and 1940s, several waves of migrants have come to Dharavi to escape caste persecution and gain secure employment in the expanding tanning and leather manufacturing industries. His father was among the first wave, settling in Dharavi in the late 1930s and sending for his new bride, Aneesh's mother, soon after that. By the 1950s the senior Shankar had built his own factory and was employing dozens of newer migrants driven by a similar set of push and pull factors. As he relayed the almost universal immigrant story of persecution, opportunity, adversity, and upward mobility—but with a distinctly Dharavi flavor—Shankar's tale also conveyed equally classic narratives of urbanization, enclave formation, and city building. Just one of more than a dozen ethnic, caste, and religious communities that have settled in Dharavi over the past century, the Adi Dravidas formed organizations and political parties, built schools and temples, and constructed homes and factories— in doing so, helping build the settlement of Dharavi and city of Bombay.

From inside Aneesh Shankar's spacious bungalow, Dharavi looked much different than slums are supposed to look. It looked more permanent, possessing a dynamic stability that comes with *pucca*,[1] or well-built, buildings, economic vitality, and established social institutions. As Shankar described his family's role in Dharavi's leather industry and later showed me his thirty-thousand-square-foot factory adjacent to his home, it seemed wealthier and less marginal to the economic life of India's richest and most global city. From here, the slum

Ground-level density along Dharavi Main Road. Photograph by Jeff Devries.

did not seem to be quite synonymous with poverty, as it is often treated in both popular narratives and dominant scholarly accounts, and Shankar did not resemble the "surplus humanity" depicted in these writings: excluded, exploited, and expendable (Davis 2006). From this vantage point, Dharavi, and the experiences of at least some of its residents, seemed to complicate the typical accounts of the slum.

The now notorious settlement of Dharavi—immortalized in several recent magazine cover stories[2] and in the popular film *Slumdog Millionaire*, which includes several iconic shots from the slum—was a prominent site in Mumbai's social landscape before it attracted the attention of film producers and magazine editors. The 535-acre area of Dharavi once contained a small fishing village and, in the eighteenth century, housed a small and relatively insignificant British fort. It made the transition to a tannery town, a working-class enclave, and later to a slum over the course of the twentieth century as Bombay grew into a major industrial city. The combination of accessible yet difficult-to-develop marshy land and limited administrative oversight fueled the settlement's growth as a site of informal housing, unregulated industries, and particularly leather tanning and garment manufacturing, that drew thousands of families like

Aneesh Shankar's. Intersecting webs of governance and political power, traversing the often-opaque lines between formal and informal and legal and illegal, fortified the burgeoning settlement and brought its residents into broader networks of political and economic power. Despite a series of slum schemes attempted once the state of Maharashtra enacted the Slum Areas Act of 1971, the government has invested very little in the settlement's basic infrastructure, and Dharavi is bursting at the seams with its expanding population and thriving (but highly polluting) industries. The area today houses upward of a million residents (although population estimates vary widely) and almost innumerable industrial and commercial enterprises in tens of thousands of buildings of varying quality—from the most *kutcha* structures in the marshy settlements of Rajiv Gandhi Nagar along the Mahim Creek to Aneesh Shankar's *pucca* bungalow in Dharavi's interior neighborhoods. Most of these buildings are technically illegal constructions, built by squatters on government-owned land. Although some communities and families—including the Shankars—claim to have legal titles to their property, the validity of most of these documents remains in dispute. Once located on the metropolitan fringe, decades of suburban sprawl and municipal agglomeration have placed Dharavi in

At home in one of the area's *kutcha* structures. Photograph by the author.

Children play cricket in one of Dharavi's few open spaces. Photograph by Benji Holzman.

the geographic center of Mumbai. Its central location and accessibility to the city's rail and highway routes has generated developer interest in the settlement and has prompted numerous government initiatives to "solve the Dharavi problem." In fact, every few decades, ambitious, "transformative" schemes have been proposed to redevelop Dharavi's infrastructure and housing stock. Yet despite the initial enthusiasm and apparent government commitment to each effort, these proposals failed to garner the requisite financial backing or political support and were left unimplemented or dramatically scaled back.

In February 2004 the Maharashtra government launched another effort to redevelop Dharavi. This $2 billion dollar project to bring consortia of international and domestic developers to the area to construct new infrastructures, housing, and office buildings for lease or sale on Mumbai's highly valued property markets has aligned with broader imperatives to attract international capital and global prestige to India and to its commercial capital of Mumbai. This time, my informants told me, it was going to happen. Aneesh Shankar, for example, recalled, "My father told me since childhood that Dharavi will develop. And now it will develop. . . . And if it's done right," he added, "it will be good for the people." An even greater sense of optimism was expressed at the project's launch, as

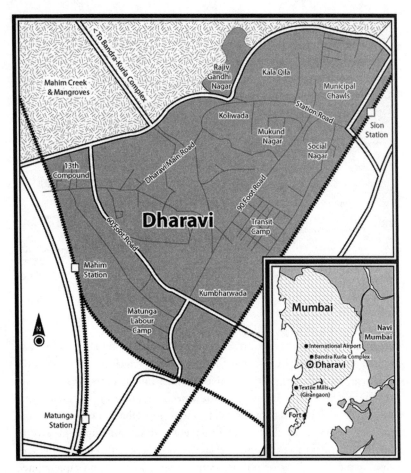

Map of Dharavi and greater Mumbai. Map by John L. Myers.

bold pronouncements were made that Mumbai would become slum-free, Dharavi would be transformed into a hub of innovation, and the world would look to India for new models of development. But nine years later, construction has yet to begin, political support for the project has waned, and investor and developer interest, once enthusiastic, has dwindled. With the fate of the project unclear, Dharavi remains intact. Its stability is rooted in Dharavi's complex political economy of labor, land, and infrastructure that helps to explain both why domestic and global property speculators have descended upon the iconic settlement and how its residents, political representatives, and community leaders like Shankar are, at least for now, keeping them at bay.

Dharavi's durability seems to contradict the dominant understanding of the effects of capital—particularly global capital—on urban space, which tends to emphasize its obliterating character. This understanding can be traced to Marx and Engels's (1978, 476) classic statement from the Communist Manifesto that "all that is solid melts into air, all that is holy profaned, and man is at last compelled to face with sober senses, his real conditions of life, and his relations with his kind." The widely quoted passage continues that "all old established industries have been destroyed or are being destroyed" with the expansion of the world market. This destruction, Marx and Engels noted, sends social and spatial relations into flux, sweeping away once fixed, fast-frozen institutions. This assessment of modernity has been cited extensively and applied by Marxist geographers and critical urban theorists to the contemporary urban condition. These contemporary theorists have conceived of the built environment of the global or postmodern city, similarly to Marx and Engels's characterization of the modern city, as "friction, fragmentation, collage, and eclecticism, all suffused with a sense of ephemerality and chaos" (Harvey 1990, 98). Although a compelling description that captures an important set of dynamics, this perspective on the contemporary urban landscape fails to account for the actually existing durabilities and the solidity of structures that refuse to melt.

This book uses the case of Dharavi and the ongoing Dharavi Redevelopment Project to explore the relationship between change and stability, ephemerality and entrenchment, in the context of global urban development. It ventures an answer to the question of how Dharavi and its seemingly marginal residents have held on, for over a century, to some of the most valuable land in this dramatically unequal city. But beyond Dharavi, it seeks to explain how cities and their residents, more generally, are responding to the potentially obliterating and totalizing forces of global capital. While these forces are locally contingent, mediated by distinctive local institutions and forms of resistance, similar sets of processes are under way in cities across the globe, from public housing transformations in Chicago, to Olympic stadium constructions in Rio de Janeiro, to new town planning throughout China. In each of these places, homes are being demolished and residents are being dispossessed as networks of global investors and local actors build new structures and create the demand to fill them. Yet it is likely that, even in these places, more remains durable than prevailing wisdom or our existing theories suggest.

Return of the Slum: The Power of Words

Given my own ambivalent use of the term "slum" throughout this book, a brief discussion of terminology is warranted. Few concepts have had as long and troubled a life in the social sciences as the slum. Emerging as a spatial form and analytic concept in Victorian England, the slum was conceptualized by Friedrich Engels and his contemporaries as a by-product of industrial capitalism and its creation of an urban working class. Yet while Engels understood the slum to be the *consequence* of capitalist relations, most sociologists, at least through the first half of the twentieth century, have viewed the slum as the *source* of such social problems as immorality, vice, and dysfunctional family forms. By the late 1960s, studies of the slum had moved from the first world to the third world. In the wake of slum clearance campaigns and national urban renewal programs, the industrial cities of the north were believed to have eradicated slums, the way they had eradicated smallpox and polio, and slums were imagined to have become the exclusive property of third-world cities. In the 1970s and 1980s, however, amid critiques about the assumptions underlying poverty research and studies of urban marginality, the word was exchanged for more neutral names like "squatter settlements," "shantytowns," and "self-help" communities. But three decades later, the slum has returned as both a term and an analytic concept, framed now as a consequence of neoliberal policy and global inequalities.

Several scholars have noted the recent resurrection of the slum in scholarly discourse (Rao 2006; Angotti 2006; Gilbert 2007; Arabindoo 2011). While its use in policy circles has remained relatively constant—due, primarily, to the array of "slum upgrading" programs promoted by the World Bank since the early 1970s—researchers and academic writers have generally shied away from the word. But with the launching of the World Bank and UN-Habitat's Cities without Slums initiative in the late 1990s and the publication of its companion report, *The Challenge of Slums*, a few years later, development agencies have sought to raise awareness about slums and, as a consequence, bring the term back into use. These efforts have succeeded, and the slum has again become an acceptable subject in academic research and popular writings. Lamenting the slum's return, Gilbert (2007), Angotti (2006), and Arabindoo (2011) have criticized it as "evocative hyperbole," a "derogatory toponym," "emotive," and "dangerous," and have charged those employing it with analytic imprecision. They assert that the attention-grabbing nature of the word—employed, in part, to shock policy makers and publics into action—ultimately stigmatizes the people who live in these settlements and can condone violent actions taken against them. In the recent history of slum clearance campaigns in the United States, Europe, and throughout the global south, labeling settlements as slums has frequently justified their demolition and the often violent displacement of their inhabitants.

These critics charge that the word lacks precision because it conflates rather diverse housing arrangements under a single evocative term. The catchall nature of the word is readily apparent in the World Bank and UN-Habitat (1999, 1) description of the Cities without Slums initiative:

> Slums range from high density, squalid central city tenements to spontaneous squatter settlements without legal recognition or rights, sprawling at the edge of cities. Some are more than fifty years old, some are land invasions just underway. Slums have various names, Favelas, Kampungs, Bidonvilles, Tugurios, yet share the same miserable living conditions.

The only common element identified across these various housing types, forms of tenure, and spatial settings is their "miserable living conditions." Yet these living conditions are relative and lack an objective set of criteria for measurement. "If slums are relational and as much a figment of the mind as a physical construct," Gilbert (2007, 700) reasons, "then it is difficult for any government or international organization to eliminate them." More than half a century ago, sociologist Herbert Gans (1962, 350) made a similar charge, noting that "the term 'slum' is an evaluative, not an analytic concept and that any definition of the term must be related, explicitly or implicitly, to the standards of the age, and more importantly, to the renewal policy in which it is used."

As Gilbert and Gans effectively argue, the definition of a slum must be understood as more a matter of politics than of science. These politics, meanwhile, are inherently local. While the designation of a slum may justify its clearance and the displacement of its residents in some contexts, it may determine the allocation of resources in others. In India, where the government, the World Bank, and other development agencies have channeled significant (although exceedingly insufficient) funds into urban areas for slum improvement programs, many localities actually *seek out* designation as a slum in order to access these funds. In a study of slum policies in the city of Hyderabad, researchers "found that labeling an area a slum is essentially a political decision, taken as a result of political pressure from residents of areas that are characterized by the non-existence of physical and social infrastructures" (Naidu 2006, 206). In fact, this research found some areas of Hyderabad with quite adequate infrastructure and housing conditions to have been designated as slums, while other areas, whose residents had less political influence, had not received the designation despite their objectively worse conditions. Consequently, local dynamics of power and place-specific policies must be acknowledged when considering the definition and designation of slums.

Remaining mindful of these concerns I contend that examinations of slums and slum policy can help illuminate local power arrangements rather than obscuring them.[3] Throughout this book I use the word "slum" to refer to the generally substandard settlements in which large segments of the urban poor live and work throughout the global south. These settlements are typically informal, illegal, or quasilegal and are supported by loose networks of residents, politicians, community leaders and crime bosses, social workers, police, and municipal officials. Although the details of their emergence and transformations differ across political, cultural, and institutional space, slums can be broadly attributed to failures or gaps in formal service provision. When markets and governments both fail to provide adequate housing to low-wage workers and their families, then slums proliferate. The concept of a slum is broad enough to accommodate the diverse forms this failure can take, and empirical examinations of them can help reveal the political and economic causes of failure.

But more important, and also more simply, I employ and engage with the term "slum" because it is used so frequently, and unselfconsciously, in my field site. The slum, and its local equivalent *jhopadpati*, has social and political significance in Dharavi and Mumbai. Despite the diverse economic conditions, forms of housing, and legal arrangements found within, the term signifies a space outside of, but tightly intertwined with, formal governance institutions and property markets. Slums exist because of these formal institutions, not in spite of them, and must be understood in relation to them.

Given this perspective, I accept the increasingly controversial claim that Dharavi is a slum, and I employ the term throughout the book. Because of its institutional density—including a multitude of schools, hospitals, pharmacies, restaurants and bars, clothing shops, electronics stores, vegetable markets, and dry goods shops—many people who know Dharavi prefer not to use the term "slum" to describe it.[4] Aneesh Shankar, in fact, never described Dharavi to me as a slum, although I am not sure how conscious the term's absence was from his language. He explained to me, "Just like Mumbai is the heart of India, Dharavi is the heart of Mumbai,[5] . . . Everything is convenient from here. From the start of birth to the end of life, you can stay within five minutes of here." Despite the completeness and economic centrality of the settlement, I maintain that Dharavi is a slum because the municipality has designated it as such and is using the state's current slum policy, the Slum Rehabilitation Scheme, as both the justification and main policy instrument for its transformation.

While identifying an informal settlement that is representative of slums in general may be impossible, Dharavi is an importantly distinctive space. The settlement's size and the diversity of its populations, activities, and industries distinguish it from almost all of Mumbai's other slum settlements, most of which house a few dozen or a few hundred families in hutments or shanties built along railway tracks or highways. Its size and scale place Dharavi in the category of settlements that Mike Davis has called "megaslums," which includes other iconic settlements like Kibera in Nairobi, Tondo in Manila, Orangi Town in Karachi, and Cité Soleil in Port-au-Prince. These megaslums are all distinctive spaces in their own right, but the economic and political power that their formal and informal leaders have amassed, which I posit contributes to their durability, requires an analytic insertion into this category. In many of these settlements, as in Dharavi today, the long-standing interests that have protected the spaces, their residents, and their mostly unregulated activities are facing a new and more powerful set of opponents, backed by both global capital and national state power. As urban property markets have expanded and demand for new commercial construction has tightened, the land on which many of these slums sit has become a potentially valuable resource, and a land grab is now under way.

Globalization and Slums

This characterization of slums as the newest strategic site of a global land grab is rooted in the assumption that globalization and neoliberalization are having new or transformative effects on slums and on the experience of residential informality. Yet while, as urban theorist Nazer AlSayyad (2004, 15) points out, it may be "easy to argue that globalization and liberalization are today giving rise to new geographies . . . the relationship between globally driven liberalization and locally based informality is often ambiguous." Some writers, such as Mike Davis (2006), posit a strong relationship, asserting that while globalization may not exactly be *causing* informality and the emergence of slums, it is certainly contributing to their planetary proliferation. This "strong program" of global slum studies suggests that as countries throughout the global south adopted structural adjustment programs in the 1980s and early 1990s, they were compelled to shift resources away from rural employment schemes as well as state-supported industrial development. As domestic markets became flooded with foreign agricultural surpluses, displaced farmers and peasants migrated to cities to seek new opportunities. But with international agencies like the IMF and World Bank pressuring these national governments to redress perceived urban biases in their political economies by halting industrial subsidies and lifting trade protections, the industrial economies that had once absorbed these new urbanites had also been decimated. Davis refers to this double bind as "urbanization without industrialization," explaining:

> Since the mid-1980s, the great industrial cities of the South—Bombay, Johannesburg, Buenos Aires, Belo Horizonte, and São Paulo—have all suffered massive plant closures and tendential deindustrialization. Elsewhere, urbanization has been more radically de-coupled from industrialization, even from development *per se* and, in sub-Saharan Africa, from that *sine qua non* of urbanization, rising agricultural productivity. (Davis 2006, 13)

The dislocated urban poor have been incorporated into the informal economy and have come to reside in slums, residential repositories of this "surplus humanity."

While Davis makes this case persuasively, his critics point out that globalization and liberalization, even the structural adjustment programs prescribed by the IMF and World Bank, are contingent and highly localized processes (Gilbert 2004; Ong 2011).[6] Alan Gilbert (2004: 52), for example, makes the important observation that "what governments say they're doing [with respect to liberalization] is not the same thing as what they often do." While officially adopted policies may resemble the liberal orthodoxy of the New Economic Program, actually existing neoliberalisms may be more loosely coupled from these structural adjustments. This recognition demonstrates the importance of supplementing Davis's broad analysis of these processes with more place-specific accounts of globalization's effects on the slum.

Neoliberal globalization in the Indian case is nothing if not ambiguous, and the notion of loose coupling aptly describes the disjuncture between discourse and practice in the regulation of many economic sectors. The year 1991 is generally identified as the watershed when India was "structurally adjusted," adopting the mix of regulatory and monetary reforms typically required to qualify for an IMF-backed loan. Liberal advocates like Jagdish Bhagwati and Gurcharan Das describe "the golden summer" of 1991 as profoundly transformative (Bhagwati and Panagariya 2012; Das 2000), but most assessments are more tempered, noting that India actually began dismantling its system of industrial licensing at least a decade earlier and continued to introduce reforms more gradually throughout the 1990s and 2000s (McCartney 2010; Nayar 2001; Nayar 2006).[7] As much as any specific reforms, however, liberalization entailed an ideological shift, reflecting and producing the sense that India had become global.

The idea of a newly globalized India could be seen in the exuberance of the country's urban property markets in the immediate aftermath of liberalization. As anthropologist Llerena Searle (2010) documented, this perception was created in part by Indian real estate firms working with global investors to generate interest in India's property sector and direct flows of speculative capital to Indian cities. Characterized by some as "casino capitalism," property prices in the commercial capital of Mumbai skyrocketed after liberalization, rising four to six times between 1991 and 1996, and fell dramatically after this peak (Nijman 2000). While some observers were quick to attribute the volatility to economic liberalization, and particularly to the entrance of foreign real estate speculators into India's newly opened real estate markets, as well as to multinational corporations clamoring for commercial space in the city, geographer Jan Nijman (2000) cautioned that the actual explanations were more complex. While acknowledging that economic liberalization, including the ideological shifts that accompanied the national-level reforms, created new demands for Mumbai real estate, Nijman found that local land-use regulations and continued restrictions on foreign ownership and investment in real estate resulted in pent-up demand and rising prices. It was less liberalization and deregulation and more the *continuation of* regulation in this sector that produced Mumbai's property price bubble in this period. The context, meanwhile, continued to shift in the 1990s and 2000s, as the property and development sectors were gradually liberalized and markets were shaped by broad-reaching networks of local and nonlocal actors (Searle 2010). As Nijman and Searle's inquiries into India's postliberalization urban property markets demonstrate, local political factors shaped these conditions as much as globalization did throughout this period.

Amid these shifts, Marxist geographers like David Harvey and the late Neil Smith were beginning to note evidence of gentrification and the dislocation of the urban poor as a consequence of this new real estate activity. In a cautious statement on the emergence of gentrification as "a global urban strategy," Smith (2002) acknowledged that neoliberal globalization can have quite contradictory consequences for large, densely populated cities like Mumbai, resulting in both the bypassing or uneven inclusion of cities in Latin America, Africa, and Asia and the pooling of capital, often in the form of concentrated luxury housing, in some of their urban cores. Although still relatively rare, he noted that "gentrification as a process has rapidly descended the urban hierarchy" and could be found in a set of cities that included Mumbai (Smith 2002, 439).

David Harvey (2008, 35), meanwhile, has recently identified a similar process under way in Mumbai's slums:

> Dharavi, one of the most prominent slums in Mumbai, is estimated to be worth $2 billion. The pressure to clear it—for environmental and social reasons that mask the land grab—is mounting daily. Financial powers backed by the state push for forcible slum clearance, in some cases violently taking possession of terrain occupied for a whole generation. Capital accumulation through real-estate activity booms, since the land is acquired at almost no cost.

While not the first to characterize the ongoing Dharavi project as a land grab, Harvey situates these developments in his framework of "accumulation by dispossession"; in doing so, he uses this case to demonstrate a broader shift away from capital accumulation through production and toward growth built on displacement and dispossession. Mike Davis, meanwhile, has referred to this process as "Haussmann in the tropics," whereby "squatters and renters, and sometimes even small landlords, are routinely evicted with little ceremony or right of appeal" (Davis 2006, 99). He notes that while slum clearance has gone on in some places for generations, Davis, like Harvey and Smith, attributes its intensification and geographic spread with the process of economic globalization under way since the early 1980s.

While these authors associate slum clearance and residential displacements with globalization and the workings of capitalism under conditions of neoliberalism, most scholars of urban India tend to ground their explanations of these processes in local politics, and particularly in the growing influence of middle-class residents in urban affairs.[8] Among these assertions that Indian cities may be "becoming bourgeois at last" (Chatterjee 2004), Asher Ghertner (2011) has characterized the process as the "gentrification of the state." "If gentrification consists of the usurpation of formerly lower-class spaces by the upper class," Ghertner explains, then the middle-class "good governance" programs he researched "achieve nothing less than the gentrification of state space, or of the channels of political participation more generally" (Ghertner 2011, 505).[9] While most studies of this political usurping, including Partha Chatterjee's (2004) now-classic framing, attribute this development to the heightened political consciousness and global ambitions of India's new middle class, Ghertner identifies a series of institutional reconfigurations within the Indian state that have allowed this population to capture urban political agendas. But regardless of how urban India's middle classes are acquiring the influence necessary to facilitate slum demolitions—and even, in one extreme case, to get away with murdering a presumed slum resident (Baviskar 2003)—this literature generally attributes the emerging geographies of informality more to internal political factors (even if those politics are rooted in global aspirations) than to neoliberal globalization.[10]

Between abstract analyses of global capital and ground-level considerations of India's emerging urban politics sits Dharavi and the Dharavi Redevelopment Project. In order to understand the current efforts under way to transform the megaslum, the account presented here demonstrates that we must consider political and economic developments also under way on multiple scales—along with the interactions between them—that include the machinations of global property investors, the liberal reformers in India's central Planning Commission, the political party coalitions that govern at the state level, and the varied local actors struggling to get or retain their piece of the slum. While it is important not to overstate the effects of neoliberal globalization, including the regulatory reforms that presumably facilitated a rush of foreign investors into Mumbai's newly liberalized land markets, neither should we overlook these developments and their potentially dramatic effects on the city.

The Right to Stay Put ← Right to the city

Amid these efforts to usurp urban space and appropriate, demolish, or transform the slum—whether with the tools of global capital, local politics, or a combination of both—countermovements to retain these spaces are also under way.[11] These counter movements have been widely recognized among those writing on the Indian city, as well as in the larger fields of urban studies and social movements, as an opposing—although admittedly unequal—set of forces. Implicit in these writings—and often made quite explicit—is an engagement with Henri Lefebvre's (1968) classic call for a "right to the city." While primarily a scholarly frame, Lefebvre's revolutionary demand to not just appropriate or retain city space but to also capture the tools or assemblages of city making (referred to in much of his writings as the *oeuvre*) has also become part of the activist repertoire in many parts of the world, particularly in urban-based struggles in

Latin America.[12] An effective rallying cry, Lefebvre (1996 [1968]: 173–74) writes, "The right to the city manifests itself as a superior form of rights: right to freedom, to individualization in socialization, to habitat and to inhabit. The right to the *oeuvre*, to participation and *appropriation* (clearly distinct from the right to property) are implied in the right to the city" (emphasis in original). Yet despite the widespread use of this framework to analyze urban claims making (and, at times, to make claims), mentions of Lefebvre are relatively scant in writings on Indian cities.[13] Poor people's politics and struggles for urban-based rights in this region have tended to be understood as less sweeping, as a series of daily transgressions—some quite unconscious—that challenge existing configurations of space and power. These actions are more likely to be framed in terms of Asaf Bayat's (1997, 2004) "quiet encroachment of the ordinary" than they are in Lefebvre's language of the right to the city.

In much of the writing on Indian cities, the act of squatting, or illegal habitation, is understood as a potentially powerful countermovement. Within the frame of urban populism, Ananya Roy (2003, 145) uses "the broad rubric of 'squatting' to indicate an ensemble of informal and tenuous rights." This rubric is employed—although perhaps less tentatively—by Solomon Benjamin (2007, 2008), in his recent writings on "occupancy urbanism." Characterizing the occupation of potentially valuable urban property as a direct challenge to the interests of global capital, Benjamin (2008, 723–24) writes:

> Master Plans designate large territories for development in higher-level policy documents, but in reality these territories remain "occupied" by pre-existing settlements and see newer ones developing. "Occupancy" refers not just to physical space but also to the appropriation of real estate surpluses made possible by the "embedding" of municipal government into popular society. Much to the dismay of globalized financial institutions and large developers, this reflects the diversion of their potential profits into an economy of small firms.

This process, which Roy (2003) has also called "informal vesting," undermines objectives of "accumulation by dispossession" both by resisting displacement and by subverting processes of capital accumulation.

Most of these scholars recognize that the question of whether these legal transgressions constitute deliberate acts of resistance is a complicated one. Roy (2004a, 165), for example, who examines the militant refusal of poor female commuters in Kolkata to purchase railway tickets as the usurpation of space, acknowledges that "these narratives of contestation

[margin note: Right to the city]

are ultimately unable to transform the structural realities of the rural-urban interface." Similarly, Nikhil Anand (2011, 557) has clarified that the establishment of illegal water connections in Mumbai's slums should not be understood as resistance but more tentatively "as politically mediated acts of unequal and inclusive settlement."[14] Despite these authors' caution—resonating with Bayat's (2004, 92) warning that these activities are carried out "not as a deliberate political act; [but rather] by the forces of necessity"—they still imbue the acts of encroachment, settlement, squatting, and illegal appropriation with a kind of political power, comparable to, but distinct from the more revolutionary claims for, the right to the city.[15]

These considerations of quiet acts of resistance are grounded in the recognition that the forms of politics and political engagement available to India's urban poor are distinct from those available to the middle class and urban elite. These political disparities are made explicit in the distinction Partha Chatterjee draws between civil society and what he terms "political society." Criticizing the imprecision with which political theorists have employed the concept of civil society, using it to describe practically every form of association outside of government, Chatterjee calls for a return to the classic understanding of "civil society as bourgeois society, in the sense used by Hegel and Marx" (Chatterjee 2004, 38). This concept, he maintains, is grounded in the liberal tradition, in which associations of citizens are endowed with equal rights ensured by a sovereign state. Although a broadly inclusive political ideal, he argues that civil society in India today refers only to "a small section of culturally equipped citizens" whose interactions with the state are shaped by the "normative values of modernity" (Chatterjee 2004, 41). The democratic politics available to the majority of Indians are more accurately captured in the concept of "political society." Part of the welfare state tradition, political society refers to the associations of the population, many of which "transgress the strict lines of legality in struggling to live and work" (Chatterjee 2004, 40). While the state *engages with* civil society through the high ideals of liberalism, government agencies—and the NGOs acting on their behalf—*administer to* political society because of the "moral assertion of popular demands" (Chatterjee, 41).

Noting that urban politics have been the almost exclusive property of political society for the past several decades, Chatterjee suggests that the bourgeois revolution under way across urban India is amplifying the influence of civil society at the expense of the urban poor. While numerous researchers have found evidence for this position, documenting successful middle-class movements to dismantle squatter settlements and evict illegal street vendors, others have noted that a more empowering set of political developments may also be under way in the neoliberalizing or globalizing Indian city. In a widely cited pair of articles, anthropologist Arjun Appadurai (2000, 2001) has identified a successful countermovement under way, which he terms "globalizing from below" or "grassroots globalization." Bringing together "highly specific local, national, and regional groups on matters of equality, access, justice, and redistribution" (Appadurai 2000, 15), he highlights an alliance of Mumbai-based NGOs that are partnering "with other, more powerful actors—including the state, in its various levels and incarnations—to achieve their goals of gaining secure housing and urban infrastructure for the urban poor in Mumbai, in India, and beyond" (Appadurai 2001, 41). Through these partnerships, Appadurai argues, globally linked but locally rooted NGOs are helping to produce a kind of global urban democracy.

Despite what is basically an upbeat assessment of these developments, Appadurai (2000, 15) acknowledges some of the contradictions entailed in this type of politics, including the ways that such groups may at times be "uncomfortably complicit with the policies of the nation-state." Roy (2009b), meanwhile, has presented a more critical assessment of some of the same groups, characterizing them not as democratic exemplars but as representative of a politics of "populist mediation." Employing the lens of governmentality, Roy (2009b, 168) argues that this new type of politics produces "governable subjects and governable spaces," and may even be helping facilitate urban renewal and the violent remaking of urban space. Despite this more critical assessment, numerous scholars have analyzed the growing influence of pro-poor NGOs as evidence of a broader movement to challenge the influence of both "Haussmann in the tropics" and urban India's bourgeois revolution.[16] Although still rarely framed in the Lefebvrian language of the right to the city, these accounts emphasize the transformative power of struggles to both inhabit the city and contribute to its construction.

Throughout this book I examine these struggles in the context of Dharavi. While I recognize the mediated forms of power entailed in the subversive act of squatting, I also find evidence of more deliberate democratic practices akin to Appadurai's "grassroots globalization." Like most of these other scholars, I choose not to ground my analysis in the sweeping frame of the right to the city. Rather, I employ the more restrained language of Chester Hartman's (1984) "right to stay put." Based on his ethnographic inquiries of land grabs and community resistance, primarily in

San Francisco, Hartman (1974, 1984) argued "that government [should] plan housing and prevent displacement instead of simply compensating the victims after the fact . . . to make government policies responsive to existing residents, not to financial interests or the mobile gentry" (Swanstrom and Kerstein 1989, 270; see also Newman and Wyly 2006). Distinct from the revolutionary aims of the right to the city, this framing acknowledges that the activities of residents and activists are usually more narrowly focused on simply resisting displacement.[17] While some housing rights groups active in Mumbai have more revolutionary and socially transformative aspirations, the near constant threat of eviction keeps these groups focused on a more immediate set of objectives.

Both historically and in contemporary Mumbai, struggles around the right to stay put are a key feature of the city's built environment and political landscape. These democratic struggles, as I demonstrate in the context of Dharavi, are waged in a variety of arenas, including in ballot box, the courtroom, and the government planning agency, and on the street. In the electoral arena, these struggles often manifest as so-called vote bank politics—as a bank into which politicians make the occasional deposit or political favor and then can cash in when elections come around.[18] Yet counter to this rather cynical narrative, electoral politics have tangible consequences for the urban poor and working classes, and participation in this arena constitutes a deliberate act of political engagement with the built environment (Bjorkman 2012; Benjamin 2008). Without regularly held, contested elections at the national, state, and municipal levels, displacements would certainly be more frequent and more violent.

Among their effects, elections can be powerfully disruptive, as resources are diverted in the lead-up to elections and all else falls by the wayside. While often lamented as an inefficiency of democracy, elections can have a much-needed slowing effect. Projects are suspended out of fear of "politicizing" development, and residents remain in place, at least for the duration of the election season. After the election dust settles, newly elected officials take their time getting up to speed, and project suspensions remain in place. Similar delays are produced by legal challenges or public interest litigations (PILs) that can hold projects up for decades, as well as by contentious street politics and more deliberative negotiations. While these delays may be protective, the uncertainty they produce can also be harmful. Residents and administrators fail to make needed repairs to homes and infrastructures, not knowing how long they will remain in place.[19] Residents and activist groups, meanwhile, work to maintain obstructions, enacting their right to stay put, rather than promoting progressive social change.

What is often gained in these struggles is the right to remain in limbo.

The empowering and exploitative dimensions of staying put were characterized to me by Aneesh Shankar during our sprawling conversation in his bungalow. Discussing the Dharavi Redevelopment Project, he reasoned, "There will be give-and-take. If they accept our proposals, we will accept theirs." Pausing for a moment, he warned that if his group's proposals were not incorporated into the plan, then "we will not accept theirs." The types of demands, or "proposals," that he and his organization were making generally concerned the interests of Dharavi's Tamil laborers, including the leather workers, garment manufacturers, and producers of *farsan*, or snack foods, made practically around-the-clock in Dharavi's questionably hygienic, windowless factory spaces. Shankar's role appeared to be one of protector and preserver of Dharavi's ways of life and avenues of upward mobility. Acknowledging that the fortunes of his own family were made in the dingy factories of the slum, he was working to ensure that similar opportunities remain available to the settlement's newer migrants and laboring communities. (And if his own businesses profit from the ready supply of migrant labor, then all the better.) Maintaining this way of life, Shankar acknowledged, requires pragmatism and the ability to situate himself in the overlapping and intersecting networks of power and sovereignty that traverse the boundaries of the slum.

Political Economy of the Megaslum

Beyond the populist politics that can undermine the ambitions of global capital, Dharavi's durability is a product of these overlapping and intersecting networks that connect the city and the slum and help keep the settlement in place. Throughout the book, I use Davis's concept of a megaslum to characterize this integration and institutional reach. Yet while the megaslum for Davis is primarily a matter of size and density—he notes that they arise "when shantytowns and squatter communities merge in continuous belts of informal housing and poverty, usually on the urban periphery" (Davis 2006, 26)—I employ the concept more as a political category. Analyzing diverse institutions and processes under way on multiple scales, I argue that Dharavi's growth and emergence as a megaslum, which took place gradually over several decades, occurred alongside and intertwined with the political and economic development of Mumbai as a whole. Institutionally embedded and politically entrenched, Dharavi has simply become (to use a catchphrase of recent years) too big to fail.

The megaslum is also a product of institutional and political fragmentations. Broadly speaking, cities are sites of fragmented sovereignties, divided loyalties, and diffuse power. Unlike the national state, where authority generally goes undisputed (except during extraordinary moments of revolution), urban space comprises multiple distinct but overlapping jurisdictions (Davis 2011; Brenner 2011). While these multiple sites of power can be useful for urban claims making—that is, appeals can be made to the most strategically relevant and sympathetic site—they also produce fragmentations and institutional gaps when lines of authority are unclear. Mumbai exemplifies this condition, particularly inside its slums, where numerous government agencies are responsible for aspects of land use, planning, and construction, each with incomplete authority and inadequate resources, and representing a distinct set of constituencies and interests. At times, the slum and its residents slip through the cracks between these administrative layers, its durability a product of institutional neglect and administrative inattention. But, as documented in later chapters, fragmented sovereignties can also manifest as fierce political contestations and result in forced evictions and other forms of political violence (Davis 2011; Hansen and Stepputat 2005).

This book considers the empowering as well as the detrimental consequences of durability. The megaslum can be an empowering place, where seemingly marginal city residents make homes and livelihoods in strategically important and potential valuable locations. Yet the right to stay put often means the right to remain in dangerous, inadequate, and inhospitable conditions. In addition to staying in poorly serviced settlements, residents make political compromises to hold their place, becoming dependent on corrupt and extractive institutions and individuals. Nor is the durability the residents experience a meaningful form of security. Rather, it constitutes a condition I refer to in later chapters as "precarious stability." With most still lacking secure tenure and legally binding protections, residents live amid uncertainty as new plans will eventually be proposed and threaten again to dispossess them.

This book examines these conditions through a political economy of the megaslum, rooted in both history and ethnography.[20] Adding ethnographic nuance and historical context to what are typically more abstract analyses of "accumulation by dispossession," it demonstrates that while cities are always changing, they do not react directly to neoliberal globalization or to emerging bourgeois politics. Rather, these macrolevel forces are mediated by the fixed structures, local institutions, and autonomous agents that give shape to particular places and strive to maintain them.

This mediation is illustrated throughout the book's first half, which traces the century-long history of the sprawling settlement frequently referred to as "the largest slum in Asia." Chapter 1 demonstrates that Dharavi grew and thrived alongside and closely intertwined with Bombay's colonial and postcolonial industrial and mercantile economy, but was not determined by these wider economic structures. Rather, local migrants, political parties, and neighborhood-level "big men" constructed this city-within-a-city and, in doing so, made illegal housing the norm for the city as a whole. The local state, meanwhile, responded with "supportive neglect," because industry thrived and the commercial city grew and prospered under this arrangement. Chapter 2 tells the sordid history of Bombay's uneven and inconsistent policy interventions in the slum. Once the Indian government articulated a slum policy in the 1950s, Dharavi, along with Bombay's other informal settlements, began to suffer under inconsistent interventions that swung from clearance to upgrading in its various forms and back again. But given the political power that had become concentrated in the settlement (along with the institutional fragmentations that undermined efforts at dramatic transformation), Dharavi and its residents weathered many of the demolition drives and resisted the effects of periodic redevelopment schemes.

By the late 1990s, however, the context of economic liberalization and global integration had become overwhelming, and new plans for Dharavi's transformation were again under way. Chapter 3 traces the multiscalar shifts underlying the formulation of the new, profit-oriented slum redevelopment that arose in this context. As the city's economic base was shifting from primarily industrial to one rooted in services and commodities, land and investment were becoming valorized over manufacturing and traditional commercial sectors. Amid these shifts, new entrepreneurial schemes for slum redevelopment began to emerge that sought to exploit the rising land values of centrally located slums like Dharavi. This chapter concludes with a description of the Dharavi Redevelopment Project (DRP) as one such scheme.

The remaining two chapters and the Conclusion highlight the complex dynamics that have worked to undermine the implementation of the DRP and keep Dharavi in place, revealing a disjuncture between the state's desire to pursue a new entrepreneurial urban agenda and its capacity to enact it. Chapter 4 begins by describing the institutional fragmentations that have traditionally undermined urban development efforts and slum housing schemes in Mumbai. Between these administrative gaps, the "political entrepreneur" who conceptualized and promoted the DRP inserted himself and appropriated the tools (or *oeuvre*) of city making. Yet despite this novel political configuration, which seemed for a brief moment that it would succeed, enduring fragmentations undermined these efforts. Chapter 5 considers the democratic configurations underlying the right to stay put in the context of the DRP, highlighting activities taking place on the street, in the courts, and around the table at the state's planning agencies. This chapter demonstrates—somewhat surprisingly—the influence that certain of Dharavi's residential and laboring communities and housing activists, connected to globally networked activist groups, garnered in the project's planning process. Despite this inclusion and the seemingly successful efforts to co-opt these groups, their activities have contributed to the project's suspension and its uncertain fate. The concluding chapter reflects upon the consequences of the DRP's suspension and the residents' state of limbo. While project advocates attribute this uncertainty to the global financial crisis and the volatility of the international real estate industry, the causes are clearly more local in nature. While these (possibly permanent) delays could be viewed as a victory for Dharavi's residents and workers, without a viable alternative vision for Dharavi, the residents continue to live in a state of precarious stability, in which the threats of dispossession remain, few investments are made, and most observers and residents simply wait for the project to be revived or replaced by an even grander scheme.

CHAPTER ONE

Becoming Asia's Largest Slum

Dharavi's early history is usually recounted with an air of nostalgia, tracing the slum of today back to the small, idyllic fishing village it was just a century ago. As its familiar origin myth goes, Dharavi was a sparsely populated village until the middle of the nineteenth century, inhabited by members of the Son Koli caste of fishing people. The Kolis are believed to have lived on India's western coast for tens of thousands of years, giving the area its sense of fragile premodern permanence. Conveying this sense, the 1909 *Gazetteer of Bombay City and Island* poetically describes Bombay's Koli fishing folk as "older than the cocoa-nut palm, older than the Bhandari palm tapper," and among whom one would find "the blood of the men of the Stone Age."[1]

Dharavi's twentieth-century development and transition to a slum, on the other hand, is decidedly less poetic, often told as the story of discarded refuse and displaced populations. Sitting in a tiny one-room office down one of the many winding lanes of Dharavi's Mukund Nagar settlement, social worker Ashwin Paul was the first of many to tell me this particular version of Dharavi's development.[2] As Bombay grew, Dharavi became its dumping ground. It was first an illegal garbage dump, he explained, when construction waste from nearby building sites was deposited on Dharavi's marshy banks of the Mahim Creek, rather than being transported to the less convenient municipal landfill. Dharavi was literately built on garbage, he mused. As Dharavi's land grew firmer, the industrial and commercial activities deemed too polluting or too much of a nuisance for the more desirable parts of South Bombay were dumped in the area. Eventually, Dharavi became a human dumping ground, as Bombay's unwanted populations of labor migrants, refugees, and others with insecure land rights were discarded here through waves of resettlements and slum clearance campaigns.

Hutments built along Dharavi's main canal.
Photograph by Benji Holzman.

Although usually unmentioned in this account of development
through dumping, Dharavi's twentieth-century growth is tightly intertwined with Bombay's broader industrial development. As the city's
textile industry expanded and spurred new areas of economic activity,
demands for space began to dramatically outstrip Bombay's land supply.
As the southern and central sections of the island grew more crowded,
the most polluting and hazardous industries, such as the slaughterhouses, leather work, pottery firing, and recycling, were pushed northward
to the marshy lands of Dharavi. Meanwhile, with the city's needs for an
industrial workforce rapidly expanding, Dharavi also attracted a steady
population of refugees and migrant workers with its available land for
squatting and makeshift housing construction. As Dharavi's residential populations and polluting industries grew denser in the 1950s and
1960s, people stopped referring to Dharavi as a village, and it became a
slum. This new designation also reflected the area's perception as a center

of criminal activity, including illicit liquor production and distribution. By the 1980s Dharavi had become "Asia's largest slum," based not on population enumerations but on the sense that the settlement needed a superlative moniker.

This chapter traces how Dharavi became a slum—and, ultimately, a megaslum. In contrast to most explanations of slum formation rooted in government ineptitude and corruption—and, to a lesser extent, demographic pushes and pulls and resistance strategies—this history demonstrates that Dharavi played a critical role in the social reproduction of Bombay's working class. While slums are usually thought to house the poorest and most marginal city dwellers, Dharavi's history reveals the economic and political centrality of such spaces and lends further support to the idea that their marginality is a myth.[3] This history, which also sheds light on more widespread processes of slum formation in Bombay and throughout urban India, reveals the tacit agreements between industry, government, and local political leaders that were central to Bombay's industrial development. Slums proliferated and spaces like Dharavi grew because they helped address the city's growing need for industrial spaces and worker housing, with minimal public- or private-sector expenditure. Through a strategy of "supportive neglect," the local state allowed illegal businesses and housing to proliferate and become the norm across the industrial metropolis. Diverging from prevailing explanations, Dharavi's history reveals that the state's actions—or, rather, inaction—on slums reflect the interests and institutions that slum formation served.

Meanwhile, Dharavi and its residents became enmeshed in local political institutions—formal and informal, legal and illicit—that provided some protection from demolitions and displacement. Amid its strategy of supportive neglect, the state has been an inconsistent presence in Dharavi. Between episodic insertions of formal state authority, informal sovereigns have consolidated the power required to get things done in the organization of daily life. As political parties, labor unions, organized crime groups, and social service organizations used Dharavi to build their constituencies and bases of power, its residents strategically used these groups and institutions to serve their own needs. Yet without a centralized node of sovereign authority, power in Dharavi has remained fragmented and diffuse. While political leaders can usually amass enough political resources to achieve objectives on a small scale, more major endeavors, such as the planning and implementation of redevelopment projects (as discussed in subsequent chapters), have proved more elusive.

Explaining Slums

Since the late 1960s, residential slums and squatter settlements have been explained primarily as a product of bureaucratic failure and political corruption. This argument can be traced in part to the prolific writings of British architect John F. C. Turner, whose benevolent view of "self-help communities" was an indirect indictment of the state. Turner's analysis and his architectural interventions in Peruvian squatter settlements shed light on the complex webs of social relations and the deep personal resolve that enable the urban poor to build their own houses and social institutions in the face of government ineptitude. Turner and his contemporaries argued that if residents were provided access to credit and tenure security, they would be best positioned to construct their own homes and improve their living conditions with limited government intrusion (Mangin 1967; Turner 1969; Turner 1976; Ward 1976). Development economists at the time, many working with the World Bank, became strong proponents of this position, due, in part, to the nonstate (and thus anticommunist) interventions it suggested (Werlin 1999). This interpretation of slum formation allowed the World Bank and other development aid agencies to bypass institutional reform and justify their work with nongovernmental organization (NGOs) and directly with self-help communities to implement slum improvement and upgrading programs over the next several decades (Werlin 1999; Davis 2006).

This antistate approach provided an alternative to the more demographic —and ultimately modernist—explanations for slums prevalent at the time. The "overurbanization" thesis, generally attributed to Davis and Golden (1954), suggested that rural migrants were being driven to cities not because of traditional pull factors like industrial employment growth but because of push factors associated with weak agricultural outputs. Because urban labor markets could not absorb these new city dwellers, they remained underemployed and concentrated in residential slums and shantytowns (Davis and Golden 1954; Sovani 1969).[4] This explanation was particularly influential in India, especially after Indian anthropologist N. K. Bose published a more Marxist variant of this thesis in the mid-1960s. Bose (1965) argued that Calcutta—and, by extension, other Indian cities—had appeared prematurely, in advance of the industrial revolution that would have naturally facilitated urbanization and urban growth. Bose contended that this premature character was manifest in the social structure of Indian cities, which more closely resembled the traditional village in which caste, religion, and ethnicity were more consequential than social class. Even as Bose's thesis remained influential, important studies of Indian slums in the 1970s questioned their premodern character by demonstrating the presence of capitalist institutions and modern ways of life (Desai and Pillai 1972; Lynch 1974; Wiebe 1975; Rao and Rao 1991). With a new focus on the internal dynamics of Indian slums, the emphasis had shifted from the causes of slum formation to the social forms found within, and slums came to be viewed as an inevitable feature of the postcolonial urban landscape.

Many of these inward-looking studies reinforced the notion that slums and squatter settlements were products of government ineptitude and political corruption. Like Turner's work on self-help communities, studies of political patronage and power brokers demonstrated the social forms and institutions developed to overcome bureaucratic neglect (Lemarchand and Legg 1972; Scott 1972; Handleman 1975; Scott 1976; Frankel 1980). These studies, rooted in classic sociological theories of exchange, highlighted the brokers who connect the urban poor with land, services, information, and security. Howard Handelman's study of Santiago's squatter settlements, for example, demonstrated these dynamics. He noted that "because the *campamento* is somewhat removed from the existing sociopolitical order and lacks basic municipal services, its inhabitants develop their own civic institutions to deal with a variety of daily problems—maintenance of law and order, criminal justice, housing, local administration and the like" (1975, 40). Beyond simply filling the gaps left by municipal oversight, this research also demonstrated that formal political systems became deeply enmeshed in these exchanges. Slums in the Indian context are frequently referred to as "vote banks" for the ready repositories of political power they provide to elected officials in exchange for these basic services.[5] Suggesting that local politicians protect their constituents' interests for the sake of their own political survival, the vote bank is often invoked to explain the presence and resilience of slums (Benjamin 2008; Ramachandran 2003).

More recently, studies of urban informality, much of it conducted in a postcolonial or subaltern framework, have also demonstrated that informal and illegal habitation can be rational responses—and even overt acts of resistance—to administrative failure (Chakrabarty 1992; Kaviraj 1997; Dhareshwar and Srivatsan 1996; Chatterjee 2004; Roy and AlSayyad 2004; Benjamin 2008; Bayat 2009). Characterizing squatting and slum formation as examples of the "quiet encroachment of the ordinary," much of this work reveals the oppression that the state's formal rules can pose for the urban poor (Bayat 1997). Partha Chatterjee (2004), for example, has argued that the Indian state withholds substantive citizenship rights by limiting legal access to housing and basic services. Chatterjee presents the problem as a vicious circle: deep inequalities preclude the urban poor from acting within liberal legal frameworks and compel them to seek unauthorized shelter in slums and in squatter settlements. Yet on account of their legal transgressions, the poor are criminalized and can justifiably be denied equal treatment under the law. Chatterjee demonstrates that their political engagements and participation in the political system (or "political society," as he terms it) become cast as subversive acts. Similarly, Solomon Benjamin (2008) has referred to such actions as "occupancy urbanism," characterizing the extralegal appropriation of land for housing and commercial activity as conscious acts of resistance, designed, in part, to undermine the ambitions of capital. While these studies differ in their interpretations of government's motivations—with some arguing that the state is directly aligned with the interests of capital against the poor, and others demonstrating a more benign form of administrative neglect—the slum is consistently treated as a product of government failure.

The narrative I present here of Dharavi's formation and emergence as a slum builds on these studies, but seeks to explain this government failure and why slums were allowed to proliferate in the first place. In doing so, this account demonstrates the ways in which city administrators treated slum settlements with supportive neglect, actions that supported and were supported by Bombay's industrial elite. While some measures were taken to construct worker housing—first by the private sector in the late nineteenth and early twentieth centuries, and then by various municipal committees and trusts in the 1920s and 1930s, and by the newly formed state government at the time of independence—these efforts were undermined by a lack of political support and insufficient financial resources. Instead, the workers' housing needs were met primarily through the government's tolerance for illegal housing construction on public and some privately owned lands. While the support of administrators and politicians was certainly bought with money and political patronage, the low-cost solution that squatting provided to this critical problem facing the growing industrial city can also explain the state's willful ignorance of slum formation.

Industrial Developments

In contrast to Bose's classic "premature metropolis" thesis, Bombay's growth and development are very much rooted in industrialization. With a profitable shipping trade well established by the 1850s, this decade is

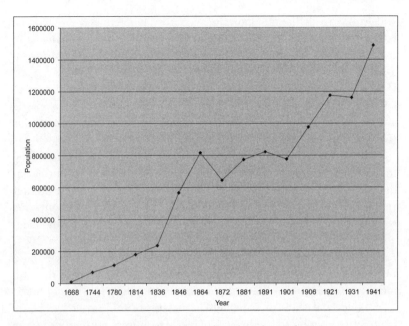

Bombay's population growth throughout the colonial period. Source: Government of Bombay 1946.

usually identified as the start of Bombay's industrial development and its dramatic population growth. The city's first mechanized cotton textile mill was built in 1854, and by the end of that decade, dozens more textile mills had been built across the city (Dwivedi and Mehotra 2001). The textile industry expanded rapidly in the 1860s, when the U.S. Civil War cut off English imports of North American cotton. Lancaster and Manchester turned to Bombay and its mills to provide short staple cotton and processed cloth. The city's textile factories and the auxiliary industries they spurred expanded rapidly. Although demand dropped sharply after the end of the Civil War, when North American cotton was again more readily available, the completion of the Suez Canal in 1869 situated Bombay in the virtual center of Euro-Asian trading networks and further fueled the city's growth.

Mirroring this emerging economic position, Bombay's population grew dramatically in this period. A census, taken at the height of the Bombay cotton boom in 1864, enumerated the city's population at over 800,000 (Kosambi 1986). Population estimates in nineteenth-century Bombay vary widely, due to the large number of migratory laborers and the periodic influx of famine victims, but with an estimated 180,000 people living in the city in 1814, it appears that Bombay's population increased four-and-a-half-fold in just fifty years (Government of Bombay 1946). After the U.S. Civil War ended and Bombay fell into economic recession, the population declined. But by the 1880s, more than one hundred new weaving and spinning mills were in operation and migrants were again returning (Dwivedi and Mehotra 2001; D'Monte 2002).

In 1867 the municipality built three slaughterhouses, or abattoirs, on the northern shore of the Mahim Creek, in the suburban town of Bandra (Government of Bombay 1882). With available land and ample water supplies across the creek in the village of Dharavi, a Parsi merchant soon set up a leather tannery in Dharavi to process and tan the animal hides and facilitate their sale and distribution (Dwivedi and Mehotra 2001; Rajayashree 1986). Other tanneries were soon built in Dharavi, and a thriving leather industry developed. Describing the activities of the Municipal Abattoirs, the 1882 *Gazetteer of Bombay City and Island* notes, "The hides and skins of slaughtered animals are sold either by private contract or auction to the highest bidder. The buyers are European and native merchants, or Dharavi tanners" (Government of Bombay 1882, 20). In the late nineteenth century, a series of health and sanitary measures were enacted by the municipality, and it was determined that industrial activities and "dangerous trades" should be kept out of South Bombay. Tanning, in particular, "which was considered to be highly polluting, was to be located in [the] distant tannery town [of Dharavi]" (Dossal 1991, 202). These measures—among the first zoning and land-use regulations enacted in Bombay—designated the village of Dharavi as a tannery town and concentrated most leather processing activities in this area. Soon migrants began settling in Dharavi, mostly Muslims and lower-caste Hindus from the southern state of Tamil Nadu (Lynch 1974, 1979; Sharma 2000). In the 1890s, Tamilian Muslims settled in Dharavi and established many of the area's early tanneries. As Desai and Pillai (1972, 44) recount, "The first batch, it appears, came in bullock carts from Tirunelveli to Sholapur, and then proceeded to Bombay." They were soon followed by low-caste Hindus from the district of Tirunelveli, including members of the Adi-Davida, Chakkilian, Pallan, Paraiyan, and Nadar subcastes who found immediate work in Dharavi's tanneries and related leather processing enterprises (Rajayashree 1986). So many people migrated from this particular South Indian district that Dharavi came to be known in some circles as "Tirunelveli North" (Clothey 2006).

During the population boom in the second half of the nineteenth century, what we now understand as slums first emerged in Bombay. Local observers in the mid-1860s observed that "wretched rows of *cadjan* (thatched) huts" were "hastily assembled by migrants to the city close to their places of work" (quoted by Chandavarkar 1994, 36). The housing situation grew severe over the next several decades, even as *chawls*, or single-room tenements, were being constructed by factory owners, municipal building committees, and private entrepreneurs to house the city's growing workforce. With an inadequate supply of worker housing constructed in this period, labor historian Rajnarayan Chandavarkar (1994, 180) explains that "some of the inhabitants of the island lived not in chawls, but in huts put together with dry coconut or date palm leaves, or sheds 'built of corrugated iron, empty kerosene tins, wood, etc.'" Meanwhile, these settlements of huts (or slums) were not evenly distributed in the city but were found in the 1901 census to be concentrated in the outlying districts of Mahim, Worli, and Sion, adjacent to the tannery town of Dharavi (Chandavarkar 1994; Dossal 1991).

Housing the Industrial City

Given the population growth and establishment of new industrial and commercial enterprises, the city's social geography and land-use patterns were undergoing significant change in the late 1800s. The strict division that had once been maintained between the European residences in the Fort area and the "native town" began to break down, as pressures for land and housing were beginning to affect all Bombay residents (Chandavarkar 1994; Dossal 1991). Land shortages in the southern part of the city prompted massive engineering projects, including efforts to reclaim low-lying coastal lands from the sea. Through waves of land reclamation projects in the late nineteenth century, "More than four square miles of valuable land [were added] to the southern half of the island" (Dossal 1991, 219). While much of this land was used for commercial purposes, such as docks, warehouses, railways, and roads, additional reclamations in the Back Bay were conceived of primarily as an effort to bolster the supply of housing for the wealthy (Chandavarkar 1994; Dossal 1991). As the southern parts of Bombay were becoming more exclusive, although less segregated along racial and ethnic lines, the northern parts of the island city, including the areas around Dharavi, had become an industrial landscape of factories, tanneries, and workshops, interspersed with chawls, rooming houses, and makeshift hutments for the workers.

Given Bombay's high land prices, pushed upward by the limited supply of land, property development became a profitable commercial activity in the late nineteenth century (Chandavarkar 1994). Many of these land investors, including the owners of factories, built private residential tenements, or chawls, as well as the shops and religious institutions that would anchor central Bombay's burgeoning working-class neighborhoods (Hazareesingh 2001; D'Monte 2002). These neighborhoods today, particularly those in the area referred to as *Girangaon*, or "village of mills," are looked upon nostalgically as bastions of civic engagement and a rising working-class consciousness. But even at the time they were built, these neighborhoods were severely overcrowded, with poorly constructed facilities (Chandavarkar 1994; Menon and Adarkar 2004; D'Monte 2002; Desai and Pillai 1972). As one concerned municipal official remarked in the early twentieth century:

> Ordinary chawl-builders generally succeeded in making a good
> profit from the capital spent on their chawls by adopting a very low
> standard of sanitation and economizing in building materials and
> supervision. . . . A private chawl-owner overcrowds his land with
> chawls, and many rooms consequently get far too little light. (quoted
> by Chandavarkar 1994, 178)

Most of this construction activity was led by the private sector, and very little government involvement took place in either housing construction or land-use planning in this period. A seven-member Board of Conservancy had been established in the mid-1840s to oversee civic works projects, including housing construction (Pinto and Pinto 2005; Dossal 1991). Despite this charge, the board—which comprised the senior magistrate of police as well as justices of both European and native origin—had no access to the municipal fund, which included revenue from taxes, fines, and licensing. The municipal fund was administered by the justice of the peace, who was usually selected from among "the city's most favored magnates" and wielded considerable influence on behalf of the city's commercial and industrial elite (Chandavarkar 1994, 28). Throughout the second half of the nineteenth century, the public sector's ability to carry out civic works projects, including new housing construction, was hamstrung by this conflict between the city's capitalist classes and its civil servants (Pinto and Pinto 2005; Chandavarkar 1994). While municipal administrators advocated for broad-reaching civic works projects and housing construction, the city's business elite pushed to maintain the status quo, in which taxes remained low, landowners could profit from the construction of private chawls, and workers could at least find accommodations in makeshift dwellings on the city's ample supply of land to the north (Dossal 1991). Housing concerns came to the fore, however, in the 1890s when the plague broke out across the city. The epidemic created a new sense of urgency about the city's inadequate housing conditions, given that it "not only disrupted the city's commerce but also brought the threat of disease and death to the doorsteps of the rich" (Chandavarkar 1994, 176). Although, as political scientists Marina Pinto and David Pinto (2005) point out, the Bombay government was well aware of the unsanitary conditions of the city even before the plague, it became the catalyst for the creation of the Bombay Improvement Trust in 1898. The trust was charged with improving the conditions of the city's overcrowded neighborhoods and constructing housing for the working classes, in addition to laying roads and overseeing the ongoing land reclamation projects (Pinto and Pinto 2005). Inaugurating the trust, its first president declared:

> We have the city filled, nay, crammed with people of various nationalities, creeds, and castes with their ancient customs, habits and beliefs which make it extremely difficult to deal with them under circumstances of such an epidemic as the plague. . . . In looking for a remedy, we must look for one to be permanent and continuous, striking at the root of evil, viz., insanitary areas and crowded localities. (quoted in Government of Bombay 1946, 159)

Consistent with this diagnosis of the problem, the trust demolished considerably more housing than it constructed in the first two decades of its existence (Chandavarkar 1994; Hazareesingh 2001).[6] Meanwhile, it invested significant resources in the construction of middle-class neighborhoods in the then suburban districts of Matunga, Sion, and Wadala.

The trust's diverted agenda has been attributed to the receding threat of the plague in the first few years of the twentieth century, as well as to the influence that the city's business elites had over its agenda (Chandavarkar 1994; Hazareesingh 2001). The trust has been characterized as "an instrument of the city's businessmen" (Chandavarkar 1994, 177), as its board comprised "leading members of the Bombay Chamber of Commerce [and] the Millowners Association" (Hazareesingh 2001, 240). Despite its failure to adequately address the city's dramatic housing shortfall, the chawls that the trust did construct before it was dissolved in 1925 are still standing in central Bombay and continue to house thousands of the city's working-class residents. These activities were carried on by the Bombay Development Department (BDD), which was established in 1920 with much the same charge as the trust. The BDD constructed hundreds of chawls in the areas around the city's textile mills, most of which are still standing today (Desai and Pillai 1972).

While municipal administrators recognized the need for worker housing throughout this period, their efforts were ultimately undermined by the city's business interests. Private developers and factory owners were profiting from the limited supply of worker chawls, while landowners and the city's elite resisted efforts to levy taxes and spend from the municipal coffers to expand housing construction. When public construction was initiated, as in the case of the Back Bay Reclamation and the Bombay Improvement Trust, these efforts did more to expand housing for the wealthy than they did to address the needs of the poor. The growing numbers of poor and working-class Bombayites, meanwhile, sought shelter in working-class districts—usually in makeshift structures—in the northward reaches of the island city.

A Working-Class Enclave

In this manner, Dharavi's population expanded rapidly. A census conducted in 1864—immediately before the municipal slaughterhouses were built in Bandra—estimated a population of 992 residents in the fishing village of Dharavi (Dossal 1991). In the mid-1940s the government of Bombay estimated Dharavi's population at around 40,000 people (Government of Bombay 1946). Naturally lowering water levels in the Mahim Creek, paired with garbage dumped along its banks, provided solid ground for the homes of Dharavi's leather workers but also for workers in the city's factories, shipping ports, and other industrial enterprises (Lynch 1979; Sharma 2000).

Given Dharavi's available land, as well as the existing concentration of polluting industries and "dangerous trades," the area was selected as the resettlement site for the Kumbhars, a pottery-making community from Gujarat, in the early 1930s. Already relocated by the municipality several times before, the Kumbhars posed a problem from an urban planning perspective, due to their needs for ample space and water and the considerable pollution produced by their kilns (Lynch 1979; Sharma 2000). Anthropologist Owen Lynch explained:

> Before coming to [Dharavi], the potters had been moved from four other locations in Bombay. Each time firing-oven smoke watered the eyes of nonpotter neighbors and occasioned the moves. Smoke remains a problem and there is talk of a move once again because it now

billows over the nearby hospital and because space is at a premium in the colony. (1979, 339)

The Kumbhars first settled in Bombay in the late 1870s when droughts ravaged their place of origin in the Saurashtra District of Gujarat (Sharma 2000). Once the Kumbhars settled in Bombay, they set up their first colony, or Kumbharwada, in the burgeoning industrial district of Dadar. Eventually they were relocated to the neighborhood of Sion. In 1932 the municipality moved the 319 families that then formed the Kumbhar community to Dharavi, when their land in Sion was taken for the construction of a British army camp (Sharma 2000). The part of Dharavi that would become Kumbharwada was sparsely populated at the time. The Kumbhars were issued leases by the municipality and assessed land grant taxes for their house plots (Lynch 1979).[7] With money raised from some of the city's wealthy philanthropic families in the early 1930s, the Kumbhars built three narrow roads, or *vaadis*, with houses and work spaces lining each side (Sharma 2000; Lynch 1979).

By the early 1940s Dharavi was part fishing village, part industrial township, and part working-class residential enclave. A report published in 1944 by the Rotary Club of Bombay and the Tata Institute of Social Sciences described this strange mix. The report divided Dharavi into five distinct settlements, defined primarily by the ethnic and industrial character of the area: Koliwada, Kumbharwada, Kala Killa (or Black Fort),[8] Matunga Labour Camp, and Dharavi (Desai and Pillai 1972). It also described the varying quality of Dharavi's housing stock between these settlements, which ranged from "the dwellings of the fishermen [which were] the best

Occupation	Kumbhars	Adi-Dravida	Muslims	Total
Dock worker	–	18.3	35.5	16.4
Factory worker	2.6	58.3	8.4	21.5
Distillery worker	–	–	13.5	4.1
Construction, laborer	1.3	6.6	18.5	8.2
Potter	75.0	–	–	29.2
Truck driver	1.3	5.0	3.3	3.0
Clerical worker	2.6	1.6	–	1.5
Carpenter	5.2	–	–	2.0
Tailor	2.6	3.3	1.6	2.5
Vendor, shopkeeper	2.6	5.0	16.9	7.6
Other	1.3	1.6	1.6	1.5
Unemployed	5.2	–	–	2.0

Occupational composition (by percentage) of three of Dharavi's largest communities in the early 1970s. Source: Lynch 1979.

among the lot, as the walls were plastered and roofs tiled" to "chawls built with corrugated iron sheets, and some single storeyed municipal chawls" (Desai and Pillai 1972, 44).

As noted in the report, the houses in Koliwada were (and still are) some of the nicest homes in Dharavi. Amid the gradual transformation of the area, Koliwada had been able to maintain some of the character of the original settlement, and its longtime residents had made significant investments in the construction of their homes and community buildings. Journalist Kalpana Sharma, who has written extensively about Koliwada, estimates that 80 percent of the Koli families living there today are descendants of Dharavi's original Koli community. Until the mid-1960s, when the pollution in the Mahim Creek rendered their catch inedible, most of Dharavi's Kolis still earned their living by fishing and crabbing as they had for thousands of years. Kalpana Sharma describes their "unique style of fishing":

> They would take on lease fishing rights which allowed them to build a dam across the creek. At high tide, the fish would enter and would then be trapped in the dammed section. At low tide, fishermen would wade into the water with nets and catch the fish alive. (2000, 46)

In addition to fishing, the Kolis also brewed a distinct blend of country liquor, made from the salty waters of the Mahim.

Throughout the twentieth century, the Kolis were joined by labor migrants arriving from all over the country. An explosion at the docks in 1944 sent many of Bombay's displaced dock workers to Dharavi in search of housing (Rajyashree 1986). Around the same time, the area known as Matunga Labor Camp came to be settled primarily by members of the low-caste Valmiki community from the North Indian state of Harayana. Many of the Valmikis found employment with the municipality, primarily in the area of garbage collection (Sharma 2000). The residents reflected the city's broad mix of industry, shipping and port labor, municipal services, construction trades, and commerce.

Anthropologist Owen Lynch (1979) noted this occupational diversity while conducting surveys with three of Dharavi's most prominent communities in the early 1970s: the Muslims, the Adi-Davidas (low-caste Hindus from Tamil Nadu), and the Kumbhars. After pottery making, the largest number of people in his sample worked in factories (one-fifth) and in the city's dockyards (one-sixth). He also found many members of these communities engaged in more middle-class professions, such as clerical work and shopkeeping. While Lynch used these findings to counter the "premature metropolis" thesis and academic and popular depictions of slums as dominated by premodern or irrational social forms, his findings also reveal that many Dharavi residents were engaged in professional activities outside of the slum. While it was typically presented as marginal to mainstream occupational and residential structures, this occupational profile demonstrates that Dharavi has long housed a wide swath of the city's working classes.

Developing Dharavi, Part One

Dharavi's character as a working-class neighborhood was recognized by those who produced Bombay's first master plan in the late 1940s. The *Outline of the Master Plan for Greater Bombay*—drafted by Nilkanth Modak, the chief engineer of the Bombay Municipal Corporation (BMC), and American architect and town planner Albert Mayer in late 1947—represents the first effort to impose rational planning on Dharavi by proposing that it be redeveloped as a working-class residential enclave. Lamenting the dearth of housing for middle- and lower-income groups, Modak and Mayer recommended that a number of residential neighborhoods be created in areas in which dense pockets of worker housing were already located. Committed to the idea, prevalent in planning circles at the time, that residential and industrial uses should be distinct and spatially segregated, these planners emphasized Dharavi's residential character over its production activities. Although the "Dharavi Layout" failed to garner the requisite political support for implementation, this experience demonstrates that the bureaucracy was not wholly neglectful and that state interventions have, in fact, been attempted in the city's slums since independence.

The idea for a Bombay Master Plan was proposed by the Post-War Development Committee in June 1945 when it met to discuss the problems of town planning, housing provision, and traffic congestion that had again become major concerns for municipal administrators and civic elites (Government of Bombay 1946). Nilkanth Modak was charged with drafting the framing document, in which he recommended that, given the small number of trained urban planners working in India at the time, an international consultant be hired to aid in drafting the city's first comprehensive master plan.[9] In January 1947 the committee extended an invitation to Albert Mayer[10] to discuss the possibility of working with Modak on the master plan project. Mayer visited Bombay in March 1947 to meet with Modak and conduct a preliminary survey of Bombay's planning resources.[11] Mayer and Modak worked together for the next five months

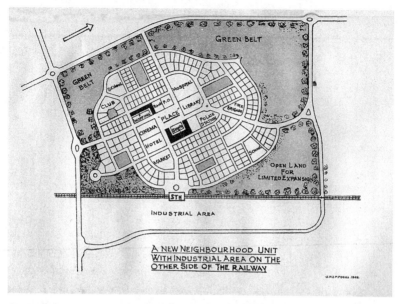

The layout for a typical neighborhood envisioned in *Outline of the Master Plan for Greater Bombay* (Government of Bombay 1946).

and, by the end of 1947, had produced the document known as *Outline of the Master Plan for Greater Bombay.*

The plan consisted of recommendations for both the island city and the broader metropolitan Bombay region, including a proposal for an underground railway, parks and playgrounds, shopping districts, housing, and several residential neighborhoods. The plan emphasized the neighborhood as the appropriate organizational unit for Bombay's urban renewal and identified a small handful of neighborhood sites to be created around the city. Justifying the neighborhood as a "modern solution" to the problems posed by nineteenth-century city building, Modak and Mayer noted:

> This principle of the neighborhood has been accepted and seems from experience in western countries to offer not only the best functional solution but also the best social and spiritual solution to City Living. Socially, it offers a cohesive organism which effectively breaks down the large amorphous City of the 19th century and of the present into constituent elements of a size where the individual is not lost, where somewhat the same social stimuli and controls prevail as prevailed in the smaller towns and villages from which the people originally came and in the case of Bombay came, to a large extent, only fairly recently. (1948, 26)

Grounded in the principle of a neighborhood unit, tracing back to Clarence Perry and Otto Koeningsberger, the plan proposed that a strict separation be maintained between industrial activities and residential neighborhoods, with "natural boundaries" like rivers or railway tracks providing the barriers between them (Vidyarthi 2010). Neighborhoods were to be surrounded by green space and anchored by social and cultural institutions, like schools, hospitals, social clubs, cinemas, and a neighborhood square (Government of Bombay 1946). Modak and Mayer identified the ideal neighborhood size at around two thousand residents.

The plan proposed Dharavi's development in line with this model. Mayer and Modak recognized that the Dharavi layout posed significant technical challenges, due to both the soft, marshy ground on which Dharavi sat, which would require landfill before construction could begin, and the concentration of highly polluting industries that would have to be relocated before a residential neighborhood could be developed. Even so, they identified Dharavi's development as a significant priority due to the dearth of adequate worker housing across the city and to the health concerns posed by Dharavi's polluting industries and inadequate basic services.[12]

The Dharavi layout proposed that a majority of the area be used for low- and middle-income housing and the remainder be set aside for public parks and recreation grounds. Acknowledging that the desperate needs for housing required that Dharavi hold many more people than envisioned for an ideal neighborhood, the plan recommended that approximately seventy-six hundred families should live in Dharavi, half of which would be lower-income families and the other half would be from middle- and upper-income groups. With the Post-War Committee estimating Dharavi's population at around forty thousand people, it was likely that alternative accommodations would have to be found for many of Dharavi's families, particularly if the ideal mix of lower-, middle-, and upper-income residents was to be achieved. Furthermore, with the family identified as the basic household unit, the plan overlooked the many single men living in Dharavi's boarding-houses or renting space in others' homes. Modak and Mayer acknowledged that 50 percent low-income residents was not "socially desirable," but they determined that such a high percentage was necessary "because so little vacant land is available and so much housing for this group is needed" (Modak and Mayer 1948, 27). If other areas could be identified, they noted, then the proportion of Dharavi's low-income families should be reduced.

The plan recommended that all of Dharavi's current industrial activities be removed, along with manufacturing facilities in other parts of the island city, and be relocated to outlying areas of Greater Bombay. The plan stated firmly, "The tanning industry will definitely have to leave Bombay Island in the first phase leaving [the] Dharavi area for development" (Modak and Mayer 1948, 12). The tanning activities would be relocated to what they referred to as "a relatively insulated location on the north side of Trombay," adjacent to the *kutchrapatty*, or municipal garbage dump (Modak and Mayer 1948, 12). In the second and third phases of the plan, all other industries would be removed from the city of Bombay, thereby freeing up at least five hundred acres of land for housing, roads, and parks. The plan did not explicitly identify the need to resettle Dharavi's potting community in Kumbharwada. But because the Kumbhars made up just a small percentage of Dharavi's population at the time, their polluting activities likely escaped the attention of the planners.

Modak and Mayer strongly recommended that parklands be integrated into Dharavi, given the dearth of green space in the island city and the physical, social, and spiritual benefits that they noted were associated with parks and open space.[13] Specifically, they proposed that the area along the shore of the Mahim Creek be designated as a "sea-wall park."[14] Modak and Mayer felt that all neighborhoods, but especially those housing working-class families, should be "insulated by a green strip from the surrounding through-roads" (Modak and Mayer 1948, 26). The plan also proposed the improvement of the sanitation infrastructure, including the construction of a sewage management facility in the northeast corner of Dharavi, outside of the proposed neighborhood boundaries.

Although Dharavi was just one of several neighborhood layouts identified in the plan, the area had a prominent placement in the master plan document. Dharavi exemplified Bombay's virtual absence of land-use planning with its organically developed districts that located leather tanning operations next to municipal chawls next to a fishing village, as well as its poorly built roads, dearth of green space, and inadequate sanitation facilities. The broader problems that Modak and Mayer identified in the city found perfect representation in Dharavi. Furthermore, the area's central location, as well as its natural boundaries of the city's railway lines and Mahim Creek, made it an appropriate place to intervene. Mayer in particular felt that the government could make a meaningful intervention in Dharavi and establish a model for planning in the Indian city.[15]

The draft master plan was completed in late 1947, but official government approval was yet to be garnered. Although both the master plan and the Dharavi Neighborhood Layout were well received by the BMC, the provincial government of Bombay, which possessed the exclusive authority and financial resources needed for implementation, was reluctant to aprove it. Although official explanations for the government's reluctance were not forthcoming, other priorities seemed more pressing for the newly independent state. By early 1948 Albert Mayer had begun working on the master plan project for Chandigarh, the capital city for the newly established state of Punjab, but he continued to campaign vigorously for the implementation of the Bombay Master Plan, writing letters to elected officials, civil society members, and municipal administrators.

Recognizing that politicians likely found the plan too vast and unwieldy to undertake all at once, Mayer and Modak discussed ways to narrow its scope. The plan offered a clear set of recommendations both for improving conditions in the island city and undertaking a broader, regionwide development strategy. As he campaigned for state-level support, Mayer emphasized the need to focus first on the central city and, particularly, on the Dharavi layout. He felt that regionwide development should be undertaken only after the inner city's most pressing needs were addressed, including the needs for low- and middle-income housing and the development of green space.[16] These recommendations put him at odds with state-level politicians and the committee that had solicited his participation, including Modak. The conflict was revealed in a letter Modak wrote to Mayer in February 1948:

> Development of the city proper will be deferred until such a time as adequate accommodation is provided in the suburban area for spilling over the population and necessary funds are forthcoming. In the present financial state of the corporation, I am afraid such redevelopment schemes within the city will have to be held over for quite a long time and it would be premature to and unrealistic to attempt to estimate for any such works. I have therefore concentrated on developing the region outside the city limits and worked out the approximate cost of the same in various stages. . . . The Committee is also not inclined to mix up the development of the City proper with that of the Suburban area as the liability for the former rests with the Corporation whereas that for the latter mostly with the Provincial Government.[17]

Citing both financial barriers and jurisdictional constraints, Modak informed Mayer that the plan's city-specific components were a lower priority, due to the lower likelihood of implementation. Mayer responded to Modak that they should continue to advocate for implementation. "I don't see how we can expect to get funds if we don't press for them in our recommendations," Mayer wrote. "Lack of funds is a relative matter, depending on what expenditures are considered more important than what others."[18] Over the next year, Mayer continued his campaigns for housing construction and increased open space throughout Bombay, writing letters and making personal pleas to municipal administrators and local elites. Although his letters remained optimistic, they dropped off sharply by the early 1950s when it became clear that comprehensive planning in the city of Bombay would not be carried out.

Mayer and Modak's master plan would be revisited a decade later by a committee charged with the problems of regional development, but the Dharavi layout was largely forgotten, even by planners and civic administrators working on Dharavi today. Meanwhile, this sordid history demonstrates the prevailing power of the status quo. Five years earlier, the Post-War Development Committee expressed a consensus that land use and planning were among the most pressing concerns facing the city of Bombay. But these issues seemed less urgent by the early 1950s. Around this time, districts like Dharavi were becoming labeled "slums" and were increasingly addressed with "slum clearance" programs (as discussed in chapter 2), rather than through comprehensive planning efforts. Meanwhile, planning endeavors across the Bombay region were mired in conflicts over appropriate spatial strategies.

Spatial Conflicts

The first major attempt to develop Dharavi became embroiled in the city's main spatial conflict: the debate over whether more appropriate planning interventions lay in the city or in its hinterlands. This debate would not only define development and land use throughout Greater Bombay but it would also give shape to the city's slums and enable Dharavi's continued transition into one. In the second half of the twentieth century, most planners working in Bombay turned their attention to the outlying districts of the region, including the planned city of New Bombay, or Navi Mumbai. Meanwhile, the ongoing practice of supportive neglect continued in inner-city "neighborhoods" like Dharavi.

As Albert Mayer found when he attempted to elicit support for implementing the Bombay-specific aspects of the master plan, Bombay lacked what sociologists now call a "development consensus" or a "growth coalition." Although Bombay was home to India's major industrial and commercial enterprises, the private sector had been more concerned with developing a national industrial policy in the years immediately following independence than they were with the more proximate concerns of urban planning and housing construction (Chibber 2003; Pedersen 2000). Because industry's needs for worker housing and basic urban infrastructures were generally being met by the haphazard and piecemeal solutions that had sustained them for the previous century, the city's industrial and commercial elite remained virtually silent on issues of town planning through the 1950s.

Meanwhile, Bombay's growing cadres of engineers and municipal administrators were becoming increasingly vocal about the need to deconcentrate the desperately crowded island of Bombay. Following the specific recommendations in the Modak and Mayer plan, the development strategies and proposed solutions to Bombay's spatial deficits were beginning to fall along two lines. On one side were groups advocating centrality and promoting downtown development in South Bombay. On the other side were those lamenting the city's congestion and pushing for development outside of the city center. With these factions working at cross-purposes, this debate ultimately undermined both efforts and hindered attempts at comprehensive planning in the postindependence period (Banerjee-Guha 1995; Shaw 2004). Among the de-concentration faction, the idea of developing satellite cities or alternative commercial districts to reduce congestion in South Bombay was gaining traction. This idea, first proposed in the Modak-Mayer master plan, was revived by a state advisory committee convened in the early 1960s (Shaw 2004). The state government decided to take action on two of the committees' proposals. One of the projects was a business complex to be built on the north shore of the Mahim Creek between the inner-ring suburbs of Bandra and Kurla, directly opposite the river from Dharavi (Banerjee-Guha 1995). The second project was the development of a new city on the east side of Bombay's harbor that would be connected to South Bombay by a causeway. This satellite city, to be called New Bombay, was proposed as a solution to the industrial, commercial, and residential density on the island city (Banerjee-Guha 1995; Shaw 2004).

Although the city's business community had not intervened in earlier debates about housing construction and comprehensive planning, industrial interests, represented primarily by the Maharashtra Economic Development Council (MEDC), played a significant role in the planning for New Bombay. The MEDC, like many of the professional architects and engineers involved in the planning process, generally favored "the idea of building a new city as opposed to patching up the old" (Shaw 2004, 74). While early plans for New Bombay proposed relocating all of Bombay's industrial activity to the new satellite city (as the Modak-Mayer plan had recommended), the business community voiced strong opposition to this idea. Remarking on the opposition, administrator N. R. Inamdar wrote in the late 1970s:

Excepting certain sections of industry, the public response to the proposal . . . was in general appreciative. . . . In Bombay [the industrialists] did not agree with the Committee's proposal about the transfer of long-established industries like textiles as well as heavy and light industries from the island to the mainland, so also about the location of future industrial expansion in centres away from over-crowded areas. (quoted in Shaw 2004, 79)

In the end, the support of industrialists was secured by employing soft language in the plan, recommending instead "that no new industry should be permitted on Bombay and Salsette islands, except for the service industry and those existing prior to 1957, and that 'the motive power for shifting industries out of Greater Bombay should be a mixture of persuasion and incentives'" (Shaw 2004, 76). The buy-in of Bombay's industrialists, which proved essential for garnering the state politicians' support for the plan, was ultimately secured by not requiring any specific action from them.

As construction began in New Bombay, the decision was made to not patch up the island city or its dense residential and industrial enclaves like Dharavi. In the midst of the New Bombay planning process, a proposal was made to "shift the tanneries in Dharavi and the slaughter houses and animal yards from Bandra" (Shaw 2004, 82), and eventually both were relocated to the eastern suburb of Denonar, not far from the location near the *kutchra-patty*, or municipal garbage dump, originally recommended by Modak and Mayer. But for the time being, Dharavi retained its particular mix of heavily polluting industries and dense working-class residential quarters. Although it may seem appropriate to attribute these missed opportunities to improve conditions in Dharavi to administrative and political failures, or to "bureaucratic neglect," the causes of deteriorating urban conditions in central city neighborhoods, including the proliferation of slums, were clearly more complex. On one hand, planners' efforts to promote housing construction and open spaces in Bombay were undermined by the prevailing planning wisdom at the time. On this point, a developer currently working in Bombay characterized this wisdom as willful ignorance:

In the 1970s, they decided that the city should only accommodate seven million people. . . . So they decided they would not provide the infrastructure to take care of the growing population. They did not think that there was a need to provide affordable housing, and there was no need to provide easy access for commuting out of the city.[19]

Second, the city's planning agencies faced structural constraints, including the administrative and fiscal division of the city and the suburbs identified in Modak's 1947 letter to Albert Mayer. With the municipal corporation bereft of funds, projects proposed within Bombay's city limits were more difficult to finance than those in the suburbs, which fell under the jurisdiction of the state or provincial government. Finally, the absence of a pro-development business community ultimately undermined efforts to address the city's dearth of housing and infrastructure. Although one might expect that industrialists and urban elites would be campaigning for investments in urban housing and infrastructure, this community continued to fear new taxes and regulations and was generally well served by the status quo. As a consequence, population growth continued and informal housing proliferated. As the city grew denser and living conditions in working-class enclaves like Dharavi continued to worsen, these areas became slums, both in the language of urban administration and in the minds of city residents.

Land, Liquor, and Dirty Politics

Dharavi's discursive transition to a slum—occurring sometime in the 1950s or 1960s—coincided with the term's entrance into India's urban lexicon and appearance in policy documents. Yet Dharavi's population growth, increasing density, and deteriorating conditions also contributed to the attachment of the label to the area. In 1946 the Post-War Development Committee had estimated the area's population at forty thousand; in 1978 anthropologist Owen Lynch cited an estimate of three hundred thousand. While both numbers are likely quite rough, given the difficulties of enumerating informal and illegal dwellings, they suggest that Dharavi's population may have increased by more than 600 percent in just thirty years. Throughout this period, labor migrants continued to settle in Dharavi, as existing residents brought their families and other relations and helped them secure housing and employment in the area.

Dharavi's particular governance arrangements and its openness to informal and illicit activities also helped facilitate its emergence as a slum. Using the pseudonym Shantinagar, Lynch made this link between Dharavi's perception as a slum and its illicit liquor trade in a 1974 article in *Economic and Political Weekly*. The area, he wrote,

> has the reputation for being one of the worst, if not the worst slums
> in Bombay. It is inhabited mainly by squatters from all over India.
> Much of the land is swampy but the squatters are slowly filling it in as
> their settlements creep across the area. Low-lying land is often flooded
> with black, swampy, garbage-laden water during the monsoon season.

> Perhaps it is this location which has made [Dharavi] notoriously
> famous for the many steaming stills which produce the bootleg liquor
> which whets many a thirsty tongue in dry Bombay. (Lynch 1974, 1657)

Dharavi's illicit liquor trade and the extralegal acquisition and development of land and housing were closely linked in this period, with both activities supported by a clientelistic political party structure and emerging
networks of organized crime groups.

Migration to the city increased rapidly in the aftermath of independence, placing even greater pressure on the city's deteriorating housing
stock and creating an opening for entrepreneurial criminal actors. The
partition of India and Pakistan, and the violence that erupted in its wake,
brought throngs of refugees and displaced persons to Bombay. Meanwhile,
the newly formed national government had initiated a strategy of state-
supported industrial development, and employment growth in Bombay's
factories was attracting workers from all over the country. The worker
housing built before independence was woefully inadequate, yet still little
new housing was being constructed by either the public or private sectors.
Recognizing an opportunity, enterprising "slumlords" began subdividing
open public and privately owned land and selling or renting out plots
to new migrants. Paternalistic community leaders amassed considerable
power in this manner by providing housing and basic services in Dharavi
and the city's other densely populated squatter settlements.

One entrepreneur who engaged in this type of land development in
Dharavi was Varadarajan Mudaliar, known locally as Vardhabhai. In
the 1950s Vardhabhai built a powerful criminal organization based on
the illicit production and sale of alcohol in Dharavi. Before prohibition
laws were enacted in Bombay in the late 1940s, alcohol had been produced legally—manufactured commercially and brewed traditionally by
members of Dharavi's Koli community. Once prohibition was enacted,
commercial alcohol production ceased and the Kolis had a virtual monopoly in this area. Yet they would soon face competition as members of
Dharavi's Tamil community entered into the illicit alcohol trade (Sharma
2000). By the early 1960s a group of Tamil liquor producers had emerged
as a powerful criminal force under the leadership of Vardhabhai. For over
twenty years, Vardhabhai ran the city's first and most powerful mafia organization out of Dharavi. Moving beyond liquor, Varadhabhai diversified
his activities with land dealings and the establishment of gambling dens
and brothels throughout the city. Reportedly a paternalistic community
leader, Vardhabhai sponsored social and religious festivals and established
informal governance structures in Dharavi.[20]

With few other policies in place to address the housing and basic needs of the growing population, public officials continued to ignore the proliferation of informal housing and illicit activities in Dharavi. The city and its local industries were thriving under this arrangement, and there was little immediate need to intervene. Meanwhile, Vardhabhai and other local *goondas*, or thugs, would work closely with local administrators to ensure that this policy vacuum remained open by registering the new residents to vote for local politicians and by paying bribes to police and officials in the BMC. Describing the role that Vardhabhai's organization played in Dharavi's growth in this period, a social worker explained to me:

> In Mukund Nagar [a settlement in Dharavi], Vardhabai's right-hand man, S. K. Ramaswamy, was in charge. . . . The goondas were in charge of small-scale criminal activities—land grabbing, selling plots. They would "catch the plots" and build huts with gunny bags. They would sell huts for five thousand to ten thousand. The BMC made a lot in hafta payments and worked closely with these goondas.[21]

As Dharavi expanded, so did Vardhabhai's organization, built in part on helping residents gain access to utilities and basic services. His men worked to establish illegal water and power connections, acquire ration cards for food and cooking gas, and get people out of jail and fines erased (SPARC 1998; in 2005). A longtime activist explains how water was accessed:

> They had to pay for water even though it was being given for free by the BMC. Goondas had a water tap in Kings Circle [an area two kilometers from Dharavi], and women would get up at four in the morning to get the water and carry it back. Getting water took five or six hours, and they had to pay money for it.[22]

With no water tap in Dharavi at the time, Vardhabhai's men appropriated the closest one in Kings Circle and charged residents for the basic service. While the arrangement was not ideal for the residents, they would not have had access to water without these enterprising, though hardly altruistic, goondas.

As has been well documented by researchers identifying similar patron-client networks in other locations, the ambiguity resulting from a neglectful state, corrupt enforcement, and otherwise powerless urban residents makes it less useful to consider these illegal acts in moral terms. Rather, such acts are situated within a broader set of survival strategies that depend—due to their dangerous and high-risk nature—on deep embeddedness in family and community networks. Although the relationships between patrons and clients are often inequitable and exploitative, these goondas provided Dharavi residents essential services in the absence of more legitimate alternatives. In exchange for the services, the criminal organizations strengthened their ties both to community networks and formal governance and political institutions. In Vardhabhai's case, these strengthened ties helped him build his liquor business and later expand into even more profitable gold and consumer-good smuggling in the 1960s and 1970s.

With neighborhood-level politicians working closely with Vardhabhai's organization and playing similar patronage roles themselves, the lines between goondas and political party representatives were blurry at best. Describing the services provided by officials with the Republican Party of India (RPI), a political party representing a broad federation of lower-caste groups, Owen Lynch discussed these arrangements:

> With help from the RPI corporators [city council members elected at the ward level], it is claimed that the Adi-Davidas chawls have been able to have water taps installed in their chawls, though at their own expense. Getting water taps in a squatter area is a big problem since most of them are there illegally. . . . Electrical connections have also been installed in many chawls through political connections and in 1970, while I was there, the RPI through its municipal corporator was able to have 10 street lamps installed. (1974, 1663)

Although these services would have been provided without charge or much fanfare in most of Bombay's municipal wards, the illegal nature of these Dharavi settlements gave electoral politics and the provision of basic municipal services a nefarious character.

> With the formal state having essentially abdicated its substantive authority over areas like Dharavi, power and sovereignty generally rested in the hands of community leaders who straddled the blurry lines between politics, instrumentalism, and criminality. The diffuse and highly localized nature of sovereignty in these areas has been recognized by political theorists, including Thomas Blom Hansen and Finn Stepputat (2005, 30), who note that "the locus [of] political authority [is] incarnated in the ubiquitous 'big men'—the tough self-made criminal-strongman-fixer-and-politician who increasingly dominate the political life in slums and townships." Meanwhile, the sovereignty of these big men is generally acknowledged within their "jurisdictions," but the absence of formal recognition means that their authority is frequently contested and must be renegotiated on a fairly regular basis.

Not only are organized crime groups and ward corporators engaged in this power struggle, but social workers and housing activists have served similar brokering functions in Dharavi; some have become "big men" in their own right. Since the early 1970s, throngs of community-based organizations, many of them affiliated with church groups, have emerged in Dharavi and sought to build their own constituencies. One of these groups, the People's Responsible Organisation for United Dharavi (PROUD), which remains part of the area's dense institutional landscape, first established itself by contesting the local authority held by Vardhab-hai's organization.[23]

This history was recounted to me by Santosh Singh, a community organizer with PROUD. Sitting just outside his small plastics recycling workshop in Dharavi's main industrial district, Santosh relayed how PROUD's founder, the late Rabial Mallick, went toe to toe with Vadhabhai over control of the Mukund Nagar settlement. After a lengthy discussion about the plastic scrap and recycling industries, Santosh began speaking about the conditions in Dharavi when he first arrived from the North Indian state of Haryana in the early 1970s. "Dharavi was a very stinky place . . . the worst area in the city," he explained.[24] He elaborated that the area had a very bad reputation. "There was a lot of crime and criminals in Dharavi, and people were scared to even come into Dharavi." It was around this time that Mallick, a community organizer from the Christian Institute for the Study of Religion and Society (CISRS) in Calcutta, came to Dharavi and began talking to the residents. Mallick went door to door talking to the people, Santosh explained, and he learned about their problems, including the absence of a water tap in Mukund Nagar and their dependence on Vardhabhai's goondas.

> Mallick and PROUD organized the people to demand water connections from the BMC. They worked to organize the women because they were the ones who were walking to get the water. PROUD recognized this problem, and they brought them to the ward officers to make their complaints there. Initially, the BMC was resistant, and there was confrontation and conflict. But eventually it was successful—the people's power prevailed—and the BMC put a water tap in Social Nagar.[25]

Santosh explained that the group's success in getting a water tap installed, paired with later successes in staving off demolitions in the early 1980s, altered the established political landscape in the settlement and ultimately diminished the influence of Vardhabhai and his associates. "After that, people made their demands to PROUD, and the social workers helped them solve their problems," he remarked. Although questions of sovereignty were far from settled, Mallick had become something of a big man—at least for the moment.

As in Howard Handleman's study of Santiago's *campamentos* or Partha Chattejee's analysis of "political society," the absence of legal recognition and a formal state presence has led to the establishment of alternative forms of power and authority in Dharavi. While some of these forms were grounded in the extractive paternalism of notorious crime bosses, others were amassed by church-based community organizers trained in the methods of Chicagoan Saul Alinsky. Yet while this informal sovereignty helped shape daily life in the settlement and entrench Dharavi in Bombay's economic and political landscape, it does not fully explain how the slum came to be. To explain Dharavi's emergence and transition to a slum, we must understand why the state chose to look the other way as unauthorized housing and businesses proliferated. Meanwhile, without the consistent presence of the state, power and sovereignty in Dharavi have remained diffuse. While big men like Vardhabhai have been able to consolidate power at certain historical moments, the fragmented nature of local sovereignty has hindered efforts to promote effective programmatic interventions in the settlement.

Making a Megaslum

A little more than a century after the municipal slaughterhouses were built in Bandra and Dharavi's first leather tannery was established, this sparsely populated fishing village had become "the largest slum in Asia."[26] Where this moniker came from is not clear, as its use is rarely accompanied by population enumerations of either Dharavi or comparable settlements across the continent.[27] Yet it is worn today as a mark of pride, as many of the residents I met in the course of my fieldwork boasted that they live in "Asia's largest slum." Largest, in this sense, seems to suggest prominence and notoriety more than demographics or land area.

The moniker appears to have been attached to Dharavi when a new superlative was needed to convey the extreme levels of population density, low quality of basic services, and degree of political entrenchment. Over this hundred-year period, Dharavi had grown into a dense settlement of at least half a million people, hailing from all over the Indian subcontinent, engaged in a multitude of industrial and commercial enterprises. Urban sprawl had stretched the city's boundaries farther northward, due, in part, to deliberate planning strategies of urban de-concentration, and Dharavi had become situated in the virtual center of Greater Bombay.

These developments are the product of decisions taking place at multiple levels+, from the nation to the neighborhood. Under a national program of state-supported industrialization, subsidized manufacturing units and related commercial enterprises attracted a steady flow of labor migrants. Meanwhile, a weak local state and an industrial elite that did not actively support public-sector infrastructure and housing improvements undermined the various proposals to address the housing shortfalls and absence of coordinated planning. The informal economy stepped in, turning housing provision and water and electricity connections into illicit commodities like alcohol during the time of prohibition. But beyond simply a story of how the informal became normal, this history also reveals how seemingly marginal settlements like Dharavi were, in fact, quite central to the economic and political life of the Indian city. Meanwhile, the intertwined development of the city and the slum foreshadows Dharavi's durability in the face of grand visions of master planners and empty promises to make Bombay slum-free.

CHAPTER TWO

State Interventions and Fragmented Sovereignties

Around the time that Dharavi became "Asia's largest slum," another attempt to transform the settlement was launched. Having been allowed to develop more or less independently and free from direct state involvement for over a century, Dharavi became the site of significant government attention in the mid-1980s, when the resources and authorities of the national government, the regional state, and neighborhood big men came together to address the problem of Bombay's worsening slums. After touring Dharavi in December 1985 and observing its conditions firsthand, India's then prime minister, Rajiv Gandhi, committed 1 billion rupees (roughly US$75 million at the time) for slum improvement in Bombay. While the move was interpreted by many to be motivated more by politics than by compassion (Mukhija 2003), the government was now making a clear commitment to Bombay's slums. Yet this financial pledge was not the central government's first intervention in this area, as slum clearance had been on the national policy agenda and was enshrined in Five-Year Plans since the mid-1950s. The state government, meanwhile, had formulated a policy for slum improvement in the early 1970s and, with the support of the World Bank, had launched a series of slum housing programs in the 1970s and early 1980s. But the 1985 Prime Minister's Grant Project (PMGP), initiated with Prime Minister Gandhi's pledge and bolstered by funds from the state government, directed unprecedented resources to this area and demonstrated that slum improvement had become a major political priority.

Yet while grand plans for Dharavi were drafted under the PMGP, the program was far from transformative. The initial plan proposed that the population of Dharavi be reduced by nearly 40 percent, with at least

55

twenty thousand families being relocated to outlying areas of the city (Mukhija 2003; Chatterji 2005). The thirty-five thousand families allowed to remain in Dharavi would be rehoused in the nearly four thousand new apartment buildings the plan proposed constructing, along with the tens of thousands of houses slated for improvement (Mukhija 2001a). New roads would be constructed, and Dharavi's sanitation and utility infrastructures would be entirely rebuilt (Sharma 2000). But opposition from within the settlement—some of it organized by PROUD, as well as by the National Slum Dwellers Federation (NSDF) and the recently formed Society for the Preservation of Area Resource Centres (SPARC)—worked to limit the planners' vision of Dharavi's transformation (Chatterji 2005; Mukhija 2003). And with responsibilities for the project handled by a small, single-purpose agency in the state's housing authority, the government "found its institutional capacity stretched in implementing such a complex strategy" (Mukhija 2001a, 798). With mounting opposition, inflating costs, and unanticipated complexities, ambitions for the PMGP were dramatically scaled back. By the time the program wrapped up in the late 1980s, the PMGP had built just a few dozen mid-rise residential buildings along Dharavi's perimeter (Mukhija 2003; Dua 1989). Some roads had been widened and other improvements were made, but Dharavi, as it was, remained intact.

As this case reveals, interventions attempted in Dharavi and Bombay's other slum settlements have failed to deliver on their grand promises. The six-decade history of state interventions demonstrates that housing provision and basic sanitation are highly contested and virtually elusive policy goals. Underlying the policy failures are diffuse power arrangements and institutional fragmentations. Limited municipal authority, inconsistent and incomplete insertions by the state and national governments, and fierce neighborhood contestations have consistently undermined the periodic and often well-meaning interventions attempted in Bombay's slums since the mid-1950s. While, in some cases, these failures have staved off potentially harmful schemes and allowed residents to retain their right to stay put, the failures have also ensured that residents remain in poor-quality housing and under the near constant threat of displacement.

The consequences of these inconsistent interventions have been more tangibly felt on the city's social structure than on its physical landscape. The various government programs have produced differentiated classes of informal residents—from the most disadvantaged "pavement dwellers" to the residents of "notified" and "non-notified" settlements—with each status conferring a different set of rights and protections. Yet all of the city's informal residents have remained vulnerable, dependent upon politicians, NGO workers, and community leaders to protect their precarious tenure and housing security. While Dharavi's residents have usually fared better than those in other slum settlements due to the area's economic might, its leaders' political influence, and a mobilized cadre of housing rights organizations, the social fissures produced by these policies remain consequential and are, in fact, being reproduced in the context of Dharavi's current redevelopment plans.

Fragmented Sovereignties

The failures of slum programs like the PMGP are a reflection of the fragmented sovereignties that mark Bombay's political and institutional landscape.[1] Here, as in many places in the former colonial world, the exercise of authority and sovereignty is uneven and incomplete, and the insertion of the state into lived spaces like Dharavi can best be understood as tenuous (Hansen and Stepputat 2005). The history of state interventions in Bombay's slums must be situated within the intersecting, overlapping, and fiercely contested scales of sovereignty that shape cities in general and postcolonial cities in particular. Defining sovereignty as "the public authority which directs or orders what is to be done," Diane Davis (2011, 229) has argued that this authority at the subnational level is invariably fractured and fragmented. On one hand, this condition can be empowering to city residents. As Davis (2011, 246) explains, "Understanding sovereignty in a more disaggregated manner means disarticulating the different components of governance and the range of rights and claims-making opportunities within each set of sovereignty arrangements." While enabling important opportunities for claims making, the fractured nature of public authority can also help us understand bureaucratic ineffectiveness and unsuccessful state interventions (Hansen and Stepputat 2005; Mbembe 2001).

The public authority of the postcolonial state is in part an extension of colonial sovereignty, which, as Hansen and Stepputat (2005, 19) remind us, was "constructed slowly and piecemeal and oscillated between confrontation and alignment, between spectacular representation of European might and culture, and incorporation of local idioms and methods of rule." Colonial powers established their authority, in part, by breaking up or fragmenting existing institutions and sites of established sovereignty (Mbembe 2001). At independence, postcolonial governments inherited an incomplete set of institutions whose contradictory missions were both authoritarian and extractive as well as benevolent

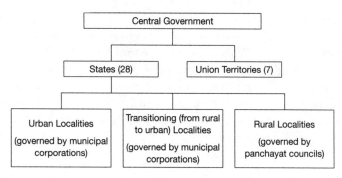

India's contemporary federalist structure.

and civilizing, and whose exercise of authority was always partial and provisional (Raffin 2011).

These contradictions were apparent in configurations of municipal authority under the British Raj. Municipal bodies—many of which, including the Bombay Municipal Corporation (BMC), became institutions of self-governance in the 1880s—were charged primarily with the oversight of basic service-delivery functions. The more substantive powers, particularly authority over land use and industrial policy—activities that would directly impact the colonial economy—were retained by provincial governments or by even more-distant colonial administrators. When power was handed to the independent Indian state in 1947, authority over urban affairs, planning, and land use was granted to regional states, while municipalities remained primarily service-delivery bodies (Pinto and Pinto 2005).

Yet more than mere path dependencies, the decision not to empower the local level upon independence was also a deliberate one, rooted in part in the antilocal bias of Indian nationalists. Although Mahatma Gandhi famously asserted that India "lives in her villages," most of the English-educated delegates to the Constitutional Assembly viewed India's villages as backward, archaic, and inherently corrupt. They believed that local elites—in villages and cities—organized power on the basis of feudal relations and communal sentiments rather than on enlightened democratic principles. The less local the political system, the more democratic many believed it would be (Corbridge and Harriss 2000).

The framers of the Indian Constitution identified federalism as one of the five core elements of the independent Indian state (along with sovereignty, democracy, socialism, and secularism), but left the three-tier federalist structure incomplete, defining responsibilities only for the central and state governments (Corbridge and Harriss 2000; Tummala 1992;

Verney 1995). Concerned about regional fragmentation along religious, ethnic, or linguistic lines, the framers granted considerable power to the regional states, in part to hold the union together (Stepan 1999). Dr. B. R. Ambedkar, the "father of India's Constitution," reportedly explained that the Constitution "instituted a dual polity, with the Union at the Centre and the States at the periphery, each endowed with sovereign powers to be exercised in the field assigned to it by the Constitution" (quoted in Frontline Magazine 1998). Urban development (including infrastructure and housing construction, economic development, and poverty allevia- tion) was a field to be financed and administered by state governments. While states could choose to devolve the responsibility for these activities to municipalities, most, including the state of Bombay, did not.

While this structure might suggest that the lines of authority between mu- nicipalities and state governments were neatly drawn, the actual exercise of power and sovereignty in the city and in informal settlements like Dharavi has always been more fraught. As discussed in chapter 1, the government generally looked the other way as residents settled and industries flourished, and "infor- mal sovereigns" were the ones who directed what was done. "Decisions on life, death, punishment, rewards, taxation, and territorial control [were] made every day by dispensers of justice that owe their standing to their own reputa- tions, the fear and respect they command, and their capacity for violence," Hansen and Stepputat (2005, 31) explain. Yet, as the history of state interven- tions demonstrates, the municipality, the state government, central authorities, and even the World Bank have stepped in at various points to attempt to insert their authority in the slum. Like the colonial state that preceded them, some of these interventions have been benevolent, while others have been vio- lent and disciplining, comprised of destructive demolition drives and eviction campaigns. These conflicting strategies often worked at cross-purposes, with one program undermining the objectives of another. Meanwhile, these fail- ures have helped the slum become more deeply entrenched in the city. They raised doubts about the state's capacity and legitimacy to intervene, and they mobilized a cadre of housing activists and organizations to resist the policy or program pursued by the state.

State Formation and Slum Clearance

Urban affairs were not a pressing concern for Bombay state in the years following independence, and the government was reluctant to expend financial resources on housing and livelihoods in the city. Compara- tively speaking, Bombay was remarkably prosperous, and the urban infrastructures built by the colonial administration remained superior to those found in most Indian cities and other parts of the state. Yet despite these comparative advantages, Bombay's civic elites and municipal administrators were becoming increasingly vocal about the problems of inadequate worker housing and the city's haphazard development. The Post-War Development Committee that convened in 1945 to propose the drafting of Bombay's first master plan included many of these concerned individuals. Nilkanth Modak's report from that meeting, which lay the groundwork for the master plan that he and Albert Mayer would draft, expressed this sentiment by borrowing language from urban administrators in the United States who were also grappling with the problems of urban decline and disinvestment. Quoting from a report prepared by the Boston City Planning Board in October 1941, Modak wrote:

> Alarm must be felt over the 'plight' of the central districts, the 'blight' of the residential areas and the 'flight' of the upper and middle income groups from the city. The time has come when the City must take vigorous action to apply an antidote. (Government of Bombay 1946, 155)

The master plan that Modak would help draft did not curry favor with state leaders at the time, but the slum clearance policies that were central to American urban renewal policy were viewed as a more appropriate antidote.

While slum clearance and evictions had been common since the late nineteenth century, they became official policy in Bombay in the mid-1950s (Singh and Das 1995; O'Hare, Abbott, and Barke 1998). The official approach to clearing slums was to demolish unauthorized dwellings and rehouse their residents in permanent structures in other parts of the city. But in practice, most eviction campaigns were undertaken without the accompanying rehousing and residents were typically rendered homeless by the actions. In fact, given its limited authority over land use and housing, the BMC was not legally empowered to acquire land or construct new housing to replace the demolished structures until a change to the BMC Act in 1954 granted the municipality this authority (Singh and Das 1995). But the city still lacked the resources necessary to construct new homes, and uncompensated evictions remained standard practice (Das 2003).

Meanwhile, slum clearance was noted as a policy priority by the central government in the Second Five-Year Plan (1956–61), and states and local authorities were encouraged to enact appropriate legislation to carry it out (Shaw 1996; Gurumukhi 2000). Consistent with this imperative, the

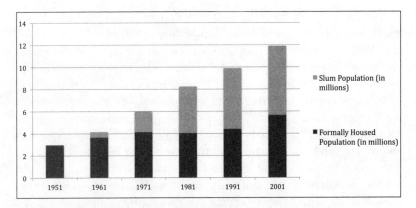

Estimates of Bombay's formally housed and slum populations, 1951_1.
Data compiled from Mahadevia 1998 and Sharma 2004.

central government enacted the Slum Areas (Improvement and Clearance) Act, 1956, to address the proliferation of slum areas in Union Territories, including the national capital of Delhi. This act, which would form a model for similar legislation adopted in Maharashtra in 1971, outlined policies for slum improvement, clearance, and redevelopment, and offered residents protections from uncompensated evictions (Bapat 1990). The central government also initiated the Slum Clearance Scheme around the same time, selecting six pilot cities, including Bombay, in which to offer financial support for clearance and improvement (Mukhija 2001b; Gurumukhi 2000).

With a mandate and modest resources from New Delhi, the BMC stepped up its clearance efforts in the late 1950s. Given the high price of land in Bombay's island city, the residents of many cleared slum areas were relocated to far-afield suburban locations. In one such clearance campaign undertaken in this period, nearly two thousand families were evicted from south and central Bombay and relocated to the Janata Squatters Colony in the Jogeshwari area in the city's northern suburbs (Youth for Unity and Voluntary Action [YUVA] 1999). In this case, resettled residents were allotted open plots of land measuring fifteen feet by twenty feet on which to construct new structures. Although they were granted a legally binding title deed called a Vacant Land Tenancy and were required to pay municipal taxes, their tenure rights remained insecure, and they were subject to police harassment and the threat of further displacement (YUVA 1999). Through resettlement schemes like this one in Jogeshwari and others in Dharavi and elsewhere, slum settlements became denser and more numerous on the outer reaches of Bombay city. Even so, slum clearance was doing little to solve the growing problem of slum proliferation. In the 1950s and 1960s the number of people living in slums and squatter settlements in Bombay grew by more than 1.5 million people (Sharma 2004; Mahadevia 1998). The population of "pavement dwellers," or those living in hutments built along roads and on footpaths, grew threefold in the 1950s, from twenty thousand to sixty-two thousand people by 1961 (Risbud 2003). This growth was accompanied by an overall worsening of housing conditions, including an increase in the number of people per household and a decrease in the average size of living space (O'Hare, Abbott, and Barke 1998). With little new housing built to replace the demolished hutments, slum clearance was proving to be a technically and politically disastrous policy, as it only served to reduce the stock of low-income housing, as well as turn voters away from the ruling political parties (O'Hare, Abbott, and Barke 1998). The practice also emboldened slumlords and goondas who would be paid again for new deeds once the land was cleared. Recognizing the ineffectiveness, the BMC wound down the practice by the late 1950s (Singh and Das 1995). In 1960 the BMC declared that structures built prior to 1956 would not be demolished unless their residents were provided alternative accommodations (Mukhija 2001b). Although demolitions continued on an episodic basis in this period, they were fairly rare in the 1960s. With few other options for addressing the city's dramatic housing shortage, the BMC returned to its long-standing practice of supportive neglect, enabling the growth of informal housing throughout this period.

Meanwhile, the challenges of municipal governance in Bombay in the mid-1950s were heightened by struggles over the redrawing of the state's political boundaries. In 1956, plans were drafted to divide Bombay state into two ethnolinguistic states, one Marathi-speaking and the other Gujarati-speaking, and debates raged over which state would administer the city of Bombay and retain its political and financial power (Arora 1956). Marathi members of the Samyukta Maharashtra movement argued that Bombay was an integral part of the state of Maharashtra, while the city's Gujarati business communities claimed the city as their own. A third group argued that the cosmopolitan city did not belong to a single ethnolinguistic group and proposed that Bombay be designated a Union Territory like Delhi (Arora 1956). In May 1960 the states were divided, and Bombay was designated the capital of the new state of Maharashtra. Although the central focus of the struggle was the politics of ethnolinguistic identity, a more subtle debate was taking place over how best to govern the city of Bombay. As the vying interests each sought control over the city's vast industrial and commercial wealth, municipal sovereignty was diminished further after Maharashtra won the spoils.

Amid India's independence and state formation, the country's commercial capital was one site of these political struggles and unclear lines of authority. Bombay's worsening housing conditions and the challenges that the BMC and state government faced in devising appropriate policy solutions cannot be separated from this larger political context, including ongoing ethnic and class tensions in the city. Colonial legacies and a series of political compromises had produced a weak municipal corporation that was not adequately empowered to carry out effective housing and land-use strategies. But the state government, which had fought for Bombay as part of the Samyukta Maharashtra movement, was a reluctant steward of the city in these early years of state formation, and the government maintained its long-standing practice of supportive neglect.

Slum Improvement and Regularization

By the early 1970s the state of Maharashtra was under renewed pressure to address Bombay's worsening housing conditions. With a mandate from Delhi and new resources from the World Bank, the state enacted slum improvement legislation and launched a series of programs over the next two decades, from the Slum Improvement Program (SIP) to the Affordable Low Income Shelter (ALIS) program to the PMGP. Yet despite the grand ambitions at the launch of each of these programs, fragmented politics and unclear lines of authority continued to hamper land use in the city and undermine the realization of their goals.

In 1971 the government of Maharashtra succumbed to pressure from the central government and adopted the Maharashtra Slum Areas (Improvement, Clearance, and Redevelopment) Act. Modeled on the 1956 slum policy enacted at the national level, Maharashtra's 1971 Slum Act established the first policy alternative to slum clearance in Bombay and created a platform for subsequent slum improvement and housing programs (Bapat 1990). Among its provisions, the act codified into law the protections against uncompensated displacements that the BMC had passed by resolution in 1960 (Mukhija 2001b). At least for those who could prove continuous residency since before a specified cutoff (or "tolerance") date, the act gave slum residents a modicum of security and a quasilegal status (Bapat 1990).[2] But the act ultimately avoided the question of legality by establishing an official definition for slums based on the area's conditions rather than on legal ownership of property or land (Bapat 1990). The act defined a slum as "any area [that] is or may be a source of danger to the health, safety or convenience of the public of that area or of its neighborhood, by reason of the area having inadequate or no basic amenities, or being unsanitary, squalid, [or] overcrowded" (State of Maharashtra 1971).[3] By defining slums in this way, the act left residents' legal status in a murky gray area.[4]

With a policy framework now in place, the state launched the SIP in 1973 and created the Maharashtra Slum Improvement Board to oversee its implementation (YUVA 1999). The SIP empowered the state government to make repairs and improve slum conditions in the city, including installing water taps and public bathing areas, constructing roads and putting in street lamps, covering drains, and building toilets (State of Maharashtra 1971).[5] By establishing an official means to extend these basic services to what were ultimately illegal settlements, the program served to diminish the power of the neighborhood big men whose networks and systems of patronage had previously been the only means for making these improvements. But the administrators charged with SIP's implementation faced technical challenges posed by the density and living conditions in these areas and found it difficult to make significant improvements (Panwalkar 1995; Sharma 2000). Reflecting upon these challenges, former BMC commissioner Gautam Chatterjee explained that although program administrators had set an initial goal of building one toilet per thirty-five people in Dharavi, they were forced to revise the goal downward to one per one hundred people once they recognized that "you could not pull down existing residential structures to build toilets" (quoted in Sharma 2000, 165). But even these more modest targets were difficult to meet because no significant funding stream was ever attached to the SIP (Panwalkar 1995).

One of the program's most important consequences was the awareness it raised about how little government officials actually knew about the city's slum settlements. Because the government had taken a laissez-faire approach to slum proliferation, administrators now found that they lacked the necessary information to implement an effective slum improvement strategy (Chatterji 2005). The state government consequently ordered in 1976 a census of the city's slums and slum residents. Although settlements had proliferated on lands owned by the state government as well as by the BMC, the central government (including the Indian Railways and the Bombay Port Trust lands), and private landowners, the state found it too difficult to coordinate with these other landowning entities and ultimately carried out the census only on lands owned by the state of Maharashtra (Sharma 2000; YUVA 1999). Consequently, the tally of 630,000 slum dwellers enumerated in the 1976 Slum Census is recognized to be a significant underestimation of Bombay's slum population at the time (Chatterji 2005).

Once the census was carried out, it was possible to provide some legal protections to at least some slum dwellers. The 630,000 slum dwellers enumerated in the census were issued photo passes or "pitch cards," and amendments were made to the 1971 Slum Act noting that those in possession of photo passes would have to be provided alternative accommodations if demolitions were carried out (Chatterji 2005; YUVA 1999). This practice, referred to as "regularization," remains the primary means by which slum dwellers are extended legal protections from displacements.[6] The policy also levied on regularized slum dwellers a twenty-rupee licensing fee and a one-rupee "land rent" charge (YUVA 1999). The legal consequences of this land rent remained ambiguous, however, as it was unclear whether the government regarded the charge as a fine for illegal squatting or as an official tax that conferred legal status (Chatterji 2005). As Roma Chatterji (2005, 203) notes, "The term rent circumvents the question of legal status articulated in terms of ownership." The ambiguity around this practice produces what Jonathan Shapiro Anjaria (2001) has called an "ordinary space of negotiation" within which residents and the state collectively normalize illegal habitation. Meanwhile, this practice created two classes of slum dwellers: the regularized and the unregularized.[7] While regularized slum dwellers would now have some sense of housing security and be protected from state-sanctioned demolitions, those deemed ineligible or lacking adequate documentation would still fear uncompensated displacement. The division between these two classes of slum dwellers would remain consequential as the state government continued to introduce housing programs that determined eligibility on the basis of regularization.

Meanwhile, the challenges that the state faced securing interagency participation in the 1976 slum census revealed the complexities and, ultimately, the fragmented nature of urban governance in Bombay that continues to hamper effective interventions in this area. Not only was landownership and administration splintered, but the Maharashtra Slum Improvement Board, charged with administering the SIP, proved unable to coordinate among the various landowning agencies to conduct the census. These challenges of coordination were heightened with the creation of several new "parastatal" agencies in the 1970s, each of which was granted certain responsibilities over land, housing, and development in the region.

These include the City and Industrial Development Corporation (CIDCO), formed in March 1970 to oversee the planning and administration of New Bombay; the Bombay Metropolitan Regional Development Authority (BMRDA), formed in January 1975 to coordinate development activities in the Bombay Metropolitan Region; and the Maharashtra Housing and Area Development Authority (MHADA), formed in December 1975 to oversee all housing activities (Pinto 2000; Pugh 1989). The BMC remained largely irrelevant in this area, as housing policy and urban development in the Bombay region fell under the domain of these new agencies. Yet rather than improving the government's ability to address housing shortfalls and the conditions of the city's slum settlements, these new agencies created additional competing agendas and undermined coordinated efforts at land management and housing construction (Pinto 2000, 2008).

A State of Emergency

Contestations over urban governance turned violent when the central government inserted itself into Bombay's housing arena during the Emergency regime of the late 1970s. Ignoring the protections enshrined in the Maharashtra Slum Act, Indira Gandhi's national government, with the support of state-level officials, undertook widespread slum demolitions across Bombay in the late 1970s. An estimated seventy-two thousand residents—many of whom were likely in possession of newly minted pitch cards—were evicted between June 1975 and March 1977 (Spodek 1983; Hansen 2001). As during the period of state formation in the 1950s, the Emergency was a politically turbulent time in Bombay, and the city's slums again became a key site of the struggles. While the demolitions carried out in the capital of Delhi have been more extensively documented, similar expressions of state violence were undertaken in Bombay in this period (Hansen 2001; Tarlo 2003; Weiner 1977).[8] The history of this politically turbulent time demonstrates that although Bombay's slum policies are generally characterized in a progressive fashion, moving from clearance to improvement, this history is actually more cyclical, comprising violent insurgencies carried out alongside and interspersed with more benevolent programmatic interventions.

On June 26, 1975, India's president Fakhruddin Ali Ahmed called a national state of emergency, enacting an order by Prime Minister Indira Gandhi. The stated purpose of the Emergency was to restore discipline across the country and undertake a program of modernization possible only with the suspension of elections and the curtailing of constitutional freedoms. But the actual objectives were starkly apparent: with the Emergency, Indira Gandhi sought to quell antigovernment protests under way across the country and deflect attention from a High Court ruling that found her guilty of corrupt election practices (Palmer 1976). Over the next twenty-one months, India experienced authoritarian rule under a state of emergency. During this time, Mrs. Gandhi consolidated Congress Party power across the country and undertook repressive programs of family planning and slum clearance. Many of these actions and the opposition they generated were concentrated in the country's cities (Mazumdar 2007; McFarlane 2008).

Tens of thousands of slum residents were victims of the central government's attempts to demonstrate its authority in the city of Bombay. Two months into the Emergency, Mrs. Gandhi declared in a speech, "We have to clean up the country. If your house is dirty, you don't leave it like that. You clean it up with a duster and a broom" (quoted in Hansen 2001, 206). The dusters and brooms used in Bombay, as in Delhi and other cities throughout the country, were bulldozers and *lathi* sticks used to demolish slums and evict poor residents. Urban planner Shirish Patel describes one such demolition incident in Bombay:

> Starting on May 22, 1976, over the next two or three days the Janata
> Colony was flattened by bulldozers. Its residents were given sites 10
> ft x 15 ft (half the size of the sites they had had in Janata Colony) in
> Cheetah Camp, a location a few miles down the road. Moving them
> just before the monsoon, without time to settle in or construct anything
> at the new location, meant that for that rainy season, living conditions
> in Cheetah Camp were horrifying. The site was under the high tide,
> and a common sight was a charpoy, protected by a plastic sheet above,
> its wooden legs in the water, stepping blocks of bricks leading to the
> charpoy, and someone lying on it with the strings and his body an inch
> or two above the water below. There were no civic amenities. Disease
> was rampant, and several children and old people died in that first
> monsoon. (1996, 1048)

In contrast to some other parts of the country, in which local officials were less willing to cooperate with the Emergency regime, the government of Maharashtra was eager to carry out the policies of the Emergency (Palmer 1977; Manor 1978; Kamat 1980). Four months before the Emergency was declared, Mrs. Gandhi had replaced the state's chief minister with her close ally and Congress loyalist S. B. Chavan (Manor 1978). Described as Indira's "hatchet man in Maharashtra during the Emergency," Chavan aggressively implemented the Maintenance of Internal Security Act

(MISA), which contained many of the Emergency's most draconian measures (Kamat 1980; Hansen 2001).

While the abuses of power were also carried out in rural areas—the vasectomies and forced sterilizations were particularly egregious—the slum demolitions and police crackdowns during the Emergency had a distinctly urban character (Weiner 1977; Hansen 2001). In Bombay, MISA was carried out by the police and by cadres of Congress Youth who were empowered to "remove anything that could be seen as abnormal, annoying, or polluting . . . [including] a halt on all new constructions, slum clearances, and rather absurd attempts to police bus queues, making it a punishable offense to step out of line while waiting for the bus" (Hansen 2001, 206–7). These actions, however, did not go unopposed, and Bombay's Emergency regime was met with significant protests and the emergence of fierce political opponents (Mazumdar 2007; Hansen 2001). The Emergency, meanwhile, had wide-sweeping political consequences, along with those experienced by the urban poor (Manor 1978). The political realignments produced by the Congress Party defeat, after Indira Gandhi reinstated elections in March 1977, would affect citywide politics and the composition of the BMC for decades to come.

The World Bank and the Slum

In the immediate aftermath of the Emergency, the Maharashtra government and the BMC took a relatively benign approach toward slums and launched a series of slum upgrading and rehabilitation schemes with central government support and World Bank financing. Although demolition drives reemerged as a political tool in the 1980s, they were pursued alongside an expansion of more benevolent slum upgrading programs. As reflected in the number of slum schemes initiated in this period, the late 1970s and 1980s constituted a period of experimentation in the field of slum improvement, supported directly by the World Bank, which had been "learning by doing" in the slums of Calcutta and Madras since the early 1970s (Pugh 1989; Mukhija 2003).

Although the first World Bank funds were not released in Bombay until January 1985, the Bank had a significant influence on slum policies in the city beginning around 1977 (Pugh 1989; Panwalkar 1995; World Bank 1997). With the Emergency still in effect, then World Bank president Robert McNamara visited Bombay in 1976 to meet with state officials and begin laying the groundwork for the Bank's involvement in the city's housing policy (Pugh 1989). The next year, the BMRDA issued a policy statement on housing that closely aligned with the Bank's emerging position in this area, including an emphasis on "'affordability,' 'cost recovery,' expressions of low-income housing in 'sites-and-services projects,' and arresting the increase in squatter settlements" (Pugh 1989, 36).

The program that first reflected this position was the Affordable Low Income Shelter (ALIS) program, which was launched by the government of Maharashtra in 1980 and received World Bank support under the Bombay Urban Development Project (BUDP) in 1985 (Dua 1989; Pugh 1989; World Bank 1997). The main objective of ALIS was to "reduce the absolute number of households living in slums by increasing the supply of affordable shelter particularly to the poor" (World Bank 1997, i). ALIS was designed both to improve the housing conditions for current slum residents and to reduce future slum growth by improving local administration and lowering land prices, primarily through deregulation (World Bank 1997). The program was rooted in the Bank's emerging neoliberal ideology, particularly its assumptions that "people's own initiative and resources" could be activated and housing shortfalls could be addressed without significant government expenditures (Dua 1989, 162). Although surveys undertaken as part of this program demonstrated that most of Bombay's slum dwellers were desperately poor, with 82 percent earning less than one thousand rupees per month and most with very low savings rates, ALIS was premised on a "user pays" model (Dua 1989; Pugh 1989). This emphasis was driven both by World Bank ideology and local necessity, as the Maharashtra government had neither the will nor the resources to make significant investments in this area.

The ALIS was made up of both a "sites-and-services" program and an "upgradation" program. The sites-and-services piece, formally called the Land Infrastructure Servicing Program (LISP), allotted low-income households "serviced" plots (i.e., those with water taps, electric hookups, and drainage facilities) on which they could construct new residential structures. During the program's nine-year run, eighty-eight thousand households were able to purchase serviced plots (World Bank 1997). In this manner, relocated households became regularized, although they still lacked legal tenure. The upgradation piece, carried out through the Slum Upgradation Program (SUP), gave residents the resources (in the form of loans) to make improvements to their existing residential structures (World Bank 1997; Chatterji 2005). SUP specified that hutments could not be rebuilt as reinforced concrete structures, but residents could use materials such as plaster and brick to upgrade structures that had originally been built of tin, mat, and plastic sheeting (Chatterji 2005). An additional floor could also be added to structures in order to create additional living space. Although it was deemed illegal to rent out these top-floor living spaces, many slum dwellers began doing so as an additional source of income.[9]

Although SUP fell short of expectations and impacted far fewer households than the sites-and-services piece, the program had significant consequences for later housing programs by establishing housing societies and undertaking slum improvement as a collective endeavor (Chatterji 2005). Specifically, SUP granted tenure rights not to individual tenants, as under the policy of regularization, but rather to contiguous clusters of approximately one hundred households that would first be required to register as a housing society (Chatterji 2005). By the program's end, approximately two hundred housing societies were registered throughout Bombay (comprising roughly twenty-two thousand households) and granted collective tenure under the program (World Bank 1997; Chatterji 2005). In fact, many of the housing societies that are registered in Dharavi today were incorporated in the 1980s to take advantage of the benefits offered through the program.

Rooted in the ideas of John F. C. Turner, whose research in Peruvian squatter settlements provided the theoretical underpinnings for much of the World Bank's slum housing activities in this period, the SUP sought to harness the collective power of slum communities to ensure collective housing rights (Werlin 1999). By granting collective tenure and making loans available to residents, the program encouraged slum residents to work together to improve their housing conditions without interference from presumably inept or corrupt bureaucracies. Although program implementation required the participation of the very same bureaucracies, it was built on the idea that because slums proliferated on account of bureaucratic failure, their solutions lay in the empowerment of "self-help" communities. At the same time, the ALIS provided technical assistance and training to the government of Maharashtra (GOM), the BMRDA, and CIDCO to improve bureaucratic performance and local governance (World Bank 1997). It also sought to remove presumably burdensome land-use regulations, such as the Rent Control Act and the Urban Land Ceiling Act—populist measures designed to expand access to affordable housing but which were believed to have the opposite effect (World Bank 1997).

Like many housing programs that both preceded ALIS and would follow it, grand expectations were met with generally disappointing results. Specifically, the World Bank had set a target of one hundred thousand households to be served by SUP, representing approximately 12 percent of Bombay's slum population in 1981 (World Bank 1997).[10] By the time the program was discontinued in 1994, only about 20 percent of this target was met. The program's disappointing outcomes were blamed on a lack of capacity and limited commitment from the local implementing agencies (Chatterji 2005; World Bank 1997). Noting that seven different agencies had been charged with implementing aspects of the program, the World Bank's self-assessment concluded that "this project has shown that the ability of BMRDA and GOM to successfully coordinate large, multi-agency programs remains weak" (World Bank 1997, ii). The report went on to note that because SUP was simply integrated into these agencies' other activities, it was not deemed a major priority by project administrators. Just one housing program among many, including SIP, the PMGP, and, later, the Slum Re-Development (SRD) program, ALIS, the World Bank's evaluation noted, "was undermined by competition from several parallel programs that financed essential infrastructure in slums, or provided new, free (or almost-free) housing to slum dwellers" (World Bank 1997, ii). As reflected in the World Bank's assessment and echoed by others who have looked at these programs, the ALIS and SUP were undermined by the competing agendas that the numerous agencies charged with their implementation pursued (Chatterji 2005; Panwalkar 1995; Dua 1989). Despite the technical assistance provided to the state government and the BMRDA to improve governance outcomes, the state lacked the authority, resources, and ultimately the interest to coordinate among these varied agencies to markedly improve conditions in Bombay's slums.

Clearance and Mobilization

Even as these programs were under way, the Maharashtra government was carrying out violent demolition drives reminiscent of the evictions of the Emergency period. Specifically, the state of Maharashtra and BMC launched "Operation Eviction" in July 1981 and "Operation Demolition" in late 1985 (Sebastian 1981; Singh and Das 1995; Mukhija 2003; Chatterji and Mehta 2007; Anand and Rademacher 2011). These clearance campaigns were undertaken amid ongoing turbulence and deep political contestations in the city, the burdens of which were experienced once again by the city's most vulnerable residents. These actions further demonstrated the halfhearted commitment the government had to the slum improvement and upgradation programs it was simultaneously pursuing. They also had the important consequence of mobilizing a wide swath of activists around housing issues and slum dwellers' rights. These mobilizations and the dense field of housing rights organizations they produced would dramatically influence the nature of housing interventions in coming decades and bolster the durability of spaces like Dharavi.

Operation Eviction was launched on July 23, 1981, at the height of monsoon season, when Chief Minister A. R. Antulay issued an order that one hundred thousand slum residents and pavement dwellers be rounded up and returned to their places of origin (Sebastian 1981; Ramanath 2005). According to an account written at the time, "The whole police force of Bombay and the top bureaucrats of the Government of Maharashtra" were called to action, while "hundreds of buses and lorries were requisitioned and special trains were arranged" to shuttle the poor out of the city limits (Sebastian 1981, 1526). But unlike during the Emergency, slum residents and activists now had recourse they could take. On the very day the demolitions began, a group of activists organized under the name the "People's Union for Civil Liberties" filed a petition with the Bombay High Court requesting that the operation be postponed until after the monsoons had ended (Ramanath 2005). The High Court granted the stay until October, but by that time, more broad-reaching petitions were filed, which claimed that "the eviction of pavement dwellers would lead to the deprivation of their livelihood and ultimately their life" (Ramanath 2005, 128). This violation of their right to life, the petitioners argued, was in direct violation of Article 21 of the Indian Constitution. The Indian Supreme Court ultimately agreed to hear the case of *Olga Tellis v. Bombay Municipal Corporation,* named for one of the journalists who filed a petition on behalf of the affected pavement dwellers. The halt on evictions remained in effect for the next four years until the Court's ruling was issued.

Meanwhile, politics in Bombay were becoming increasingly fractured in the early 1980s. The Congress Party was still experiencing the political fallout of the Emergency and was facing significant competition at the national level, even as the state of Maharashtra remained a Congress stronghold (Manor 1978). The Congress Party faced more direct challenges in the city of Bombay, which is not surprising given the Emergency's deeper impact on the city and its residents. While opposition parties—most notably, the Shiv Sena—had been gaining ground in Bombay since around 1970, the Congress Party lost control of municipal politics only in April 1985 when the Shiv Sena won a majority of seats in the BMC elections. Once the Shiv Sena took control of the BMC in the summer of 1985, the party's leaders made a vow to step up clearance and slum demolition activities (Mukhija 2003; Weisman 1988; Associated Press 1985). These actions were justified with the party's campaign slogan, "Green Bombay, Beautiful Bombay," and with statements from its leader, Bal Thackeray, announcing that pavements "are meant for pedestrians and we will see that those living on the pavements will be removed" (quoted in Associated Press 1985; Times of India 1985; Singh 1986). Although demolitions had continued in the city throughout the Supreme Court's four-year stay on evictions, the BMC launched its demolition campaign in earnest only after the stay was lifted in late 1985.

On July 10, 1985, the Supreme Court issued its ruling in the case *Olga Tellis v. Bombay Municipal Corporation*. The unanimous opinion of the five justices ultimately supported the petitioners' claim that evicting slum residents and pavement dwellers, whose livelihoods depended on their appropriation of shelter near their places of work, denies them their livelihoods and right to life. Yet the Court also found that the government had the right to evict those unlawfully dwelling, or "trespassing," on public roads, pavements, and footpaths. "The existence of dwellings on the pavements is unquestionably a source of nuisance to the public," the ruling stated, "at least for the reason that they are denied the use of pavements for passing and repassing" (Supreme Court of India 1985, 77). Furthermore, the Court ruled that the government was not obligated to provide alternative accommodations to those they evicted, unless they were regularized residents, possessing pitch cards and included in the 1976 slum census. Lifting the stay, the Court ruled that the government could resume evictions, but stipulated that it must wait until after the monsoon season.

One of the more consequential pieces of the judgment was the distinction it made between slum residents and pavement dwellers. In the Court's ruling, delivered by Chief Justice Chandrachud, pavement dwellers were explicitly maligned:

> Those who have made pavements their homes exist in the midst of filth and squalor, which has to be seen to be believed. Rabid dogs in search of stinking meat and cats in search of hungry rats keep them company. They cook and sleep where they ease, for no conveniences are available to them. Their daughters, come of age, bathe under the nosy gaze of passers by, unmindful of the feminine sense of bashfulness. The cooking and washing over, women pick lice from each other's hair. The boys beg. Menfolk, without occupation, snatch chains with the connivance of the defenders of law and order; when caught, if at all, they say: "Who doesn't commit crimes in this city?" (Supreme Court of India 1985, 63)

This characterization of pavement dwellers and the differences it engendered between them and the (if only slightly) more respectable residents of slums or *bastis* further reinforced distinctions between the city's informal residents and justified the differentiated sets of rights they were afforded. In doing so, the Court put pavement dwellers at the bottom of an implicit hierarchy of extralegal city residents, in which groups were stratified by length of tenure, possession of specific forms of documentation, and whether the government had officially recognized (or "notified") their settlement.

Focusing most explicitly now on pavement dwellers, the Shiv Sena led–BMC began demolishing hutments again in December 1985 (Mukhija 2003). By February 1986, Operation Demolition (also referred to as "Operation Slum-Wreck") was in full force (Mukhija 2003; Singh 1986). Writing at the height of the campaign, Bombay-based journalist and activist Gurbir Singh described the government's approach to the operation:

> Phase I of Operation Demolition involves the eviction of 15,000 families. The strategy adopted is a low profile one. There are no widespread simultaneous demolitions being carried out all over the city. Each earmarked slum or pavement settlement is demolished singly, with an overwhelming show of force, and without fuss or press publicly the residents are carried off in lorries to the resettlement sites or just driven off and dispersed. After each demolition, public reaction is tested. If there is some commotion, the next demolition is held off for some time. If things go smoothly, the next target is set upon soon after. (1986, 684)

In this manner, the BMC undertook dozens of demolitions, many of them quite violent, throughout early 1986.

Meanwhile, as Gurbir Singh and others documented at the time, settlements and pavement colonies were frequently razed even when their residents met the qualifications for protection under the state's regularization policy. Writing about the March 1986 demolition of the Sanjay Nagar slum in South Bombay, which had been established in 1974, Singh described the difficulty of residents to demonstrate their length of tenure:

> To prove residence before 1980, your name must figure in the 1980 voters' list. Sanjay Gandhi Nagar residents have produced bulky piles of documents like 1975 pay slips, 1979 demolition notices, correspondence of 1979 with Sharad Pawar, the then chief minister, as proof of pre-1980 occupation. But for the state government, collective proof is not sufficient. Individual documents must be furnished. For a slum that has been ravaged by fire in the previous year, and demolished, according to housing secretary Afzalpurkar, 44 times in the last one year, can its residents be still expected to hold on to their little chits so grandiosely referred to as "documents"? (1986, 685)

Yet this time, as during the 1981 clearance campaign, activists were mobilized to oppose the government's actions. By the mid-1980s, numerous NGOs and activist groups had formed to demand justice and housing security for Bombay's slum residents and pavement dwellers, many of which—including Dharavi-based PROUD, the National Slum Dwellers Federation (NSDF), the Slum Rehabilitation Society, Youth for Unity and Voluntary Action (YUVA), the Society for the Preservation of Area Resource Centres (SPARC), the Committee for the Right to Housing (CRH), and Nivara Hakk Suraksha Samiti (NHSS)—remain active today. While some of these groups (such as PROUD and NSDF) were formed in response to earlier evictions or to the various programs launched since the early 1970s, others came together in the mid-1980s to explicitly oppose the 1985 Supreme Court ruling and the evictions carried out during Operation Demolition.[11] NHSS, for example, was organized in 1982 as a coalition of more than twenty-five groups representing slum residents, trade unionists, and youth groups demonstrating against the numerous violations of the Supreme Court's stay on evictions and demolitions (Ramanath 2005). But after the particularly violent demolition of the Sanjay Nagar slum in March 1986, NHSS became a highly mobilized agitator for slum dwellers' rights across the city (Singh 1986; Ramanath 2005). CRH, meanwhile, was formed in 1985 when YUVA and other social work organizations came together in the immediate aftermath of the Supreme Court ruling.

These groups represented distinct ideological positions (NHSS, for example, adopted an explicitly communist platform) or advocated using certain tactics to accomplish their aims (SPARC did not see the utility of directly confronting demolition squads, for example), and found it difficult to collaborate despite their common interests (Ramanath 2005). As a consequence, the field of housing rights activism became a densely populated and highly contested terrain comprising numerous groups representing various ideologies and promoting distinct modes of action. Even after Operation Demolition wound down in mid-1986, most of these organizations remained vocal advocates for the rights of slum and pavement dwellers to stay put. As new programs for slum improvement and housing construction were launched over the next two decades, program administrators now had to contend with these mobilized groups and with more general resident opposition.[12] The opportunity for these groups to directly shape housing policy came about almost immediately, as the Prime Minister's Grant Project was launched on the heels of the BMC's 1986 demolition drive.

The Prime Minister's Grant (Developing Dharavi, Part Two)

When Prime Minister Rajiv Gandhi visited Bombay in December 1985 to celebrate the centennial of the Indian National Congress (the precursor to the modern-day Congress Party), he arrived in a city rife with political conflict and mobilizations around slums. With the BMC's renewed eagerness to clear pavements and slum settlements, the Supreme Court's recent decision in the Olga Tellis case, the World Bank's slum interventions beginning to take hold, and opposition mounted by the myriad new housing organizations, slums and squatters' rights had risen to the top of the city's political agenda. Finding it impossible to ignore these concerns on his December visit, the prime minister included a tour of Dharavi in his itinerary, which he ended with a financial pledge of 1 billion rupees to improve conditions in the settlement.

Because the announcement of the grant coincided with the Congress Party's centennial celebration, many interpreted the prime minister's financial pledge as part of an effort to rebuild populist support for the Congress and to counteract recent political gains made by the Shiv Sena party (Weintraub 1988; Mukhija 2003). Once again, the city's slums had become a focus of political conflict. The history of Bombay politics demonstrates that slums tend to attract political attention when politics are most contentious, as they were in the mid-1980s. While the political attention is often unwanted, coming in the form of bulldozers and demolition squads, in the mid-1980s it arrived as a 1 billion-rupee grant.

The grant was transferred from the central government to the state of Maharashtra, which was also ruled at the time by the Congress Party.[13] The Maharashtra government supplied additional funds and assembled an exploratory committee, chaired by noted architect Charles Correa, to make recommendations for Dharavi's redevelopment (Mukhija 2003). Recognizing the need for information about Dharavi's social and physical composition, one of the first actions the Correa Committee took was to collect these data (Sharma 2000). Although the committee's population estimates were vigorously contested and widely recognized to be low, they formed the basis for a planning process. Somewhat less contentious but equally consequential, the committee recommended that a sole, relatively autonomous planning authority, called the Prime Minister's Grant Project (PMGP), be created and given singular responsibly for planning and implementing Dharavi's redevelopment under the program (Mukhija 2003; Sharma 2000). This recommendation emerged from the recognition that institutional fragmentation, competing agendas, and the absence of clear leadership had undermined earlier housing programs (Sharma 2000).

In other important ways, the Correa Committee (and, later, the PMGP) drew upon the cumulative knowledge acquired from three decades of interventions in this area. First, the program maintained the collective approach to slum improvement developed in the context of the SUP. Although the SUP, and the ALIS program more broadly, were not recognized as particularly successful, the practice of collective regularization through the formation of housing societies had been deemed both technically viable and politically popular (Chatterji 2005). Furthermore, the policy of regularization itself, and the determination of program eligibility on the basis of a specified "tolerance" date, had been a key feature of housing programs since the adoption of the 1971 Slum Areas Act (Bapat 1990; Mukhija 2003). As with each new program since 1971, the PMGP maintained a division between those deserving and undeserving of tenure security, as determined by length of tenure (Sharma 2000; Chatterji 2003). Also building on ALIS—and particularly on the World Bank's emphasis on self-help—the PMGP mandated that residents be responsible for a significant share of construction expenses. As under the World Bank program, housing assistance for the PMGP would come primarily in the form of low-interest loans to slum residents.

Meanwhile, the PMGP represented a break from these earlier schemes in two key ways. First, for the first time since the Modak-Mayer plan was drafted in the late 1940s, the program proposed slum improvement or redevelopment at the scale of a township (or "neighborhood unit" in the language of the earlier plan). Although it fell far short of these expectations, the PMGP was remarkable for its ambition, envisioning a Dharavi-wide project that would coordinate sanitation and infrastructure improvement, housing construction, and commercial development. Second, the PMGP attempted to achieve this goal through a new strategy of in situ redevelopment, rather than through improvement, upgrading, or sites-and-services (Sharma 2000). The SUP program, for example, had allowed for the upgrading of existing clusters of hutments, but had specified that homes could not be rebuilt as reinforced concrete structures (Chatterji 2005). Under PMGP, homes could now be rebuilt on site, replacing *kutcha* hutments with mid-rise *pucca* apartment buildings. Employing this new approach to slum "redevelopment," the PMGP proposed that upward of four thousand shanties in Dharavi be replaced with middle-class-style apartments, complete with indoor plumbing and in-unit toilets (Mukhija 2003).

As Modak and Mayer had suggested four decades earlier, the Correa Committee concluded that comprehensive redevelopment could only be achieved if Dharavi's population density was significantly reduced. While the committee's official enumeration put the area's population at fifty-five thousand families, it recommended that Dharavi had space to accommodate only thirty-five thousand families (Mukhija 2003).[14] Thus, at least twenty thousand families would have to be relocated outside of Dharavi. The proposal of evictions on this scale brought back recent memories of the government-sponsored demolition drives and mobilized housing rights activists to oppose the plan (Mukhija 2003). Employing many of the same tactics they used during Operation Demolition, these groups, which included SPARC, NSDF, and PROUD, worked not just to halt the evictions but also to undermine the whole project. According to Chatterj (2005, 206), "PROUD claims that its initiative in organizing a public protest led to the withdrawal of the proposal [to relocate families] made by the Correa Committee." Meanwhile, SPARC and NSDF drafted an alternative redevelopment plan for Dharavi that they called the "People's Plan" (Mukhija 2003; Sharma 2000). Among the lasting legacies of the PMGP was the direct involvement of mobilized NGOs and grassroots organizations in slum improvement and redevelopment efforts. While earlier schemes, such as SIP and ALIS, had vocal critics, project planners and administrators had not had to contend with and ultimately address the concerns of housing activists and resident groups to the extent that they did under the PMGP. While their involvement certainly shaped the outcome of this particular project, it also altered the way that subsequent housing programs would have to be planned.

Contested Numbers

Much of the conflict around the PMGP's planning process entailed disputes over the enumeration of Dharavi's population. As revealed during the 1976 slum census, the collection of household-level information in areas like Dharavi is a technically difficult and politically fraught activity. And as the Correa Committee worked to compile this information for Dharavi, groups like SPARC and PROUD contested not just their numbers but also the means by which they were collecting them and even whether they had the right to collect them. In fact, the collection of data about informal residents in Bombay has become a key site of conflict between bureaucrats, developers, and housing rights activists, with some observers characterizing these conflicts as a struggle between "governmentality" and "counter-governmentality" (Appadurai 2001; Chatterji 2005; McFarlane 2011).[15]

Soon after its formation, the Correa Committee hired the Hyderabad-based National Remote Sensing Agency to conduct an aerial survey of Dharavi and derive estimates of the settlement's population from aerial photographs. With pressure to begin making recommendations, the committee selected this admittedly imprecise data collection method for its efficiency (Sharma 2000). Using this approach, the Committee estimated Dharavi's population at 250,000 people, or about fifty-five thousand families (Sharma 2000; Mukhija 2003). Meanwhile, with concerns mounting that mass evictions would soon be under way in Dharavi, NSDF and SPARC vocally criticized the committee's methods and expressed skepticism about their numbers. Bringing together SPARC's professional resources with NSDF's Dharavi-based networks, these housing rights organizations soon launched an alternative enumeration of Dharavi, employing a community-based technique that SPARC had refined during its earlier organizing efforts (Sharma 2000; Chatterji 2003). This approach entailed training community residents, particularly women, to count huts, draw rough maps, use chalk to mark house numbers, and conduct interviews with household residents (Patel, D'Cruz, and Burra 2002). Accurate population numbers were just one of several objectives of the survey. As SPARC's founding director has written, such surveys can be "important tools in educating communities to look at themselves and in creating capacities for communities to articulate their knowledge of themselves to those with whom they interact" (Patel and Mitlin 2002, 6). Information came to be viewed as a resource that could be deployed by residents in negotiations with government officials. The Dharavi survey became the basis for such negotiations and for drafting an alternative "People's Plan" for Dharavi's redevelopment (Mukhija 2003; Sharma 2000). While Dharavi was already a mobilized community, with groups like PROUD engaged in community organizing campaigns for over a decade, the SPARC-NSDF survey further deepened the residents' sense of collective efficacy and strengthened their resolve to resist displacement.

The SPARC-NSDF survey produced an estimate of 530,225 people, or 106,000 families, living in eighty-six thousand residential structures (National Slum Dwellers Federation [NSDF] 1986; Sharma 2000). Although some government officials claimed that these numbers were too high, the social profile gleaned from the survey was widely accepted (Mukhija 2003). One of the most significant insights it offered was that although planners and bureaucrats treated Dharavi as a single slum settlement, its residents saw themselves as living in smaller, semiautonomous settlements within Dharavi (Sharma 2000). Survey collectors with NSDF identified eighty-four such settlements (referred to as *chawls, nagars, wadis,* or colonies) by asking residents where they lived (National Slum Dwellers Federation 1986). The survey also found that while most residents lived in family units, many individuals had come to work and send money back to their home villages. While some of these labor migrants rented first-floor rooms in the chawls, many lived in *pongal* houses, or dormitory buildings housing between thirty and one hundred men. The survey enumerated sixty-two pongal houses in Dharavi (Sharma 2000). This finding underscored the problems of determining program eligibility on the basis of documentation of tenure, given that the most disadvantaged of Dharavi's residents would be the first ones evicted.

The SPARC-NSDF survey also revealed that despite the PMGP's emphasis on housing improvement, Dharavi was as much an industrial and commercial enclave as a residential one. The survey enumerated 43 large industrial units and 244 small-scale ones, engaged in such activities as leather work, printing, video editing, packaged-food making, recycling, scrap dealing, and garment manufacturing (National Slum Dwellers Federation 1986). These findings contradicted widely held perceptions about slums, not only on the part of the general public, but also by the PMGP planners. Despite the Correa Committee's somewhat innovative recommendation that Dharavi be redeveloped on a large scale—as an integrated township—program administrators continued to treat Dharavi as a housing problem and to direct the majority of PMGP resources toward housing construction and improvement.

State Capacity and Diminished Expectations

Despite the Correa Committee's recognition that political fragmentations and administrative weaknesses had undermined earlier attempts to address Bombay's worsening slum problem, as well as their recommendation that a new agency be created to administer the program (Sharma 2000; Mukhija 2003), most assessments of the PMGP have concluded that the program's rather limited success was a product of political fragmentation and administrative weakness (Pinto 2000). Urban planning scholar Vinit Mukhija (2001a, 798), for example, asserts that the state's institutional capacities were stretched too thin when a single agency was given the responsibility for implementing such a complex program. Mukhija elaborates that the state's decision to administer the program wholly at the state level, without support from the BMC, reflected the Congress Party's efforts to maintain distance between the program and the Shiv Sena party (Mukhija 2003, 28). Meanwhile, a Washington Post correspondent reporting on the program's slow implementation at the time quoted a local activist making a similar point: "The Congress Party wants credit for the grant program and won't cooperate with Shiv Sena, which controls the city government, and Shiv Sena won't cooperate with Congress," the activist stated. "This 'my party' business has to be stopped somewhere" (Weintraub 1988).

Beyond institutional capacities and political conflicts, the grand ambitions of the PMGP were scaled back almost immediately when the 1-billion-rupee grant for Dharavi's redevelopment was reduced by almost two-thirds. Based on conversations with Gautam Chatterjee, an IAS officer who was charged with administering the PMGP,[16] journalist Kalpana Sharma (2000) notes that certain factions within the government had argued against giving the entire grant for Dharavi. Chatterjee recalled:

> It was argued that the major problem in Mumbai is not slums but the old dilapidated buildings. Rs 41 crore [410 million rupees] went for reconstruction of old dilapidated tenanted buildings. After deducting the Rs 37 crore [370 million rupees], the remaining [220 million rupees] was for slum upgradation in the rest of Mumbai. (quoted in Sharma 2000, 163)

With reduced funds available for Dharavi, the PMGP decided to focus its activities in three main areas. First, a relatively small amount of the funds were used to clean up the heavily polluted Mahim Creek that formed Dharavi's northern border. Second, around half of the funds were used to improve Dharavi's infrastructure, including widening roads and laying sewage lines, primarily along Dharavi's perimeter (Sharma 2000; Chatterji 2003). This left roughly half of the Dharavi funds, around 150 million rupees, for housing construction.

Adopting a novel approach to housing construction, the decision was made to redevelop much of the housing stock, rather than improving it, by replacing clusters of hutments with mid-rise apartment blocks. Gautam Chatterjee claims that this decision was made after speaking to Dharavi residents, who "wanted to get out of this so-called informal settlement syndrome and move to mainstream formal housing" (quoted in Sharma 2000, 169). Given the limited resources now available for housing construction, initial proposals that called for redeveloping most of Dharavi's housing stock were replaced with a more modest pilot project that would redevelop just thirty-eight hundred units across Dharavi (Mukhija 2001a). With the government providing generous subsidies and interest-free loans, there was intense competition to be among the housing societies selected to participate. Yet once construction began, it became clear that participation would place a significant financial burden on the residents. In fact, many of the residents were already in debt, still paying back loans on their hutments, and could not afford the monthly payments for the new PMGP tenements (Sharma 2000). Moreover, because the buildings had indoor plumbing, it was only possible to construct them along the newly laid sewage lines. Consequently, PMGP buildings were built almost exclusively on the main roads along Dharavi's perimeter, leaving the settlement's interior largely untouched (Mukhija 2003). While some funds had been made available for improving the existing housing stock, density in the perimeter made such improvements virtually impossible in these areas (Chatterji 2003). Also although the Correa Committee had recognized this would be a problem, any proposals to reduce Dharavi's density by relocating residents outside of the settlement were deemed unfeasible once the residents were mobilized.

In the end, the PMGP implemented a considerably scaled-back version of its initially ambitious proposals. Major thoroughfares had been widened, new sewage lines were laid, and some mid-rise buildings were built along Dharavi's perimeter, enabling a few hundred residents to shift out of the "informal settlement syndrome." But as with the various housing schemes that preceded it, the PMGP's most significant legacy lay in the cumulative knowledge it produced about slum improvement. Two aspects of the program in particular would become central to future schemes: redevelopment and cross-subsidization. Although redevelopment on a large scale was not achievable under the PMGP, the replacement of clusters of hutments with mid-rise apartment buildings was found to be exceedingly popular. Although more appropriate financial models would have to be developed, residents and project administrators both now saw apartments as a viable alternative to hutments. The more appropriate financial models, meanwhile, would be found through cross-subsidization. When the apartments became too expensive for residents, even with direct subsidies and no-interest loans, the PMGP administrators determined that the commercial tenants could pay a higher rate for their units and subsidize the residential units (Mukhija 2001a). Under the program, ground-floor spaces in the new apartment buildings were being allocated for commercial occupants, such as dry goods shops, clinics, and office spaces. Because these uses were ultimately revenue-generating, project administrators determined that they could pay 50 percent more than the residential occupants were paying, thereby subsidizing the residential apartments (Mukhija 2001a). Although this approach did little to alleviate the financial burden on residents, it demonstrated to administrators that potentially profitable components of the project could be used to finance the less profitable parts. New housing could be provided to slum residents for a relatively lower price and at no additional cost to the government (Mukhija 2003). Over the next two decades, these two discoveries would transform the terrain of housing policy and Bombay's physical landscape, as mid-rise buildings like those being built in Dharavi would begin to spring up across the city.

Legacies of Entrenchment

Although the various interventions in Bombay's slums were designed to improve and ultimately eradicate them, these programs had the opposite effect of further integrating and entrenching informality in Bombay's urban fabric. Living conditions in some of the city's slum settlements did gradually improve with the service provision, infrastructure building, hut improvements, and redevelopments undertaken as part of each program, even while the programs as a whole failed to achieve their usually ambitious objectives. But each of these interventions, along with the episodic demolition drives carried out intermittently throughout this period, established and deepened social rifts between already disadvantaged groups. The stratification of the city's informal residents by location, length of residency, and possession of documentation exacerbated vulnerabilities and ultimately deepened residents' dependence on politicians, NGOs, and neighborhood big men. These experiences also resulted in the mobilization of numerous housing rights organizations to use the courts, the street, and the tools of self-enumeration to establish the residents' right to stay put. These mobilizations have, at times, staved off disastrous outcomes, such as the mass eviction of tens of thousands of Dharavi residents under the PMGP, while strengthening the durability of spaces like Dharavi, making them resistant to each new effort to transform them.

The forty-year history of government interventions in Bombay's slums also demonstrates entrenchment as a product of bureaucratic weakness and political fragmentation. While I have argued that slums proliferated in Bombay not simply because of government ineptitude but also because of more deliberate support for industrial growth and the supportive neglect of slums as a solution to the need for workers' housing, the state's limited capacity and authority to intervene in this area remains a critical piece of the city's experience with residential informality. Despite the participation of often well-meaning and competent program administrators, shortfalls of resources and political authority undermined each slum scheme. Without clarity about which agencies or levels of government were authorized to design and implement appropriate housing interventions, each program suffered from unclear and inconsistent objectives, competing agendas, and a lack of coordination.

Yet despite these inconsistencies, this history also demonstrates the iterative nature of the city's housing interventions. Each subsequent effort has built on the programs that preceded it; the supposedly innovative solutions proposed today thus have their foundations in more than a half-century of experiments. While this history may appear to be linear, moving progressively from clearance to improvement to redevelopment, it is also cyclical, as seemingly abandoned ideas like clearance and relocation are periodically revived in this turbulent political context.

CHAPTER THREE

From Labor to Land

An Emerging Political Economy

In the 1980s and 1990s Mumbai[1] underwent a major economic transition, shifting from a mostly manufacturing city to one increasingly dependent on services and consumption. With changes to India's industrial policy and increased competition from abroad, manufacturing facilities, particularly those associated with the city's historically powerful textile industry, began to shut their doors and relocate to the rural hinterland. As labor demands shifted, so did the place of slums and slum dwellers in the city's political economy. At the same time, Mumbai's land prices were soaring. Unleashed by a series of national-level industrial and monetary reforms, demand for Mumbai real estate intensified among local investors and global speculators. As political interests around land and labor were shifting at the national, state, and local levels, new actors, interest groups, and political parties were emerging to help shape Mumbai's agenda for slums and slum redevelopment. Slums were becoming more valuable for their land than for the labor provided by their inhabitants, and centrally located settlements like Dharavi came to be viewed as the latest development opportunity.

In broad strokes, these dynamics reflect structural transformations under way in cities throughout the world. Analyzed in other contexts under the framework of deindustrialization, neoliberalization, or a shift from *Fordism* to *post-Fordism*, similar developments have been recognized in cities in Europe and North America and in much of the former colonial world. While these transformations partially reflect global shifts, they are also shaped by local political, economic, and cultural institutions, resulting in distinct experiences and outcomes in each city. In Mumbai, the burdens of these shifts have been borne most directly by the millions of slum residents, pavement dwellers, and inhabitants of other informal

Despite its general condition of durability, Dharavi has not been immune to development pressures under way across Mumbai. This photograph shows new construction in the Kala Kila settlement of Dharavi. Photograph by Benji Holzman.

settlements. This population has experienced the most direct impacts of job losses in the formal manufacturing sector, the informalization of labor, the pressures placed by land speculation and development, and new forms of political violence that have accompanied these turbulent transitions.

This chapter traces these transformations. While demonstrating that the government's emerging response to slums is rooted in shifting economic conditions and, more specifically, the dramatic exodus of manufacturing employment from the city center, the chapter also situates the new priorities and policies in broader (even global) changes under way since the early 1980s. The most consequential developments include the reforms adopted to liberalize the Indian economy; the breakdown of Congress Party dominance in the state and the shift of power toward Maharashtra's more urbanized coastal districts; the volatility (and increasing criminality) of Mumbai's land markets, bolstered by economic liberalization and the new urban coalitions gaining power in the state government; and the alignment of public and private interests around a new, globally oriented urban development agenda. After detailing these multiscalar shifts, and noting, in particular, their effects on the increasing marketization of the city's slum lands, I move on to discuss the latest plan for Dharavi's redevelopment. Situating the plan in this emerging political and economic context, I conclude that while the Dharavi Redevelopment Project shares many features with the earlier slum schemes attempted within and outside of Dharavi, the DRP reflects a new set of imperatives associated with neoliberalization and the promotion of capital accumulation through land development.

Political Economies of Land

David Harvey (2003, 2008) has provided one of the clearest analyses of the effects of neoliberalization on labor and land in his more recent writings on "accumulation by dispossession." Identifying dispossession as a core feature of capitalism under conditions of neoliberalism, Harvey explains that, since the 1970s, forms of accumulation rooted in expanded production have given way to accumulation by dispossession. The privatization of water, electricity, and other utilities, as well as new and aggressive forms of urban renewal, reflect an effort to commoditize and infuse new value into once-public goods (Harvey 2003). This process is inherently violent, Harvey explains, as the state employs its monopoly on the legitimate use of violence to facilitate capital extraction. "Surplus absorption through urban transformation has an even darker aspect," Harvey (2008, 33) writes. "It has entailed repeated bouts of urban restructuring through 'creative destruction,' which nearly always has a class dimension since it is the poor, the underprivileged and those marginalized from political power that suffer first and foremost from this process."

While Harvey's analysis draws directly upon Marx's notion of "primitive accumulation" and later Marxist theories of "creative destruction," he is not referring to the initial transition to capitalism. Rather, Harvey demonstrates that accumulation by dispossession is a response to the crisis of overaccumulation that arose in the early 1970s. In this sense, his argument is consistent with those who draw upon Karl Polanyi's classic work to argue that the current phase of globalization can be understood as a "second great transformation" (Burawoy 2000, 2010; Hettne 1999; Howard-Hassmann 2010). If the first great transformation, as Polanyi argued, entailed the fundamental restructuring of state and society to enable the commodification of land, money, and labor, then globalization and its associated neoliberal reforms can be understood as efforts to infuse new value into these "fictitious commodities" (Burawoy 2010). While Harvey's earlier writings on "flexible accumulation" put more emphasis on the changing nature and locations of production and labor in this process (Harvey 1990), his more recent analyses emphasize the extraction of surplus value from land and property (Harvey 2003, 2008).

Harvey and a number of other urban political economists have also analyzed recent shifts in urban policy, including the retrenchment of support to industry and workers in cities, as part of this transformation (Harvey 1989; Brenner 2004; Jessop 2002; Brenner and Theodore 2002). Amid the de-concentration of manufacturing and broader promotion of flexible accumulation, city leaders began to adopt neoliberal—or what Harvey (1989) terms "entrepreneurial urban governance"—strategies to attract new forms of investment. Among these strategies, cities have increasingly turned to property development as a way to bolster revenues. Harvey and others writing on these shifts in Europe and North America note that this process began in the 1970s and 1980s, as other transformations associated with neoliberal globalization were beginning to take hold.

Scholars writing on Indian cities point to the adoption of a similar set of strategies, but note a shorter history and an otherwise distinct experience of neoliberal urban governance reforms in the subcontinent (see Shatkin and Vidyarthi 2013; Ong 2011). As neoliberalization has spread as both a global ideology and a set of concrete reforms, its manifestations in any one place are historically contingent and rooted in local actors and institutions. Furthermore, despite what appears to be a political consensus emerging in Mumbai to carry out land development strategies to facilitate surplus value extraction, these aspirations frequently go unrealized. As detailed in subsequent chapters, even as new entrepreneurial schemes like the Dharavi Redevelopment Project gain momentum, institutional weaknesses, political fragmentations, and popular resistance continue to limit the aspirations of neoliberal reformers.

Deindustrializing Mumbai

Mumbai's changing economic context since the early 1980s is reflected in the shifting composition of workers in the region's formal economy. Manufacturing employment declined 5 percent per year throughout the 1980s—from 600,000 workers in 1980 to just 450,000 workers a decade later (Harris 1995, 49). The share of workers in the Mumbai Metropolitan Region (MMR) employed in manufacturing declined from 36 percent of the total workforce in 1980 to just over 17 percent eighteen years later.[2] While the share of workers in all other major sectors increased in this period, communication and services, and finance, insurance, and real estate (FIRE) had the most significant gains of 15 percent and 7 percent, respectively. While banking and financial services have been significant components of the city's economy since the early days of East India

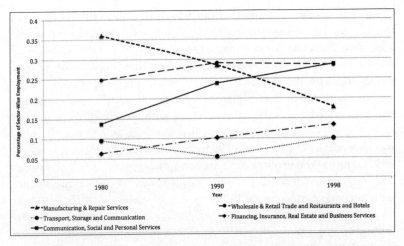

Employment by sector in the Mumbai Metropolitan Region. Data compiled from Pendharkar 2003.

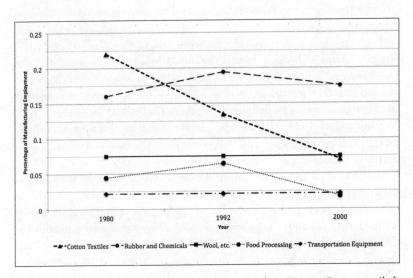

Manufacturing employment in the Mumbai Metropolitan Region. Data compiled from D'Monte 2002.

Company control, their share of the overall economic mix increased in this period. The sharpest employment losses in this period were in textiles, with a decline of more than 14 percent. All other manufacturing sectors experienced combined job losses of less than 3 percent of the total workforce, with the rubber and chemical industries experiencing slight employment growth in this period. Although Mumbai's textile industry had maintained relatively stable levels of employment through the early 1980s, a general consensus exists that the industry had been growing weakly since the 1960s (Harris 1995; Bhowmik and More 2001; D'Monte 2002). The backbone of the city's economy throughout the colonial period and into the first few decades after independence, cotton textiles—along with other export commodities—were de-emphasized in the national-level five-year economic plans of the 1960s in favor of heavy industry (D'Monte 2002; Rudolph and Rudolph 1987). The industry grew weaker in the 1970s when India's textile exports began facing increased competition from Hong Kong and China, which were pushing down the global prices of cotton textiles (Harris 1995; D'Monte 2002). With diminished profits came fewer capital investments, and the already outdated mills fell into further disrepair.

Problems in the textile industry were taking their toll on industry-worker relations throughout this period (D'Monte 2002). Strained relations reached a breaking point in January 1982, when the mill owners refused to meet the workers' demands for pay increases and the extension of labor protections to temporary workers (Bhowmik and More 2001). In mid-January 1982, a strike called by the union leadership was enthusiastically supported by the 250,000 workers in all sixty of the city's major textile mills (Menon and Adarkar 2004). Although most workers believed it would reach a quick resolution, the strike lasted eighteen months and ultimately achieved none of the workers' objectives. The mill owners had taken the opportunity provided by the strike to subcontract with power loom factories outside of the city and did not face significant reductions in production (Bhowmik and More 2001). In the meantime, many workers returned to their home villages and sought other sources of employment (Dandekar 1986; Van Wersch 1995).

When the strike ended in August 1983, the size of Mumbai's workforce in the textile industry had declined by 40 percent. Between retirements and mass layoffs, fewer than 150,000 workers returned to work after the strike, and ten of the city's textile mills were permanently closed (Bhowmik and More 2001). Although mill owners blamed the closures on the striking workers, it is generally agreed that the strike simply provided owners the opportunity to downsize the long-suffering industry (D'Monte 2002). Although the national-level industrial policy had imposed strict prohibitions on layoffs, the strikes gave the factory owners the opportunity to close without consequences. Once the strikes ended, the less profitable mills simply shut their doors. Many of the workers who were brought back were hired either as new employees without seniority or as temporary workers in the unprotected informal sector (Bhowmik and More 2001).

Economic Liberalization and the Criminalization of Land

As Mumbai's textile industry went into further decline in the 1980s, the sector most directly impacted by these shifts was real estate and property development. Given the city's continued expansion northward over the twentieth century, the mills that had once been located on the city's outskirts came to be situated in the virtual center of Mumbai. By the end of the century, the former mill compounds, concentrated primarily in an area of Central Mumbai called Girangaon, or village of mills, had been transformed into a landscape of shopping malls, television studios, and residential high-rises, becoming some of the city's most sought-after real estate. These cases of Mumbai's mill land conversions demonstrate the criminal involvement, violence, and abuses of state power entailed in the city's emerging political economies of land.

By the early 1990s the state government was under considerable pressure from the mill owners to allow the sale and redevelopment of the centrally located mill lands. Yet given the symbolic position of the city's textile industry and the continuing power of labor unions, simply rezoning the lands and preparing them for sale was politically unfeasible. In 1991 a political compromise was reached, and a new policy was written into the city's Development Control Regulations. According to the policy, referred to as DCR 58, one-third of the land was to be given to the state government to rehouse displaced mill workers and construct other low-cost housing, one-third was to be given to the Bombay Municipal Corporation for park space and other public amenities, and the textile mill owners could sell the remaining one-third for redevelopment.

The state's decision to undertake these industrial reforms and allow the lands to be sold at this time reflected a broader set of changes under way in India's economic policy. In the early 1990s the central government had succumbed to pressure from the International Monetary Fund and undertook a structural adjustment program that would have significant effects on land development and the city's property markets. Although most political economists date the first phase of India's gradual and inconsistent economic liberalization and integration into the world economy to around 1975, when the central government began deviating from its long-held import-substitution strategy, domestic industry remained highly regulated and foreign imports remained restricted throughout the 1980s (Denoon 1998; Corbridge and Harriss 2000; Nayar 2001, 2006). More deliberate reforms were enacted in the mid-1980s, initiating modest industrial deregulation and allowing for some technology imports. Most significant in this period, however, was an ideological shift regarding national development, signaled by the young, cosmopolitan prime minister Rajiv Gandhi "proclaim[ing] his faith in a new India that would 'seek to do a Korea'" (Corbridge and Harriss 2000, 150–51; Nayar 2006).

By the beginning of the 1990s India found itself in the midst of a deep recession. The war in the Persian Gulf had led to a spike in oil prices and a halt on worker remittances from the region. With significant foreign debt accrued over the previous decade, India was forced to negotiate a loan with the IMF. The terms of the loan included the adoption of structural adjustment reforms.[3] A new economic policy was adopted by the central government in January 1991, which included the reduction of industrial licensing controls and other industrial reforms, changes in trade policies, and increased allowances for foreign direct investment. The policy's most direct effects on Mumbai's political economy included new allowances for firm closures, which enabled mill owners to move out less profitable industries and leverage their centrally located lands as their most valuable asset.

Despite mounting pressure from mill owners and other private-sector interests to turn all of the six hundred acres of Mumbai's mostly defunct mill land into developable properties, competing pressures from labor unions, affordable housing advocates, and environmental groups compelled the state to take a more balanced approach to development. The government allowed some of the privately owned mills to begin selling off excess land in 1992, provided that they secured permission from the workers. These competing pressures between labor and land interests created an opening that was seized by some of the city's most notorious criminal actors, and redevelopment took a somewhat violent turn. As Mumbai-based journalist Darryl D'Monte explains (2002, 153), "The loss of industrial jobs was a grim reality; prices of real estate were going through the roof; and the ugly face of the underworld was emerging."

This ugly face became all too apparent in the case of the Khatau Mills. In this case, Sunit Khatau, chairman of one of the city's oldest textile mills, wanted to sell a factory that was sitting on prime real estate and relocate to less valuable land in the north of the city. Taking his case to the state government, the sale was approved, provided that the labor union gave its consent. When Khatau recognized that the union president would not agree to the sale, he employed the help of mafia leader Arun Gawali to engineer a union coup and install a more "sympathetic" president. With a new union president in power, Gawali helped gather the requisite worker support to approve the sale. For his part, Gawali was allegedly promised 5 percent of the sale price of the land (D'Monte 2002).

Offers were made on the land, but before the sale could be finalized, Sunit Khatau was shot while sitting in the backseat of his car. The assassins managed to escape, and Khatau died on the way to the hospital. It is widely believed that the murder was ordered by one of Gawali's main criminal rivals, anticipating the power that Gawali's gang would acquire if the sale went through and he received his share of the profits. An unsuccessful assassination attempt was also made on the union president who had worked with Khatau and Gawali to secure union support for the sale. Meanwhile, a longtime worker advocate who had been a leader in the 1982–83 strike and who had fought against the sale of the mill lands was murdered in January 1997 (D'Monte 2002). Because of the murders and alleged mafia involvement, the government eventually nullified the sale of the Khatau Mill. The union, the mill owners, and the state government are still fighting the case in court. Meanwhile, after the ruling Congress Party lost the 1995 election to the more populist Shiv Sena party, all mill land sales were halted and industrial land conversions were further banned as a measure to appease working-class voters (Raval 2000). The mill lands sat idle until the Congress Party returned to office five years later.[4]

The criminalization of land development revealed in the Khatau case is nothing new in Mumbai. Enterprising slumlords and goondas have long played important roles in the construction of low-cost housing and the proliferation of slums, when dramatic housing shortages throughout the twentieth century were met with minimal state response. While these activities received state support due, in part, to the payment of bribes and the use of goondagiri (strongarm tactics), the state also chose to supportively neglect these activities because they addressed the city's housing shortage with limited public expenditure. Yet in the early 1990s, amid the city's shifting political economy, the nature of both criminal involvement and the government's interests in land development began to change. Unlike earlier eras in which the state turned a blind eye to these nefarious development practices, state involvement became more direct. As the stakes of urban development, housing construction, and slum redevelopment increased over the coming decade, criminal involvement would become a stable feature of property development in Mumbai's emerging political economy.

The Urbanization of State Politics

The new context of deindustrialization, land conversion, and heightened urban violence had significant effects on the political landscape of Maharashtra in the 1980s and early 1990s. At the same time, the rise of new political groups and the statewide ascendance of a Mumbai-based political movement was helping to shape these emerging political economies of land and housing.

Since its formation as a linguistic state in 1960, Maharashtra has been recognized as one of the country's clearest Congress strongholds. With the exception of the 1978 election, which marked the end of Emergency rule—in which the Janata Party took the largest share of seats in Maharashtra's Legislative Assembly—Congress Party rule (in its various incarnations and splinter parties[5]) has remained stable (Vora 1996). But more than just a "typical example of the 'Congress system,'" Maharashtra's politics have also effectively illustrated the "dominant caste" thesis,[6] which identifies the enduring influence of a single political community (Vora 1996, 171; Lele 1981). Generally speaking, positions of leadership in the state have been held by members of the predominantly rural Maratha caste, given the community's dominance in local village councils (*panchayat raj*) and its control over the state's powerful agricultural cooperatives (Vora 1996). With the exception of a few brief periods, Maharashtra's political leadership has generally hailed from either the rural eastern regions of Vidharbha and Marathwada or from the central Desh. Given that most urban development and housing programs are coordinated at the state level, this rural bias in Maharashtra politics helps explain the rather limited state support garnered for earlier slum schemes and development efforts in Mumbai.

Amid the broader economic and political shifts under way at the time, this political landscape also began to change in the late 1980s and early 1990s. These shifts culminated in 1995 with the statewide electoral victory of a coalition of right-wing parties, led by the Bharatiya Janata Party (BJP) and the Mumbai-based Shiv Sena party. While scholars and political

FROM LABOR TO LAND 95

analysts have written extensively on the underlying causes and significance of their exclusionary and violent politics, there has been little focus on the implications of these electoral shifts for the new politics of land that emerged in the 1990s.[7] Rather, these studies have emphasized the "saffronization"[8] of party politics (Lele 1995; Katzenstein, Mehta, and Thakkar 1997; Hansen 2001); the political implications of deindustrialization and shifting class politics (Sharma 1995; Huezé 1995); the Shiv Sena's neighborhood level organization (Katzenstein 1979); the participation of women in the party (Bedi 2008); and the Shiv Sena's strategic use of violence (Banerjee 2000; Sharma 1995). Yet in addition to these other features of the political environment at the time, the 1995 election also signals a political shift from the rural to the urban regions of the state and helps explain the political support garnered for new agendas of land development (Vora 1996).

The Shiv Sena party—formed by the staunchly anticommunist journalist Bal Thackeray in Mumbai in 1966—has had a significant presence in the BMC since around 1970 and has held a majority of seats in the municipal corporation since 1985. Despite the party's electoral successes, the Shiv Sena did not begin as a political party, but rather as a single-issue movement, resisting the perceived dominance of South Indians in Mumbai's professional positions. Amid an acute recession in the late 1960s, Thackeray garnered grassroots support for his movement by whipping up anti–South Indian (primarily anti-Tamil) sentiments and drawing upon centuries-old myths of Maharashtra's Hindu warrior history (Lele 1995). Despite the Shiv Sena's highly centralized authoritarian structure, controlled exclusively by Thackeray, the movement grew using local networks and neighborhood-level committees or *shakas* throughout Mumbai's predominantly Maharashtrian neighborhoods (Hansen 2001). By the early 1970s, the Shiv Sena had established a significant presence in city politics and began building a statewide network with aspirations for seats in the Maharashtra Legislative Assembly. These efforts, however, proved largely unsuccessful in the 1970s. Citing Mary Fainsod Katzenstein's 1979 study, Jayant Lele (1995, 196) notes that, by the close of the decade, "the Shiv Sena had no member in the state legislature or the national parliament and its strength in the Bombay Municipal Corporation declined from 42 in 1968 to 21 in 1978."

Despite the Shiv Sena's poor electoral showing in that decade, the party's shaka structure remained strong in Mumbai's neighborhoods and slums, recruiting disaffected youth with its message of physical strength and its occasional use of violence (Lele 1995; Hansen 2001). Working-class Maharashtrians, many of whom remained active in the textile mill

Political Party	1990	1995
Congress Party	141	80
Shiv Sena	52	73
Bharatiya Janata Party (BJP)	42	65
Others and Independents	53	70
Total Seats	288	288

Outcomes in the Maharashtra Assembly elections, 1990 and 1995. Data compiled from Mukhija 2003.

labor unions, generally maintained their support for the Communist Party and the left-leaning Congress Party. Given Thackeray's anticommunist position, his party initially had little success mobilizing this population. But after the textile mill strike ended, and the promises of union activism seemed largely unrealized, the Shiv Sena's discourse became more compelling to young, working-class Maharashtrian males (Huezé 1995). The Shiv Sena's cultural content also underwent transformation in this period, as the party traded its anti-Tamil message for the increasingly popular discourse of Hindu nationalism (Lele 1995). By reframing their message in terms of Hindutva, the Shiv Sena was able to build a much larger constituency in other parts of Maharashtra, where there were much lower levels of Tamil migration, and this population was not seen as an economic threat. Its new anti-Muslim message also enabled it to forge a coalition with the right-wing BJP, which had been building a nationwide Hindutva movement (Lele 1995). Running alongside the BJP, the Shiv Sena gained significant ground in the 1990 Legislative Assembly elections, acquiring its first major bloc of non-Mumbai seats (Vora 1996). While the coalition had failed to win the majority in 1990, scandals in Maharashtra's Congress Party over the next few years, paired with the Shiv Sena's strategic use of violence, sealed the coalition's electoral success; they won enough seats to put together a government in 1995. The coalition partially owes its statewide victory in 1995 to the Shiv Sena's deep entrenchment in Mumbai's neighborhoods and slums, along with its strategic use of violence. This entrenchment became all too apparent when the city erupted in communal riots in December 1992 and January 1993. Muslim youth initiated the first set of riots on the night of December 6, just hours after Hindu fundamentalists had destroyed the Babri Masjid, a north Indian mosque that had been built on land believed to have deep Hindu significance.

In the aftermath of the 1992–93 riots, a Dharavi-based Mohalla (peace) committee created this image of a Christian boy, a Sikh boy, a Muslim boy, and a Hindu boy to demonstrate the settlement's diversity and religious tolerance. The making of this image and the activities of the Dharavi Mohalla Committee are depicted in the film *Naata*, directed by Anjali Monteiro and K. P. Jayasankar. Photograph by the author.

A month later, rival Hindu gangs, organized through Shiv Sena shakas and relying on support from the local police and major organized crime figures, carried out a more orchestrated series of attacks, targeting Muslim homes and businesses (Sharma 1995; Hansen 2001; Mehta 2005). In March 1993, in what was seen as retaliation for the January riots, a group of primarily Muslim men, most associated with the D-Company, a notorious organized crime group, carried out more than a dozen coordinated bomb blasts in hotels, corporate offices, and public spaces across Mumbai, killing more than three hundred people (Sharma 1995). The riots and bombings had deep cultural and political effects on the city, helping to deepen the rifts between Hindus and Muslims and solidify support for religious politics, not only in Mumbai, but also throughout the state.

The coalition's 1995 electoral victory can also be attributed to the state's shifting political geography. In addition to several high-profile scandals, the Congress-led government lost public support after its seemingly inept response to a 1993 earthquake in the state's eastern Marathwada district (Vora 1996). Agricultural outputs, meanwhile, were declining across the state, while investments in urban-based services were on the rise, leading political scientist Rajendra Vora (1996, 172) to suggest that "the urban sector is acquiring greater significance in the state and, therefore, the rural-based Congress is becoming irrelevant." These changes were discernable in the 1995 election results. Although the Shiv Sena and BJP made gains throughout the state, the coalition's most significant victories were in the more heavily urbanized western areas—the regions traditionally marginal to state politics.

The government put together by the Shiv Sena–BJP coalition reflected this new political geography and the coalition's urban constituency. Mano-har Joshi, the new chief minister, was the first Mumbai-based leader of Maharashtra since the state's formation in 1960. In fact, Dharavi was situated within his constituency, which would have consequences for the government's support for slum redevelopment in the coming years. Eleven out of his twenty-two cabinet ministers came from urban constituencies, and six out of sixteen state ministers came from urban areas (Vora 1996). Major Shiv Sena figures took leadership positions in the ministries and authorities with responsibility for urban development, and Chief Minister Joshi took control of the state's urban development portfolio. In contrast to previous governments that had most directly represented the rural sector, Maharashtra's government in the mid-1990s was—for the first time—of the city.

As development activities in Mumbai were overseen largely by Mumbai-kars, the ruling government now had unprecedented ties to Mumbai's business community. The Shiv Sena's leaders had close ties to builders and property developers, many of whom had open connections to organized crime groups (Hansen 2001). Also, leaders in the BJP were closely integrated in the city's pri-marily Gujarati industrial and commercial communities and had strong ties to the Bombay Chamber of Commerce and Industry (BCCI) (Vora 1996). These new alliances between government and a pro-development business commu-nity helped facilitate a new opening for real estate and property development. Meanwhile, with manufacturing on the decline and new opportunities emerg-ing for real estate development, both public- and private-sector tolerance to-ward slums was dwindling. While civic groups and municipal officials had long railed against the proliferation of slums, reflected in the violent demoli-tion drives undertaken by the BMC throughout the 1980s, these interests co-alesced into a clearer anti-slum agenda once the Shiv Sena–BJP coalition took control of the state government.

Turning Slums into Gold

The new interest in slums became apparent soon after the new government took office in 1995. One of the first actions they took (after changing the city's name to Mumbai) was to institute a housing scheme for slum dwellers to be financed with private incentives. Campaigning on a message of populism, as well as one of Hindu nationalism, the Shiv Sena ran in both 1990 and 1995 on the campaign promise of providing free homes to nearly all of Mumbai's slum dwellers. With the party's strongest support found in the city's slums, this promise appealed directly to its poor and working-class urban constituents. Yet the notion of a comprehensive solution to the slum problem also garnered support from the business community, middle-class urbanites, and those outside of Maharashtra's major cities.

The promise of free housing was made possible by the growing demand for land on the island city. Recognizing that the impacts of the Prime Minister's Grant Project (PMGP) and earlier slum housing schemes had been diminished because of the financial burden they placed on slum dwellers, the new government devised a strategy for providing the units to residents free of charge. While campaigning in the 1990 election, the Shiv Sena leader first outlined the financing formula of the plan. Thackeray suggested that given the city's high land prices, private developers would be willing to finance the reconstructed housing in exchange for the right to build on the cleared slum lands (Mukhija 2003, 29). Despite the Shiv Sena's loss in 1990, this proposal was enormously popular, and the newly elected Congress government clearly could not ignore housing issues after the election.

In 1991 the Congress-led government introduced the Slum Re-Development (SRD) program based on the financing model first proposed by Thackeray. The SRD was intended to be a voluntary program in which slum residents could participate by first forming a housing society. Housing societies could then solicit an architect and builder to carry out the construction work, as they had under the PMGP. Although the financing formula under the SRD did not allow the newly constructed units to be provided for free, as had been promised by the Shiv Sena, residents were expected to pay less than 40 percent of the construction costs (Mukhija 2003). In exchange for shouldering this significant expense, the builders had the choice of constructing market-rate housing units either onsite or in another part of the city through a practice called floating Transferable Development Rights (TDR). TDR was included in the financing formula in order to entice builders to work with housing societies located in less desirable parts of the city where there would be limited demand for the market-rate units. Without floating TDR, builders had an incentive to redevelop slum settlements only in areas in which they would see the highest return on their investments. Fearing that the program would be perceived as a giveaway to builders, significant restrictions were put in place, stipulating where the builder could use TDR and what types of buildings could be constructed on the space (Mukhija 2003). Given these restrictions, the SRD failed to generate considerable interest from builders, and few buildings were built under the program. Furthermore, the 60 percent subsidy did not provide the slum residents enough of an incentive to participate, given that they would still be likely to pay as much as twenty-five thousand rupees per housing unit (Mukhija 2003).

During the 1995 campaign, the Shiv Sena vowed to expand the program and eliminate some of these restrictions. Soon after the election, the newly elected Shiv Sena–BJP government dismantled the SRD and replaced it with the Slum Rehabilitation Scheme (SRS), which was to be overseen by a newly created parastatal agency, the Slum Rehabilitation Authority (SRA).[9] The SRS more closely reflected Thackeray's original proposal, providing the housing units to current residents free of charge. The program also had the benefit of timing, with the election coinciding with the mid-1990s peak in Mumbai's property prices. The year that SRS was launched, the cost of office space in the city's central business district surpassed the price of real estate in London and Tokyo to become the most expensive in the world, while land in other parts of Mumbai and the suburbs also reached record levels (Nijman 2000). The SRS provided builders a clear way to access land in the city's highly lucrative land markets, providing enough of an incentive to justify their now complete subsidization of the redeveloped housing units.

The program details were a blend of new features, like TDR, and familiar elements. As under the SRD and PMGP, participation in the Slum Rehabilitation Scheme was voluntary and could only be initiated when a cluster of roughly one hundred contiguous hutments organized themselves into a housing society.[10] The housing society was to select an architect and builder, and the SRA would oversee the arrangements. The SRA stipulated the building specifications and the rules governing resident eligibility, which employed the same moving tolerance date as earlier programs. When the SRA was launched, slum residents who could demonstrate continuous eligibility since before January 1, 1990, were eligible to participate.

Residents of a rehabilitation building would be given ownership of their unit, thereby providing them with secure tenure. Although they now possessed legal ownership, they would be barred from selling their unit for a period of ten years. Meanwhile, recognizing that building maintenance can create a significant financial burden for the new residents, the builder was expected to provide an additional twenty thousand rupees per unit for the building's initial maintenance costs. In exchange for these significant expenditures, the builder would receive land at a ratio of 1:1.33, which could be used either on-site or in the northern and eastern suburbs through the practice of floating TDR. In other words, for every 100 square feet of rehabilitated space the private developer constructed for former slum residents, he would receive 133 square feet of property to develop and sell at market rates.

Consistent with the 1971 Slum Act, the state government would acquire ownership of the land under the SRS, regardless of whether the slum land had previously been owned privately or by another government entity, such as the BMC or the national-level Indian Railways. After construction was completed, the government would retain ownership of the land on which both the rehabilitated housing and the market-rate buildings were built and lease it to the new occupants under a thirty-year lease. After this period, the terms of the lease were to be renegotiated.

Despite the tenure security and the dramatic subsidization, local activists initially resisted the SRS, pointing out the significant profits that builders could garner through the scheme. Eventually, broad-based support emerged for the plan, reflecting the growing acceptance that market mechanisms could be used to finance housing construction and urban development (Risbud 2003). Yet given the wild opportunities for profit, the program has been marred since its adoption with charges of corruption and illicit activity. While previous Congress-led governments certainly had their share of criminal connections—reflected, for example, in the Khatau Mill murders in the early 1990s—criminal involvement in land development became even more apparent once the Shiv Sena–BJP coalition took power. While becoming more invested in development activities in the city, the state government has also become increasingly dependent on criminal actors to help carry out its objectives.

Although the SRS stipulates that the scheme should be initiated by the housing society, builders frequently approach slum residents to propose rehabilitation projects. In some cases, residents have to be "persuaded" to accept the plan, and many builders employ goondagiri to help coerce residents to participate. These tactics have been apparent in the case of the Janata Housing Society, located in the virtual center of Dharavi. In this case, an SRS construction project was left unfinished in the late 1990s. Although the residents had moved into the building, they had to temporarily share flats because the upper floors were still uninhabitable. After this "temporary" situation went on for more than seven years, the residents began working with activists and government officials to pressure the builder to complete construction. A resident explained to me, "This is when Babu began coming around. He is the builder's right-hand man. Once we started complaining, the builder started using goondagiri. We haven't seen the builder; he is nowhere to be found. But Babu has been threatening to evict us and use violence against us if we don't stop complaining."[11] The builder's use of goondagiri proved an effective strategy for some of the residents, who are now patiently waiting for the builder to complete construction. But other residents claimed that Babu did not intimidate them, and they continued to press for the building's completion. With significant profits to be made from slum redevelopment, and given the builders' questionable business practices and professional connections, goondagiri has become an enduring feature of the new housing policy.

Despite reports of resident intimidation, the SRS has remained popular with both residents and builders. Even after the coalition lost the 1999 election and the Congress Party resumed control of state government, the SRS was continued. More than simply a scheme to provide housing to the city's most disadvantaged residents, the SRS created a way to push centrally located lands onto Mumbai's lucrative property market, thus enabling the residential and commercial developments and helping to fuel the city's property boom. The program's model for financing public initiatives has since become an accepted mechanism for funding public projects, including the construction of housing, schools, parks, and infrastructure. While similar land-sharing arrangements have been used in Southeast Asia since the late 1980s (see Sheng 1989), the cross-subsidization of land for development has proved a particularly attractive approach in Mumbai, where land prices are high and government's supply of land is greater than its financial resources to undertake development (Mukhija 2003). Meanwhile, the marketization of slum lands has been supported by neoliberal urban policy shifts in which local government has devised strategies to facilitate private-sector land development and capital accumulation.

A Man with a Plan

Among the investors and developers who recognized the opportunities entailed in this approach was Mukesh Mehta, a Mumbai-born architect and property developer who had been living and working in suburban New York. Like many nonresident Indians, or NRIs, observing the political reforms and economic growth under way in their country of origin, Mehta made the decision in the mid-1990s to return and explore business opportunities in the "new India." More specifically, Mehta saw the possibilities entailed in Maharashtra's new slum housing policy and Mumbai's increasingly lucrative property markets. Just one of many builders and developers who recognized these opportunities, his ambitions were larger than originally envisioned in the slum policy. Up to that point, the SRS had been used only on a piecemeal basis, to rehouse single housing societies, comprising roughly one hundred families, at a time. Although many builders were working on several SRS projects simultaneously, none had sought to redevelop contiguous housing societies as part of a larger development project. Yet Mehta could see no reason why the program could not be implemented on a larger scale, allowing for the redevelopment of larger plots concurrently, thus freeing up much larger amounts of space for market-rate developments. A consultant working with Mehta explained:

> The SRA had just been formed. And they were going about—well, they still do today—going about it in this piecemeal kind of approach. So he met with political people at that time and said, look you are going about this all wrong. When you have large areas, you should try to develop them as suburbs. . . . They were like, like what, areas like Dharavi? And he said, well, yes, areas like Dharavi. And it sort of took off from there.[12]

Although it is unlikely that Mehta's decision to redevelop the entire settlement of Dharavi emerged from a single conversation, this story has taken on something of a mythical quality, as Mehta has worked to portray himself as Dharavi's accidental developer.

Determined to redevelop the entire 535-acre settlement of Dharavi within the framework of the SRS, Mehta set to work on land-use plans and financing formulas. His initial plan proposed rehousing Dharavi's current residents in high-rise buildings along the settlement's perimeter, while building up its interior with luxury housing, office buildings, and a golf course. Yet he soon came to realize that his plan entailed too great a financial risk for him to take on alone. "A project of this size needs money," he explained. "If it got obstructed by government, I could have lost a lot of money. The finances had to come from somewhere else. And government needed to put a guarantee on the financing."[13] In addition to the financial risk, he recognized that the state's development regulations would have to

be amended. Consequently, he determined that the project could only proceed if it secured government sponsorship. He began selling his Dharavi
plan to the government of Maharashtra.

By the end of the 1990s Mehta was receiving some encouragement
from government officials, but he was yet to garner an official pledge
of support. With the new government's political base found primarily in
Mumbai for the first time in the state's forty-year history, housing and
urban development initiatives were more prominently on the state agenda
than they had been during previous administrations (Vora 1996). In fact,
the state's chief minister, Manohar Joshi, represented the Mumbai constituency that included Dharavi. Although Mehta recalls that Joshi remained
skeptical of his plans, the project was beginning to elicit support from
others within his government. Yet in October 1999 the ruling coalition
lost the statewide elections, and the opposition, led once again by the
Congress Party, formed a new government. The political ground Mehta
had gained was lost. Because the previous government had begun express-
ing support for the scheme, the newly elected Congress government took
steps to publicly distance itself from it. Mehta went to work again to build
political support within the new government. Not aligned with any of the
state's political parties, Mehta felt free to work with whatever party was
in power.

Mehta's efforts began to pay off in 2001 and 2002 when his plan won
favor with the state's housing secretary Suresh Joshi. Mehta recalls:

> We had been petitioning them for years. Every housing secretary that
> came in, we would go straight to him and say, "Why don't you get
> involved? Why don't you do this?" And then Dr. Suresh Joshi came
> to us. They were interested all of a sudden. Maybe it was destiny, or
> whatever. . . . Right then the government had taken this huge initiative
> for infrastructure projects, so I guess it all fell into line.[14]

Housing Secretary Joshi encouraged Mehta to approach government as
a partner rather than simply an enabler for his plan. Taking Joshi's advice,
Mehta claims that he was able to present the project as a "win-win" situation.
"Politicians got a new way to look at slums, and I got the project I wanted."[15]

Although Mehta had begun building support throughout the government, Chief Minister Vilasrao Deshmukh still refused to officially sponsor
the project. Over the next two years, however, as a new urban agenda
came together, premised on transforming Mumbai into a "world-class
city," Dharavi's redevelopment would rise to the top of this agenda and
would eventually garner state sponsorship.

Dharavi's Place in a "World-Class" City

With the city's manufacturing base in steep decline, new markets emerging for land and property development, and politics in the state having taken an urban turn, a new set of political and economic interests were coalescing in the early 2000s. These interests gained voice in late 2003, in a report commissioned by a policy organization named Bombay First. The report, referred to as the "McKinsey Report" for the international consulting firm commissioned to prepare it, did not reveal new findings or present novel policy proposals for improving the city's competitive position. Rather, the glossy thirty-page report voiced anxieties that the business community had felt for years and made familiar recommendations for improving the city's economic position and quality of life. The report suggested that Mumbai could make "jumps toward achieving world city status" within ten to fifteen years if a variety of development projects were undertaken, including improved transportation infrastructures, deregulation of the city's land supply, and the construction of new housing (Bombay First 2003). Given the congruence between Mehta's Dharavi plan and the recommendations outlined in the McKinsey Report, the state government eventually adopted and promoted the two plans side by side.

In the mid-1990s, members of the Bombay Chamber of Commerce and Industry (BCCI) formed a new organization to press for economic development objectives. Modeling itself on London First, a similar effort launched by London's business community to address that city's declining competitive position, the BCCI created Bombay First in 1996. As the former director of Mumbai First explained:

> People felt the business was going away, out of Mumbai. There was not much business coming into the city. It was moving to Hyderabad, to Bangalore. . . . It was learned that Mumbai was going down in two major ways. One was that economic growth in the city was going down. And secondly, economic growth was reducing the quality of life in the city. So in order to bring Mumbai back onto the business map of the country, several models were looked into. The New York model was looked into. And London was looked at too. It was going down twenty years ago, when the organization London First had emerged. And we picked up the London First model and we became Bombay First.[16]

Representatives of most of the large foreign and domestic companies with headquarters or offices in Mumbai joined the effort. Upon its formation, Bombay First began lobbying the newly elected Shiv Sena–BJP government to support reforms and make investments. With the new administration amenable to urban development and willing to work with private investors to secure financing, Bombay First found government generally receptive to its concerns. These lobbying efforts, meanwhile, were bolstered by the existing ties that the BJP's political leaders had with members of the BCCI.

Even after the Congress Party returned to office in 1999, the state government retained its commitment to urban affairs, continuing the SRS and moving forward with the Mumbai Urban Transport Project (MUTP), a World Bank–financed infrastructure project launched by the previous administration. Bombay First continued to organize seminars and produce reports on such issues as the regulatory barriers to housing construction and the state of Mumbai's entertainment industry. Despite the government's rhetorical support, Bombay First's members were growing frustrated with the slow pace of action on this agenda.

In mid-2003, Bombay First hired the global management consulting firm McKinsey & Company to conduct an analysis and make recommendations to improve its competitive position. The civic leaders recognized that recommendations from international consultants may carry more weight and bring more attention to their agenda. Over a period of five months, McKinsey & Company conducted interviews and held focus groups with government officials and representatives from business and civil society. They conducted case studies of other cities that had apparently bolstered their competitive positions—including Hyderabad, Cleveland, Bangalore, and Shanghai—and concluded that, with investments from the public and private sectors totaling approximately $40 billion, Mumbai could make a similar transformation in a decade. Upon its release, the McKinsey Report generated debate among academics, opposition from civil society organizations, and a rhetorical commitment from the government—demonstrating that the international consulting firm did indeed lend weight to the recommendations.

At the report's public release in September 2003 Vilasrao Deshmukh, Maharashtra's chief minister, announced his commitment to carrying out its recommendations. Within weeks, he established a task force to investigate the feasibility of specific recommendations and created subcommittees to work on each of the issue areas. In early 2004 the "Chief Minister's Taskforce" released its own report with plans for "transforming Mumbai into a world class city" within ten years (State of Maharashtra 2004). The government's version adopted many of the recommendations of the McKinsey Report essentially verbatim. In an effort to bring even greater recognition to this agenda, the state hired McKinsey & Company to oversee the implementation of the task-force plan. Over the next three years McKinsey would be paid roughly two hundred thousand dollars to conduct an audit of the government bureaucracy and document the implementation of the recommendations (Marpakwar 2006).

The release of the McKinsey Report came in the lead-up to statewide elections, helping to give it a public platform and to help shape the message of the Congress Party's reelection campaign. Campaigning for state officials in Maharashtra in October 2004, India's prime minister Manmohan Singh employed the language of the McKinsey Report to advocate for Mumbai's transformation. Leaving aside the models of Cleveland, Bangalore, and Hyderabad, Singh promoted the idea that Mumbai could be transformed in the model of Shanghai:

> When we talk of a resurgent Asia, people think of the great changes that have come about in Shanghai. I share this aspiration to transform Mumbai in the next five years in such a manner that people would forget about Shanghai and Mumbai will become a talking point. I have a dream that we can do it. I believe we can become number one through modernization, expansion and development and make Mumbai the number-one city in our country. (Quoted in Srivastava 2005)

Singh's statement soon became the rallying cry of Maharashtra's Congress Party and formed the core platform for the newly elected chief minister, Vilasrao Deshmukh, in November 2004. Over the next several months, politicians and bureaucrats made pronouncements that Mumbai would be "transformed into Shanghai." Although few specific proposals were made for how this could be achieved, statements about the transformation were accompanied by bold language about state-of-the-art infrastructures and slum-free cities. How the government planned to undertake the transformation became clear within weeks after Chief Minister Deshmukh took office.

In early December 2004 Chief Minister Deshmukh ordered the BMC to begin demolishing unauthorized hutments. Despite the emphasis on authorization, the BMC demolition squads did not ask for documentation of "authorization" or tenure. Rather, residents were given immediate orders to take their belongings and vacate their homes. As one resident of the Bhimchaya settlement explained to a newspaper reporter, "In the morning when the policeman and the bulldozers came and told us get out, there were women bathing. They were not given time even to dress properly. We lost everything. We had papers to stay here. Where should I move now?" (Ramesh 2005). In a similar manner, settlements were demolished across the city. In early January 2005 Miloon Kothari, independent special rapporteur with the UN Commission on Human Rights, visiting the sites of the cleared hutments, described the campaign under way as the "most brutal demolition drive in recent times" (Srinivasan 2005). By the time the campaign ended in February 2005, due to mounting protests and increased pressure from the national-level Congress Party, upward of four hundred thousand people had been evicted from their homes (Committee for the Right to Housing 2006).

At the height of the campaign, Chief Minister Deshmukh unveiled his plan for transforming Mumbai into Shanghai. In February 2005 Deshmukh outlined a roughly 6.5-billion-dollar plan that included the construction of new roads and bridges, upgrading the international airport, constructing an underground metro, and continuing to remove "encroachments" (*Indian Express* 2005).[17] His plan simply adopted and gave greater specificity to many of the proposals outlined in the McKinsey Report. In fact, Deshmukh credited McKinsey & Company with helping provide the vision and framework for his new Shanghai plan and his ongoing demolition drive. Although the McKinsey Report did not explicitly advocate the use of bulldozers to carry out these objectives, representatives of Bombay First affirmed its support for the government's actions. "If Mumbai has to be a World Class city, then the slums have to go and . . . strong and urgent steps need to be taken" (quoted in Mahadevia and Narayanan 2008, 551). And as news outlets around the world reported on the demolition campaign, the government's strong and urgent steps had been made starkly visible.

Although Mehta's plan for Dharavi was not explicitly mentioned in either the McKinsey Report or the Chief Minister's Taskforce document, the Taskforce did include the redevelopment of Dharavi among both its short-term and longer-term goals. Specifically, the document recommended the development of "at least three sectors of Dharavi for commercial or office use, and [the extension of] the Bandra-Kurla Complex to Dharavi" (State of Maharashtra 2004, 14). From the perspective of the state government, Dharavi's redevelopment could be an extension of the Bandra-Kurla Complex (BKC), and state government pushed for changes to Mehta's plan to reflect this emphasis.

The BKC, seen as one of the most significant development successes of the Maharashtra government in recent years, is an office complex, directly opposite Dharavi on the north shore of the Mahim Creek. For the better part of the 1990s, the state government's Mumbai Metropolitan Regional Development Authority (MMRDA) oversaw construction of hundreds of acres of office space in the Bandra-Kurla area, much more accessible to Mumbai's international airport than the traditional business center in South Bombay. Although the project took more than a decade to construct and has faced significant political and technical hurdles, the project is now viewed as a success for the state. In a series of auctions in the mid-2000s, developers and the MMRDA both made significant profits, with each auction securing record-high prices (Business Standard 2007). The high land prices in the BKC are generally attributed to the limited supply of space in the area, which would be bolstered by extending the complex into Dharavi. Dharavi's redevelopment would improve the connectivity of the BKC to South Bombay's traditional business districts, as the current route between the BKC and the island city now passes through Dharavi's narrow and congested roads.

With the DRP aligned with the development objectives presented in the McKinsey Report and the Taskforce document, Mehta was able to secure the state government's support for his plan in early 2004. In a cabinet meeting in February 2004 Chief Minister Deshmukh committed his political support to the comprehensive redevelopment of Dharavi's housing, infrastructure, industries, and commercial spaces. Amid media fanfare and bold proclamations that Mumbai would be slum-free and Dharavi would be transformed into a cultural, business, and knowledge center, a new public commitment was made to slum redevelopment in general and to Dharavi in particular. As Mehta stood at the podium, detailing the DRP in a PowerPoint presentation complete with color-coded land-use maps and catchy acronyms, the meeting resembled the launch of a new product more than a cabinet discussion of a low-income housing program. Framed now as a part of the state's efforts to transform Mumbai into a world-class city, this presentation revealed the new objectives of slum redevelopment, facilitated by the economic and political shifts of the previous decade. Soon after the state government's endorsement of Mehta's plan in 2004, it began promoting the sale of BKC land and Dharavi's redevelopment alongside one another.[18]

While the timing of the state's endorsement of the DRP was due, in part, to the plan's congruity with the broader agenda of improving Mumbai's competitiveness and world-city standing, the project's profile was also raised by growing support from New Delhi. In January 2004 the project won an important victory when the central government committed roughly one hundred million dollars for Dharavi's redevelopment. Although the pledge was reminiscent of the PMGP, it was made without consultation of officials in the Maharashtra government. In fact, the intervention of the central government into Mumbai's urban affairs was interpreted as a direct challenge to the state government's authority. Given that urban development is a constitutionally defined "state subject," it was remarkable that New Delhi would pledge its financial support to a scheme that had still not garnered official state approval. More than an intergovernmental conflict, the subversion of the state's authority also represented interparty conflict, given that the central government was ruled by a right-wing coalition that included the Shiv Sena party and had former Maharashtra chief minister Manohar Joshi in the position of Speaker of Parliament. Meanwhile, the Congress Party was in power at the time at the state level. Now shamed into offering its own support, the state government announced the following week that it would partner with Mehta on the project and provide financial backing for this project. Although the national government's support had put pressure on the state, New Delhi eventually rescinded the pledge after the ruling government lost the next election and the Congress Party took control at the center.

Developing Dharavi, Part Three

The physical plan of the Dharavi Redevelopment Project (DRP) has gone through many incarnations since it garnered state approval in early 2004 and is certain to change again before implementation. The official version endorsed in 2004 divided Dharavi into ten sectors of roughly equal size. Each sector would continue to house most of the current residents and much of the commerce and industry currently located in that sector, in addition to the market-rate commercial constructions. Eventually, the number of sectors was reduced to five, due to both political and technical challenges mounted against the plan.

The approved plan stipulated that each household deemed eligible for rehabilitation would receive an apartment in a mid- or high-rise building located in the sector in which the household currently lives.[19] Regardless of the size of the household's current home, all rehabilitation apartments would be 225 square feet, made up of a main room, a kitchen, and an attached bathroom. As discussed in the next two chapters, this policy regarding housing standardization has been a source of significant conflict throughout the planning process, given that some of Dharavi's residents currently inhabit much larger dwellings. Consistent with SRS policy, apartments will not be rental units, but leases will be given to the tenants. Earlier stipulations barring residents from selling units in the rehabilitated buildings for ten years would continue. Although the apartments would be given free of charge, residents are expected to pay municipal taxes and maintenance fees, which are anticipated to have significant effects on the housing expenses for most Dharavi residents.

The plan stipulated that the constructions would be financed by five private developers or developer consortia, each of which would be responsible for constructing the infrastructure, amenities, and housing for a single sector. As compensation, the developers would receive additional land and increased height allowances to develop market-rate commercial properties, yet in contrast to the SRA, developers would not be able use floating TDR to construct the market-rate properties outside of Dharavi. Given Mumbai's high land prices and the desirability of Dharavi's location, the developers were expected to recoup their expenses and make considerable profit from the sale of the market-rate constructions. These expectations were revealed when expression of interest (EOI) documents were invited in June 2007 and seventy-eight development firms applied to bid on the project.

While most of the project features, including the cross-subsidization financing formula, simply continue the SRS policy devised by the Shiv Sena, the most significant difference is the types of developers sought for the DRP. Most SRS projects are constructed by small-scale local builders who specialize in housing for Mumbai's rehabilitated slum dwellers. When the DRP plan was approved in 2004, it was slated to be the first government-sponsored scheme allowing and encouraging bidding by foreign investors and international real estate development firms. Although the project's administrators claimed that the most qualified developers would be selected for the project, regardless of their location or size, there has been a clear preference throughout the planning process for large, international developers. The project administrators have taken steps to elicit interest abroad, making frequent presentations about the project around the world, particularly in the United States, Canada, the United Kingdom, Dubai, and Singapore. When developer interest was invited in June 2007, the tender was published in newspapers in more than twenty countries as well as throughout India. Of the seventy-eight developers who submitted expression of interest documents to bid on the scheme, over a third were non-Indian firms (Deshmukh 2007). The remaining two-thirds were made up of India's largest development and construction firms, not the smaller-scale builders that typically participate in slum rehabilitation projects.

Beyond the project's scale and the interest it has garnered from large domestic and international developers, the DRP's aims reflect a new set of objectives, namely the conversion of land to market-rate properties in support of the state's ambition to make Mumbai a more globally competitive city. While this shift toward the marketization of slum land to facilitate urban development has been gradual—having first been identified as a potential strategy in the PMGP—the DRP reflects its culmination. It reflects the embrace of entrepreneurial approaches to urban governance, in which local policy agendas shift toward supporting capital accumulation by the private sector. Although the process by which the Mumbai government embraced this strategy is rooted in changes under way in the local and national political economies—as much as a global transformation—it resonates with Harvey's analysis of similar shifts under way in a diverse set of cities since the late 1970s. Harvey writes:

> Deindustrialisation, widespread and seemingly 'structural' unemployment, fiscal austerity at both the local and national levels, all coupled with a rising tide of neoconservatism and much stronger appeal (though stronger in theory than in practice) to market rationality and privatisation, provide a backdrop to understanding why so many urban governments, often of quite different political persuasions and armed with very different legal and political powers, have all taken a broadly similar direction. (1989, 5)

In the case of Mumbai, the particular political persuasions have been reshaped by a series of multiscalar shifts that include economic liberalization, the challenges to long-standing Congress Party power, the rise of Hindu nationalist politics and associated urban violence, the criminalization of land development, and the emergence of a pro-growth coalition comprising the city's business elite and officials in the state government.

From Labor to Land

The changing objectives from slum improvement to property development have paralleled the city's shifting political economy. Amid Mumbai's deindustrialization and changing economic composition, the state has become less accepting of slums. While the presence and proliferation of slums had been "supportively neglected" throughout the city's hundred-year period of industrial development, tolerance for residential informality has diminished as the land on which slums sit has become more and more valuable. In addition to deindustrialization and the movement of manufacturing facilities out of the city, this shift has been facilitated by the creation of a new political economy of land. Land speculation has long been a part of Mumbai's economic geography—given the island city's limited supply of land and its poor transit linkages to the main-

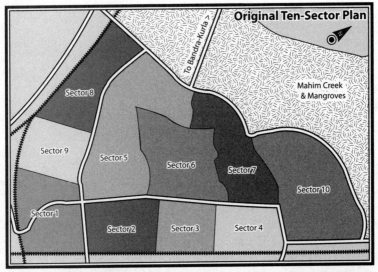

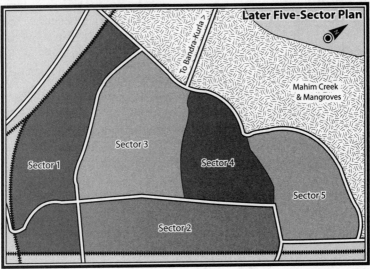

Maps depicting the original ten-sector Dharavi layout and the later five-sector plan. Maps by John L. Myers.

land. Yet begining in the early 1990s, a new urgency for land conversion and property development has arisen alongside economic liberalization and a greater openness for global investment. Land speculation took hold among both local and global investors, and some Mumbai properties became the most expensive real estate in the world. Along with legitimate investors, organized crime groups have entered into Mumbai's lucrative property sector, and goondagiri have become a predominant feature of these new politics. Within this context, the objectives of the city's slum housing programs began to change.

The government's new perspective on slums came into sharp focus when Desmukh's administration launched the violent demolition campaign in late 2004, premised on turning Mumbai into Shanghai. Yet while the state may wish to simply bulldoze slum settlements, these accumulationalist aspirations have been tempered by the political and institutional entrenchment of slums in the city of Mumbai. Given this entrenchment, Harvey's concept of accumulation by dispossession may not be the most appropriate frame for understanding the shifting place of slums in Mumbai's global economy. Even as slum settlements are being bulldozed and plans are being developed to transform Dharavi into an extension of the Bandra-Kurla office park to the north, these spaces retain some of the durability that has made them an enduring feature of Mumbai's complex social landscape.

CHAPTER FOUR

Political Entrepreneurship and Enduring Fragmentations

I had been trying for weeks to set up a meeting with Satish Sheynde, the elected BMC councilor for Dharavi's 176th Ward and a longtime member of the Congress Party. I had heard that Sheynde had been criticizing the Dharavi Redevelopment Project (DRP) in private conversations and public forums. Meanwhile, these accounts conflicted with official statements about uniform Congress backing for the project. In fact, politicians at all levels of government had assured me that the DRP's success was virtually guaranteed because "this is a Congress plan" and all party members support it.[1] I finally reached Sheynde by phone, and he told me to come right over to his ward office in the industrial warehouse district on Dharavi's northern edge. When he arrived more than an hour later, accompanied by six large, somewhat intimidating men, he apologetically ushered me into an office and instructed me to take a seat. We sat in facing chairs, and his entourage sat on benches behind us, quietly listening to the conversation.[2]

Without much prompting, Sheynde began listing his complaints with the project and its planning process. First, he explained, "The public is confused about the plan. Mukesh Mehta is not explaining it very clearly." He elaborated that the residents in his ward were primarily businesspeople—industrialists, leather workers, and tailors—and that many of them currently have much more space than the 225 square feet that was then being promised under the plan. He added that some of the residents in his ward currently have as much as 2,000 to 3,000 square feet of space. He estimated that 65 percent of the households have about 225 square feet; 5 percent have less than that; and the remainder has more. "If 30 percent of my constituents are going to be harmed by the plan, then how can I support it?" he asked rhetorically. He explained that those with the larger units are businesspeople who use the additional space for productive activities. "Mehta's plan looks nice, with its gardens and hospitals," he acknowledged. "But how will the people live if they cannot do their businesses?"

I had also been meeting with some of these businesspeople and small-scale manufacturers and had heard about their space concerns, but Sheynde was the first elected official I had met who was raising these issues publicly. Curious about the mechanisms of Dharavi's ward-level politics, I asked how he learns of his constituents' concerns. Do they seek him out to discuss these space issues? And does he then bring these concerns directly to officials in the Slum Rehabilitation Authority (SRA), the government agency charged with designing the plan? He replied emphatically that yes, his constituents come to him to discuss these and all manner of issues. But he quickly clarified that there is little point in raising them with the SRA, as they would not be addressed in the planning process. "Mukesh Mehta and the SRA will not change the plan. They are making all the decisions themselves." He further explained that, as a ward councilor, he has little say in "how the city gets run." The city is run by Maharashtra's chief minister, he explained, and local politicians are not very involved. Sheynde seemed more or less resigned to the limited influence he had over the DRP and in municipal affairs more generally. But as was evident by the brazen way he spoke about the project, as well as by the entourage that accompanied him, Sheynde clearly commanded respect within Dharavi, and there were domains over which he had influence.

While Sheynde's candor and vocal opposition were distinctive, his characterization of a centralized planning process for the DRP was widespread. Working closely with the SRA and the state's chief minister, Mehta appeared to have consolidated the authority and resources required for Dharavi's redevelopment. The concerns Sheynde raised had an urgency to them because he believed implementation was imminent. This belief that development was finally coming to Dharavi was pervasive among the project's advocates and its critics. What development would mean for the settlement's hundreds of thousands of residents and productive industries was unclear and subject to fierce negotiations. But something was happening. In addition to an altered political context and new economies of land and property, the DRP appeared to have something that earlier development schemes in Dharavi and elsewhere had lacked: centralized authority. Since its early conceptualization in the late 1990s, Mehta had advocated for the project in the face of bureaucratic neglect and political opposition. When the state endorsed the project in early 2004, Mehta received the

National Level
1. Mumbai Port Trust
2. Indian Railways
3. Mahanagar Telephone Nigam Limited (MTNL)

State Level
4. Government of Maharashtra (GoM)
5. Mumbai Metropolitan Regional Development Authority (MMRDA)
6. Slum Rehabilitation Authority (SRA)
7. Maharashtra Housing and Area Development Authority (MHADA)
8. Maharashtra Industrial Development Corporation (MIDC)
9. Maharashtra Pollution Control Board (MPCB)
10. Public Works Department (PWD)
11. Road Transport Office (RTO)
12. Maharashtra State Road Development Corporation (MSRDC)

Municipal Level
13. Municipal Corporation of Greater Mumbai (MCGM) or BMC
14. Mumbai Police
15. Bombay Electric Supply and Transport (BEST)

Agencies with planning and land-use powers in Mumbai. Adapted from Bombay First 2003.

legitimacy and resources he needed to pursue his vision, along with the promise of some of the financial spoils of development. In return, Mehta would help the government overcome the structural inertia and resource gaps that had hindered earlier schemes.

Yet while Mehta consolidated the authority he needed to get the DRP onto the state's political agenda and redirect administrative resources to support its planning, he proved unable to bring either local political leaders or citywide elites on board with his vision. Although Mumbai's business community and civil society organizations had been advocating the types of developments that would make Mumbai globally competitive, or a "world-class city," these groups never explicitly endorsed Mehta's project as a way to realize this vision of a "world-class" Mumbai. A virtual outsider to the city's political networks and civil society groups, Mehta proved unable to forge an effective development coalition, and the DRP has remained the property of a single individual. Meanwhile, Mehta seemed to underestimate the importance of ward councilors like Sheynde and their Dharavi-based networks. As a consequence he proved unable to shield the DRP from political debates and public scrutiny, and both the project and his role in it came under sharp criticism. More than a decade into the DRP's planning process, municipal authority remains weak, power in both Mumbai and Dharavi remains fractured, and the iconic slum remains entrenched in the city's social and spatial landscape.

Fragmentations and Partnerships

Given the hundreds of administrative and elected positions within the Municipal Corporation of Greater Mumbai, or MCGM,[3] as well as the dozen or so other agencies responsible for land use and planning in Mumbai, it seems strange to emphasize weaknesses in local administration. Yet despite this administrative complexity—and ultimately because of it—substantive authority for urban planning is fragmented and overly diffuse. Although the MCGM is the body formally responsible for governance in Mumbai, many substantive powers, particularly those around urban planning and land use, rest with the state of Maharashtra. Within the MCGM, chief executive authority continues to be held by the municipal commissioner, a senior-level member of the Indian Administrative Service (IAS), appointed by the state government. Serving at the favor of Maharashtra's chief minister, Mumbai's municipal commissioner is an extension of state-level power in the city. And although the MCGM has a mayor elected from among its ward councilors, the mayor's authority is minimal and his duties are largely ceremonial. The activities of town planning, land-use regulation, and building construction are spread among roughly fifteen agencies that straddle the local, state, and national levels of government.

Although most substantive land-use powers rest with the state government, the government of Maharashtra has historically exhibited a reluctance to devote significant resources to this area. Even though Maharashtra is one of India's most urbanized states, a majority of its residents live in rural areas, and its politics have generally been centered outside its major cities. Until the mid-1990s, none of Maharashtra's chief ministers had represented a Mumbai-based constituency, and elected officials had little incentive to expend political resources in the state's largest city (Vora 1996).

The state's "politically neutral but professional policy bureaucracy" has also failed to provide the leadership and centralized administrative power needed to promote urban development (Rudolph and Rudolph 1987, 79). Observers have remarked that, with positions in the bureaucracy assigned by state politicians, bureaucrats tend to collaborate directly with the political leadership and are susceptible to similar political pressures (Rudolph and Rudolph 1987). Mumbai-based political scientist Marina Pinto and former municipal officer David Pinto have been scathing in their critique of bureaucrats in Maharashtra's parastatal planning agencies:

Often they lack transparency in their functioning and are ridden with corruption. They are highly bureaucratised and lack knowledge and experience of grassroots problems. They not only weaken the MCGM, which is a multi-functional body, but also give rise to problems that result from an overlapping of civic and urban functions between them. Besides, their field officers show very little interest in coordinating their activities with others at the local level. Often, their functional autonomy is reduced because of State controls and statutory constraints. Although each quasi-governmental organisation has a logic and history of its own which can justify its existence, their proliferation aggravates the problem of coordination, diffuses responsibility and weakens citizen control over local affairs. (Pinto and Pinto 2005, 494)

These additional administrative layers add further complexity and do little to overcome the political and administrative weaknesses that undermine effective urban planning and land use in Mumbai.

The movement to decentralize political authority, which culminated in the adoption of the Seventy-Fourth Amendment to the Indian Constitution, reflects an effort to redress this situation. Beginning in the 1980s, pressure to devolve resources and authority to the local level began to emerge from two disparate corners: pro-democracy social activists and pro-liberalization economic reformers. Development economists and social activists had begun to make the connection between India's rampant inequalities and the lack of political representation at the local level (see, for example, Drèze and Sen 1995). Development schemes and social service provision were perceived to be carried out by technocrats disconnected from local affairs. Reflecting this sentiment, Pranab Bardhan notes:

For far too long . . . large-scale technocratic development projects have been directed from above, administered by a distant, uncoordinated and occasionally corrupt bureaucracy, insensitive to local community needs and concerns. These projects have not involved the local people and simply treated them as objects of the development process. Vast sums of money have been spent in the name of the poor, but very little has actually reached them. (1996, 152)

The decentralization of authority, advocates argued, would improve political participation and ensure more equitable resource allocation. Responding to this movement, members of the Indian Parliament proposed the Sixty-Fourth and Sixty-Fifth Constitutional Amendments in

1989, outlining the devolution, of certain aspects of political representation from state governments to rural and urban local bodies respectively (Tummala 1992). Despite popular support for the amendments, they failed to garner the requisite political backing, due primarily to opposition from the states.

In the wake of India's adoption of economic liberalization reforms in 1991, however, the movement to politically empower India's municipalities was reinvigorated, this time recast as a component of structural adjustment. Included in the package of reforms advocated by the IMF, political decentralization was identified as a structural precondition for liberalization and a way to improve government performance through greater local accountability. With support now from advocates of democratic deepening as well as economic reformers, the Seventy-Third and Seventy-Fourth Amendments, defining a wider scope of authority for rural localities and urban municipalities, were adopted in 1992. The Seventy-Fourth Amendment stipulated the devolution of substantive powers and resources to municipal governments and charged state legislatures with devolving "powers and responsibilities upon the Municipalities with respect to preparation of plans for economic development and social justice, and for the implementation of development schemes as may be required to enable them to function as institutions of self-government" (Government of India 1992). Although predictions were made that urban governance would be transformed, local democracy would be invigorated, and municipal representatives would be empowered, the amendment appears to have had little real effect on the planning for development projects like the DRP.

Few states have actually devolved the powers over urban development, given the opportunities for revenue often generated from land development activities. Allowing this limited compliance was the amendment's weak wording, which specified that states should simply "[put] on a firmer footing the relationship between the State Government and the Urban Local Bodies," as well as "recommend principles for" instituting greater revenue sharing (Government of India 1992). Although the government of Maharashtra made some reforms, most observers agree that the Seventy-Fourth Amendment has done little to alter the distribution of power between the state and municipal levels in Mumbai.[4] Most important, no reforms for fiscal devolution have been adopted in Maharashtra. As urban economist Abhay Pethe explained, "Localities cannot be politically empowered unless they are either given the resources to implement programs or are allowed to raise resources through taxation." While Pethe speculated that these changes have not taken place out of fear by state-level politicians that resources will be diverted from rural areas, others cite interparty and interscalar conflicts (Pinto and Pinto 2005; Harriss 2007).[5] Given these conflicts, India's urban planning institutions have been characterized as dysfunctional and even pathological. Noting the informalities and popular insurgencies that "undermine the possibilities of rational planning," planning theorist Ananya Roy (2009a, 80) has made the provocative assertion that "India cannot plan its cities." Rather, India's planning institution may be better described as a collection of complex and nontransparent networks whose members straddle the lines between public and private, formal and informal, and even legal and illegal. These failures of rational planning can be attributed, at least in part, to the structural weaknesses of city government.

Yet in spite of these weaknesses, things do get built in Mumbai, and development does take place. One of the principal ways the city's political leadership and development bureaucrats have overcome these fragmentations is by forming strategic partnerships with institutions and actors that possess the necessary political (and, in some cases, financial) resources to carry out development. As public-private partnerships have become a central feature of Mumbai's entrepreneurial or neoliberal strategies of urban governance, observers note a "paradigm shift from state-run infrastructures to infrastructure that is built and managed by private developers, often granted monopoly powers by the state" (Roy 2009a, 77). Meanwhile, Nainan (2006) has demonstrated that these partnerships, such as those between the Mumbai Metropolitan Regional Development Authority (MMRDA) and the private-sector construction industry, are long-standing and have been buttressed by professional networks in the city. As demonstrated in earlier chapters here, these partnerships have, at times, been forged with illicit actors and organized crime groups that are less compelled to work within formal regulatory frameworks and are more likely to have cash on hand.

The remainder of this chapter describes the strategic partnership between Mukesh Mehta and the government of Maharashtra, detailing how he was granted the "monopoly powers by the state" to carry out the DRP. It describes how he sold his project to the government, embedded himself within the state's planning bureaucracies, and collaborated with (and, in many cases, bypassed) local elected officials. Although he was a virtual newcomer to Mumbai's development field, he attempted to position himself as a central node in the city's webs of domestic and global capital and political and administrative power. Yet in the absence of deeper institutional change and broader-based support from civil society, these efforts proved insufficient to overcome the institutional fragmentations that have given Mumbai's planning institutions their pathological character and have helped keep spaces like Dharavi entrenched in the city's social and spatial landscape.

The Political Entrepreneur

The endorsement that Chief Minister Deshmukh gave to Mehta's plan in February 2004 can be attributed to the plan's congruence with the new agenda to transform Mumbai into a world-class city, as well as to broader shifts in the city's political economy. However, the garnering of official state backing must also be attributed to Mehta's perseverance and his political entrepreneurship. For the better part of a decade he worked tenaciously to elicit this support. Reflecting upon these efforts, Mehta mused,

> I am an entrepreneur. I first decided I was going to do it myself, but eventually I had to contract with a developer—in this case, the government. When I sold it to them, I said, only pay me if I'm successful. I should only get paid on the success of the project. . . . There will be two measures of success: first, government had to accept the plan. Then the builders have to give money to redevelop it. Only once the builders make the investments can the project be deemed a success.[6]

Interestingly, his measures of success did not include benchmarks for development or the well-being of Dharavi residents, only that the deals had been made.

Once the government endorsed his plan, Mehta created MM Project Consultants Pvt., a private entity subcontracted by the government of Maharashtra to support the planning for the DRP. Mehta was appointed the project management consultant (PMC) for the DRP, and most of the activities associated with the physical designs, regulatory changes, and community relations for the project were coordinated through his office. For these efforts he would be paid a consultancy fee of 1 percent of total project expenditures. With the project costs initially estimated at $2 billion, Mehta's fee was expected to be roughly $20 million (Kamath 2010a, 2010b). Although he noted that his payment should be contingent "on the success of the project," as of mid-2010 Mehta had reportedly been paid an estimated $3 million even though the work had not yet begun and the builders were yet "to give money" (Kamath 2010a). Meanwhile, Mehta's role as PMC and the payments he received would become a contentious political issue in the coming years, leading to calls for his removal and the withdrawal of government support.

Mehta's activities as PMC have been closer to those of a salesman than to a technocratic planner. After he successfully sold the project to the government, he then worked to sell it to the domestic and international developers, as well as to the public and the residents of Dharavi. This salesmanship has been (mostly) successful because of his unwavering commitment to the project. This commitment resonates with Max Weber's description of the political entrepreneur in his classic essay *Politics as a Vocation*. While Weber was describing the work of being a professional politician, his analysis holds for political deal making entailed in development planning. Emphasizing the intrinsic relationship between an entrepreneur and his enterprise, Weber (1946 [1921], 85) writes that "it is precisely the entrepreneur who is tied to his enterprise and is therefore not dispensable. . . . It is very difficult for the entrepreneur to be represented in his enterprise by someone else, even temporarily." This commitment and irreparability have been central to Mehta's political entrepreneurship.

The project-specific nature of the enterprise has also supported his activities. Mehta's political entrepreneurship has been enabled by a shift, noted by anthropologist Arjun Appadurai, from comprehensive planning efforts to an increased reliance on discrete projects. "Whether it be the World Bank, most Northern donors, the Indian state or other agencies," Appadurai (2001, 30) writes, "most institutional sources of funding are strongly biased in favour of the 'project' model, in which short-term logics of investment, accounting, reporting and assessment are regarded as vital." Beyond these short-term logics, discrete projects like the DRP are also sites of consolidated power. With a focus on just a single enterprise, Mehta was able to consolidate the power needed to coordinate between the various public agencies and private entities whose involvement was deemed vital to the project.

Equating project management with "deal making" and a development plan with a "business model," he explained:

I am filling a void. That void is of coordination function, to make people talk to each other and make deals. I start by asking the question: What do we need to do to redevelop Dharavi? . . . And I am coordinating with groups to meet these needs. We need urban designers, entrepreneurs, service providers. We need the best of the best, and my job is to bring them into the project. I am bringing a business model to work through these issues.[7]

These entrepreneurial activities were supported by his NRI status, professional experience in the United States, and general global acumen. Selling

the project to the state government and the city's business community as
a "global" endeavor, Mehta relied heavily upon his experience abroad to
convince these audiences that he could bring together capital and power
from India and abroad. As he pitched the project at industry conventions
and private meetings with potential investors abroad, he presented himself
as someone who possesses an insider's understanding of the complex layers of India's bureaucratic and political systems and could render them
comprehensible for those on the outside.

The Consultant and the Bureaucracy

The institution of the PMC represents a novel configuration of power
and authority in the area of development planning for Mumbai. Although
the state has a long tradition of hiring consultants to design town plans
or advise politicians on development projects, the position that Mehta
crafted for himself entailed a more significant scope of authority than a
private consultant has typically held. Mehta even acknowledged that his
role should probably be performed by a government official, but he maintained that only he could see the project through to completion.

> That's where the bureaucracy would come in. But I don't think we have
> creative bureaucrats. We have very few of them. We have the Dharavi
> project. It's virtually one-man-handled. . . . I even type letters for them,
> interdepartmental letters! Why? Because Mukesh Mehta is the only one
> in the entire universe who wants Dharavi to go on![8]

Mehta attributed this lack of commitment, along with other weaknesses
in the state's development agencies, to the system of placing bureaucrats
in positions and providing them rewards.

> The typical government officer won't do this. They generally believe
> that if you don't do anything, you can't lose your job—which is true in
> the current system. They also don't have deep knowledge on the issues
> they're working on. They move from position to position. They may
> work on education and then housing and then environment. Those run-
> ning ministries should be experts in those areas of work, but
> they're not.[9]

While his criticisms were more targeted, Mehta's discussion of India's planning bureaucracies resonates with a general loss of confidence in the Indian
bureaucracy, long referred to as the "steel frame" of the Indian state.

The contemporary pathologies of India's planning institutions are often attributed to problems with the Indian Administrative Service (IAS),

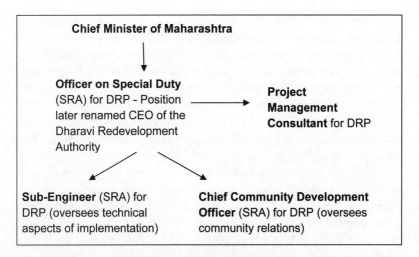

Official organizational structure for the Dharavi Redevelopment Project's planning process. Source: Author's field notes.

the core institution of India's bureaucracy, even as IAS officers continue to garner respect in Indian society. India's civil service was established by the colonial state to facilitate administration of the colony, and while the constitutional framers debated abolishing the imperial institution at the time of independence, they ended up retaining it with few structural changes (Taub 1969). Embraced by Prime Minister Jawaharlal Nehru and other advocates of development planning as a "politically neutral but professional policy bureaucracy," IAS officers were believed to possess both the generalist knowledge and technical expertise required for modernizing the Indian state and undertaking large-scale development planning (Rudolph and Rudolph 1987, 79). Although the IAS suffered from weak direction and an unclear mandate following Nehru's death and amid the emerging political populism of the 1960s and 1970s, it was generally regarded as a stable yet progressive force, due to its impartiality and perceived freedom from partisan strife.

IAS officers posted to state and local positions, however, have not generally enjoyed the impartial image associated with national-level bureaucrats. As Lloyd Randolph and Susan Rudolph have noted (1987, 81), "The ways in which civil servants are posted have enabled local politicians to appropriate administration to partisan and personal ends." They note that the personal challenges associated with frequent transfers typically make IAS officers more likely to align with the state-level politicians who have the power to move them. They argue that bureaucrats placed in state- and local-level offices are more engaged in party politics and more susceptible to the corrupting forces that plague local politicians. Baken (2003) has made a similar point but notes that bureaucrats often retain the upper hand in clashes with politicians at the local level. Emphasizing the layered nature of urban governance and the complex lines of administrative control, Baken claims that local decision making often appears idiosyncratic and nontransparent, but IAS officers as heads of local bureaucracies often make unilateral decisions.

Mehta, for his part, emphasized the idiosyncratic nature of these decisions and bureaucrats' concerns about "turf." Even so, Mehta acknowledged that the support of the IAS officers posted to the SRA was critical to the project's success. At the time the project received state backing in early 2004, the SRA was headed by an IAS officer who, Mehta noted, "had an agenda to stop the project."[10] He claims that turf battles and concerns about whether he would be recognized led the former SRA chief to stall the project. Eventually he was replaced with someone whom Mehta saw as an initial ally but who he claims proved similarly unhelpful. In mid-2005 IAS officer Iqbal Chahal was appointed by the chief minister to head the SRA and was given the designation of "Officer on Special Duty with Responsibilities for the Dharavi Project." Mehta described Chahal as "very supportive," noting that he viewed the DRP as "the most important project of his career."[11]

Despite Mehta's characterization of the project as "one-man-handled," administrators in the SRA were assigned to fulfill certain duties on the project. While Mehta may have been filling a coordination function, Chahal's official role was to communicate between Maharashtra's chief minister, Mehta, and the SRA staff assigned to help design and implement the project. Two SRA officers, reporting directly to Chahal, were given responsibilities for the project's political and technical dimensions. Roopa Shinde, the DRP's chief community development officer, was charged with community relations, while Rajeev Talreja was assigned to the project's technical aspects, including land use and building regulations. Mehta and his staff at MM Consultants worked closely with Chahal, Shinde, Talreja, and others within the parastatal planning agencies on all aspects of project planning.

Speaking to Rajeev Talreja in his office at the SRA headquarters, he confirmed the central role that Mehta had played throughout the project's planning process. Even before the government had endorsed the project, Mehta had done much of the technical work, including many of the activities that would typically be performed by Talreja's office, he admitted. For example, Mehta had acquired materials from the city surveyor at the MCGM, including the records of land ownership and the surveys of slum encroachment. This information, Talreja explained, was being used to determine the areas of Dharavi that could be designated slum areas and thus included in the redevelopment plan. Mehta was also using building surveys he had conducted to determine the appropriate mix of residential, commercial, and industrial activities under the development plan.

As the project's plans were being developed, the SRA's primary role had been simply that of a regulatory agency, to ensure that Mehta's project complied with the state's Development Control Regulations and that the needed changes were made to those rules. But even these activities, Talreja acknowledged, had been undertaken "in close consultation" with Mehta. Once the revised rules were approved by a group of secretaries in the chief minister's cabinet, an Expression of Interest (EOI) document would be issued and developer bids would be solicited. As these activities were under way, Mehta remained central in the process and kept the project moving forward. Meanwhile, conversations with Roopa Shinde and her staff confirmed that Mehta played a similarly central role on the community relations side of the planning process (discussed in chapter 5).

Discussing these institutional arrangements with Mehta, he suggested that the centralized authority he maintained throughout the planning process was necessary to the project's survival. Speaking primarily about project delays, he explained:

> Dharavi is just one of the million projects the government is working on. So from their point of view, why is Dharavi more important than something else? The government claims that it is a hyper-priority project. This is their claim. But what happens is that the claim might not be percolating to all the people from the lowest to the highest rungs. So it might be a super-high priority for the prime minister or the chief minister and the secretaries, but their deputies and the deputies of their deputies might not think it's that important.[12]

For Mehta, on the other hand, Dharavi was his only priority. By overseeing every step of the planning process, he might not be able to prevent delays but he could ensure that the project moved forward in spite of them.

More than simply a matter of priorities, Mehta also attributed the lack of support he had received to concerns about "turf stealing." He explained that not only are bureaucrats unwilling to undertake large-scale development planning but they also want to undermine others' efforts to do so. He explained that the opposition he had received from bureaucrats was "not based on the merits of the plan, but on what they perceive as turf-stealing. Powerful people are accepting my model," he added, "so these people are beginning to feel marginalized."[13] Mehta spoke with such a clear sense of ownership over the project that it was easy to forget that the DRP was officially a government initiative, but by this point Mehta had devoted nearly six years of his life to Dharavi's redevelopment. Determined not to let the project fall between the cracks of administrative authority, Mehta has carved out space for himself and his project within one of the state's fragmented planning agencies.

Politics at the Margins

Although he had embedded himself in the state's development bureaucracies, Mehta maintained considerable distance from the local political networks that reach into Dharavi. While municipal politicians have typically been excluded from development planning, the Seventy-Fourth Amendment offered the promise of decentralization in development planning. Yet, despite their intimate knowledge of constituent need and their ability to communicate directly with local communities, Dharavi's ward-level politicians have remained marginal to the DRP's planning process. This marginality reveals the ongoing divisions between electoral politics and development planning and the distance that project managers (consultants and bureaucrats) have attempted to maintain from localized sites of power.

Sitting in a large conference room in the Bandra offices of MM Consultants overlooking Mumbai Harbor, I once asked Mehta to describe the involvement of Dharavi's six elected ward councilors in the DRP's planning process. He replied flatly that their role was "negligible."[14] He elaborated that the municipal corporation only matters when "speed money" is involved, referring to the payment of bribes that can help get permits approved or stalled projects moving again. But, he went on to explain, speed money isn't an issue in this case because the chief minister has made this project a priority. Mehta quickly clarified that local politicians "do not operate on conviction, only on what they can get." But because the chief minister supports the project, the municipal commissioner supports it, and the rest of the MCGM will eventually do so as well. "The municipal commissioner will make everyone fall in line."

Speaking more specifically about Satish Sheynde and Dharavi's five other ward councilors, he conceded that they matter because their constituents matter. But, after thinking for a moment, he clarified that even they can be "managed." Citing intraparty hierarchy, he elaborated that "they operate on the kick-and-lick theory [kicking down and licking up]. You can manage them by managing the top party bosses." This mode of party management seemed possible in Dharavi, where a single party held power at all levels of government. Each of Dharavi's elected representatives, from the ward councilors to the state-level Member of the Legislative Assembly (MLA) to the national-level Member of Parliament (MP), were (at the time) members of the Congress Party.[15] Holding a majority of seats in the MCGM, the Shiv Sena party leads most local wards in Mumbai, which can result in interparty conflict and make management of local representatives more difficult. But because all of Dharavi's ward councilors were Congress members, Mehta expressed confidence that they would eventually toe the line. He elaborated that the MP and MLA, a father-and-daughter pair who support the project, would make that happen.

Although Sheynde seemed resigned to the little say that he and his constituents had in Dharavi's development plan, he appeared frustrated by the situation. In our first meeting in Dharavi's municipal warehouse district, he described some of the particularities of land ownership, as well as the local social structure, which he suspected would undermine the success of the DRP and make life more difficult for the residents.[16] He noted specifically challenges that residents face when they move to the transit camps—or temporary accommodations built during the construction period of slum rehabilitation. "But Mukesh Mehta and the SRA don't know or care about these problems," he said angrily. "They haven't thought through these problems. They are sitting in air-conditioned offices and aren't thinking about how it will actually work." Noting that his familiarity with these issues should make him a resource, Sheynde speculated that the project will run into problems because Mehta has not valued the knowledge of local politicians.

This intimate knowledge was revealed one evening as I sat in the ward office of Vishnu Damle, the corporator for Dharavi's 177th Ward.[17] His office was a small, unornamented room adjacent to the Gandhi Municipal School on the dirt path alongside Dharavi Main Road. Damle sat behind his desk while I sat to the side, leaving room for his constituents on the other side of the desk. An older, soft-spoken man, Damle turned to me and mused about Mehta and his project between these constituent visits.

The first person to enter the office was a petite woman whose worn, tired face made her look much older than her years. She explained in Marathi that her husband had left her with no money and no family here in Mumbai. She wanted to return to her village, where she had family and people who would help her, but she had no money even for the train ticket home. She explained that her children were hungry and had nothing to eat. As Damle listened to her story, he wore a look of mild frustration rather than one of concern. As he asked her questions about her predicament, it was clear that he was trying to find the contradictions in her story. After the exchange, Damle said that he would buy some food for her and her children, but he would not give her money for the ticket. She thanked him as she was escorted out by Damle's assistant and taken to a nearby dry goods shop. Once they left, he told me that he did not believe her story but acknowledged that she was clearly facing other hardships. I asked if he frequently heard similar requests. He explained that, yes, this is the majority of his "political work." His assessment seemed accurate as I listened all evening to his constituents sit down and describe personal hardships.

Referring to these conditions, Damle explained between meetings that the promises being made by Mehta and the other promoters of the DRP did not match the needs of Dharavi's residents. He described the troubles that his constituents have faced because of their quasilegal status and the government's lack of interest in addressing their basic needs. He explained, "Government has opposed the people and not allowed them to construct a nice space. There are no markets in Dharavi or colleges or even footpaths. But now they are making a full plan for Dharavi, a big plan. But it would be nice if they just did small things to improve the conditions here. . . . But," Damle sighed as he elaborated, "that type of development would not make the kind of money that this big project will." He commended Mehta for getting the government to go along with his plan when earlier Dharavi schemes had failed to progress this far. Even so, Damle explained, it is not the type of thing his constituents need.

While Sheynde and Damle expressed concern that the DRP would not adequately address the needs of their constituents—in Sheynde's case, the larger property owners who operate businesses from their homes; in Damle's case, the poorer residents who need basic services more than high-end developments—most of Dharavi's councilors were more neutral about the scheme. Several of them saw their role as the government's representative in Dharavi, helping to make the residents feel comfortable with the development plan. This role was explained to me by Subash Kale, an MCGM bureaucrat assigned to the DRP. Sitting in the G-North administrative ward office[18] about three miles from Dharavi, he explained that the MCGM as a whole is playing a very small role in the project's plan-

POLITICAL ENTREPRENEURSHIP 131

ning process.[19] He stated that his only role was to work with the SRA to help it determine which residents qualified for eligibility under the 1995 "tolerance" date and whether they had the necessary documentation. He acknowledged that neither the MCGM administrators nor the elected councilors have much say about the features of the plan or the policies governing eligibility. The councilors' role, he explained, is to convince the residents that the project is "a good thing." "First, the corporators [councilors] will convince the activists and the community leaders. And then the activists will convince the people." Like Mehta, Kale expressed confidence that both the elected officials and "the people" would eventually support the plan.

Alka Korde, Dharavi's 178th Ward councilor, concurred with this characterization. She explained that her role on the project was to "explain it to the people." Unlike Sheynde and Damle, she believed that the project served the best interests of Dharavi, and she explained that her role was to help her constituents understand this. She suggested that it would not be too difficult to do because the project is perceived as a Congress Party project, and "the people trust the Congress Party."

> They know that Congress will do a good job for the people. From
> about 1985, this has been an all-Congress area. . . . The Shiv Sena and
> BJP are saying that Congress wants to pull you out of Dharavi. But
> people have full trust in the Congress Party. So there will not be a prob-
> lem. They will not be successful.[20]

Despite this perceived role as project translator and advocate, it struck me how little most ward councilors seemed to know about the plan itself. They spoke in broad terms about the project's features and changed the subject when I asked for clarification, expressed most clearly in a conversation with Shivdas Mane of Dharavi's 175th Ward. After avoiding several questions about the eligibility rules or how much space eligible residents would receive, I asked how he learns about the project's rules and features as they change. His assistant immediately jumped in and explained to me, in English, "He's the ward councilor. He knows these things."[21] After a bit more prodding, Mane explained that the MLA attends the meetings and keeps him informed about the project and policy changes. While it was not clear that they were operating on the kick-and-lick theory, it did appear that information was trickling down through the party hierarchy. But when I asked the same question of another of Dharavi's ward councilors, Seema Joshi, she acknowledged that no one shares information with her. She stated plainly that the government keeps a tight hold on project details and keeps it out of the hands of politicians or the public.

Calls for Authority

The limited role the ward councilors play in most development planning efforts reflects a broader division of authority between Mumbai's municipal corporation and the government of Maharashtra. While most municipal officials seem resigned to this role—with several simply stating, as Satish Sheynde did, that the city is run by the state's chief minister—a small movement has emerged to empower the municipal corporation and centralize authority in the hands of a mayor. The Seventy-Fourth Amendment has largely gone unimplemented in Maharashtra; some reforms were made to the organization of ward-level administration, carving out a larger role for NGOs in municipal affairs. But as financial resources and substantive authority have remained with the state government, the reforms have done little to empower the municipality. Meanwhile, critics charge that the reforms that have been made have simply resulted in further fragmentations and continued weakness in urban governance (Pinto and Pinto 2005). In order to carry out effective housing programs and social policies, the critics say, the city cannot continue to be governed by rural politicians representing far-removed constituencies.

While calls for centralized authority are made on a relatively regular basis, these calls had grown louder a few months before I arrived in Mumbai in the fall of 2005, immediately following the worst monsoons the city had experienced in generations. Beginning on July 26, 2005, thirty-seven inches of rain fell in a twenty-four-hour period. The banks of the Mahim Creek overflowed, and the city was submerged in water—a scene that seemed to foreshadow the hurricane-induced floods that would engulf New Orleans just one month later (Anjaria 2006). During the deluge, Mumbai came to a virtual standstill: roads were blocked, railway lines were under water, and more than 150,000 people were stranded from their homes for days. Some parts of the city were entirely surrounded by water, and area residents were unable to access drinking water, food, or requisite medications.[22] The municipality proved unable to deliver services and address residents' needs, but local NGOs and social service agencies that were located in affected communities and could connect to one another via email and cell phone proved better able to reach citizens and communities. This event focused attention on the MCGM's limited capacities as well as the unique position of NGOs as service delivery bodies. Describing the political implications of the floods, an organizer for Lok Satta, an advocacy organization pushing for local governance reforms, explained, "After the deluge, people thought a lot about how the government failed to serve the people's needs. The crisis raised the urgency of municipal reforms in people's minds."[23]

One of the areas identified was the need for a single person accountable for the city of Mumbai. A number of groups began advocating for a "strong mayor" system. While Mumbai does have a mayor, elected from among the MCGM's 227 ward councilors, it is mainly a ceremonial post. Referred to as "the first citizen of Mumbai," the mayor's primary responsibility is to meet dignitaries and "honored guests on behalf of the citizens."[24] One of the groups pushing for the empowerment of this office was Bombay First, the organization that had published the McKinsey Report two years earlier. "The deluge illustrated that there is no one accountable," explained the group's director.[25] He blamed the MCGM's poor response on the lack of clarity around which individual—or even which of Mumbai's fifteen governance agencies—should be leading the relief efforts. "Bombay needs a single point of governance to coordinate all of the agencies that govern some aspect in Mumbai," he explained. He cited Mayor Rudy Guiliani's strong response to the 2001 terrorist attacks in New York, indicating that Mumbai needed someone who could govern with that kind of clarity. Other groups, including Lok Satta and Bangalore-based Janaagraha, made similar recommendations.

Having heard these calls for a strong mayor, a World Bank official who had been charged with overseeing Mumbai's recommended governance reforms met with the mayor on his first official visit to Mumbai. "I tried to include him when I first came in March. But he didn't seem interested. He didn't speak much English, and he deferred instead to the municipal commissioner."[26] The state government ignored these calls for governance reform and retained municipal authority in the office of the municipal commissioner. The calls, frequent in the immediate aftermath of the floods, dried up soon after the floodwaters receded.

Although these advocates were unsuccessful, they highlighted a general frustration with the governance situation in Mumbai. Mehta was often commended in this context, and his accomplishment of focusing the government's attention on Dharavi was acknowledged. Although the push for a strong mayor centered on daily governance issues and a general distance between Mumbai's residents and their local government, many— even the DRP's most ardent critics—commended Mehta for centralizing authority and bringing a sustained focus to Dharavi. Unlike municipal ward councilors who have limited access to the state government, Mehta brought the attention of the chief minister and the resources of the planning bureaucracies to bear on the problems of Dharavi. While recognizing

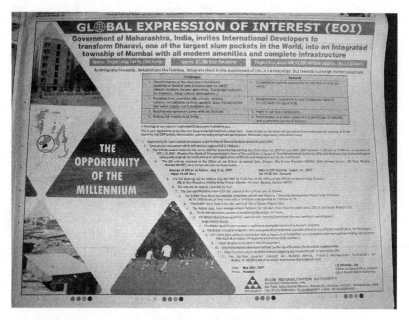

Advertisement announcing the opportunity to bid on the Dharavi Redevelopment Project. This ad ran in newspapers around the world on June 1, 2007, including the *Times of India.*

this accomplishment, his critics charged that he did not fully understand these problems because he did not represent Dharavi's residents and was not accountable to them. Furthermore, because he was working in the capacity of a consultant, his position lacked the legitimacy of either an elected representative or a bureaucratic officer. While the advocates of a strong mayor were pushing for centralized authority, they emphasized that this authority must be legitimately recognized and democratically accountable.

Challenging the Strategic Partnership

The legitimacy of Mehta's authority came into question when a small but influential group of housing advocates and retired bureaucrats began voicing concerns about the DRP's planning process in mid-2009. Petitioning the chief minister to remove Mehta from his post and speaking candidly—although mostly anonymously—to newspaper reporters about their concerns, many within Mumbai's advocacy community publicly challenged the position that Mehta had established for himself. Despite his efforts to keep the DRP planning process outside the public's gaze, criticism had become pervasive and was threatening to derail the project. Although the chief minister maintained his support for Mehta and the DRP amid this criticism, these debates exposed the limits to Mehta's centralized authority and shed light on the still fragmented nature of power in Mumbai.

In mid-2007 it appeared that Mehta's decadelong effort to redevelop Dharavi would finally be realized. In January of that year, the state government had finalized the necessary revisions to Mumbai's Development Control Regulations, thus putting the Dharavi redevelopment plan into a formal policy framework. A few months later, an Expression of Interest (EOI) document was drafted, outlining the project's objectives, financing arrangements, and the details of the international bidding process that would select the five developers to carry out the work. On June 1, 2007, the EOI document was made public when newspapers throughout the world carried a half-page color advertisement inviting "international developers to transform Dharavi, one of the largest slum pockets in the world, into an integrated township of Mumbai with all modern amenities and complete infrastructure." The advertisement promised that the scheme would provide both an opportunity for profit and a chance to participate "in a noble cause with a plentitude of rewards" (State of Maharashtra 2007). Over the next two months, seventy-eight firms submitted EOI forms to the government of Maharashtra, with about a third of them submitted on behalf of international developers. When the invitation period closed at the end of August 2007, it appeared that Mehta's second measure of project success would be realized; the builders, it appeared, would give the money to redevelop Dharavi.

As domestic and international developers were preparing EOI documents that summer, Mumbai's housing advocates and political opposition leaders began mobilizing against the DRP. Chief among the activists' concerns was the unprecedented position that Mehta held in the project's planning process. In August 2008 a delegation of Dharavi residents, led by the right-wing political leader Uddhay Thackeray, raised these issues in a meeting with the chief minister. The chief minister agreed to meet some of the delegates' demands at that meeting. He announced that a committee would be established, comprising Dharavi residents, that would advise the government on the project, thus bringing greater accountability into the planning process (*Times of India* 2008).

Later that month, a ten-person committee was convened, called the "Committee of Experts." But rather than comprising Dharavi residents as promised, it was made up of prominent housing activists and retired bureaucrats, including the state's former chief secretary and a former chief planner from the Mumbai Metropolitan Regional Development Authority (MMRDA) (*DNA* 2008). Simply an advisory committee without a mandate or a clear set of powers, the Committee of Experts became another layer in an increasingly fractured planning process. Furthermore, because the committee comprised ardent opponents of the project as well as more neutral observers, it did not represent a clear position but offered somewhat conflicting advice on how Dharavi's redevelopment should proceed.

While Mukesh Mehta's relationship with the Committee of Experts was never an easy one, their conflicts came to a head the following year when the committee reportedly sent a letter to the chief minister requesting Mehta's removal. The letter was never made public, but members of the committee discussed its contents in a June 2009 article published in the *Times of India*. According to the article, the letter expressed concerns about the way that Mehta had been selected as the PMC, as well as his qualifications for the position and the size of the consultancy fee he was promised by the government (Bharucha 2009a).

> The standard procedure of good governance requires a transparent process of selection, which includes an invitation of expression of interest by agencies which fulfill certain basic pre-qualifications and experience, a rigorous process of scrutiny and objective evaluation. We were, however, shocked to find that no such procedures had been followed and the present consultants were arbitrarily and hastily appointed on a colossal fee to be paid from the public exchequer. (quoted in Bharucha 2009a)

Noting that Mehta's "further continuance will be detrimental to the interests of the project and the city," the committee members asked that he be removed from this position (Bharucha 2009b).

The following month, the Committee of Experts raised a new set of concerns in a second letter to the chief minister. Choosing to make this letter public, the committee acknowledged that "earlier letters to Government regarding our strong reservations about the Dharavi Redevelopment Project (DRP) have not been acknowledged."[27] Mentioning neither "the present consultants" nor Mehta by name, the July 2009 letter detailed the committee's concerns about the features of the plan and identified revisions that they claimed would better address the residents' needs. Apparently unmoved by the committee's recommendations, the chief minister issued no response to the second letter.

Relations between the government, Mehta, and the committee continued to sour over the next several months. Reports began to surface of newly strained relations between Mehta and the CEO of the Dharavi Redevelopment Authority (the successor to Iqbal Chahal) (Mehta 2009a), and some political leaders began publicly criticizing the Committee of Experts (Mehta 2009b). The MP for the area reportedly raised concerns to the chief minister that the committee was obstructing the DRP's planning process. The MP explained to a newspaper reporter that "if the committee is fulfilling its role for which the members were appointed, I have no objection." He continued, "The project is meant for the people's benefit and the local residents have reposed their trust in me by electing me from this constituency"(Mehta 2009b).

In October 2009, when the fourteen developers who had been approved to bid on the project were expected to submit their final documentation, half of them abruptly withdrew from consideration (Bharucha 2009c; Mehta 2009a). Although no public explanations were given, one of the developers, speaking to a *Times of India* reporter on the condition of anonymity, simply stated, "It's a messy affair and we've decided to stay out" (Bharucha 2009c). By early 2010 the state government had placed the DRP on hold. With public fights under way between the Committee of Experts, politicians, bureaucrats, and Mehta himself, few developers seemed interested in moving forward with the bidding process. Yet the chief minister maintained his public commitment to Mehta; he and the administrators in the SRA were charged with finding another way to bring the plan to fruition. Although it has not been completely abandoned at this time, the grand plans for Dharavi's redevelopment had become once again snared in political fragmentations and institutional weaknesses.

The Limits of Political Entrepreneurship

Despite charges from Mehta's critics that his continued role would be detrimental to the project, his participation has clearly been essential to its survival thus far. Unlike more typical examples of strategic partnerships in which the government seeks out private-sector involvement, the DRP is Mehta's project. Even as calls grew louder for Mehta's resignation, Maharashtra's leadership retained their support for him, recognizing that his continued participation was critical if the plans for Dharavi's redevelopment were to move forward. A reluctant (and usually inept) urban planner, the government saw Mehta's project as a way to undertake a massive development scheme without committing significant public resources and without having to address the structural weaknesses that have traditionally plagued local administration and development planning. Yet while the chief minister's support, along with Mehta's entrepreneurial acumen and single-minded commitment to the project, helped push the DRP over these institutional barriers, his failure to win over local political leaders and civil society members may ultimately prove these barriers to be insurmountable.

In broad strokes, this case resonates with the governance shifts identified in the larger literature on neoliberal governance and global cities, which has identified the increased centrality of private actors in domains that had been the exclusive or primary domain of the state. Yet while much of this literature has associated privatized authority with a decline in state power—with the extreme variations even suggesting that such initiatives represent "politics beyond the state" (see Wapner 1995)—this case reveals the reconfigurations and rescaling of institutional power required for the promotion of globally oriented urban development. The manner in which Mehta inserted himself into structural gaps in the state's development planning bureaucracies—even writing interoffice letters on department stationery—reveals the state's porous boundaries and the relocation of state power to where it can most effectively carry out urban restructuring activities. If not for Mehta's administrative centralization, the DRP would almost certainly have slipped into the cracks between the numerous agencies with responsibility for land use and planning in Mumbai. The conflicts that now threaten the project demonstrate that these efforts were largely unsuccessful and that the state transformations remain incomplete.

With changes under way in Mumbai's political economy—including new economies of land and labor and the emergence of a governing coalition that, for the first time, gave voice to city-level concerns—it seemed that the institutional reforms would soon follow. The adoption of the Seventy-Fourth Amendment calls for a strong mayor, and even the consolidation of state authority by a private consultant reflect efforts to reconfigure and rescale state power to facilitate new development initiatives and make Mumbai a world-class city. Yet the reform efforts turned out to be more contested than observers may have anticipated. Existing fragmentations, the absence of empowered and coordinated leadership, and ongoing turf battles have continued to undermine these efforts to consolidate the state power required to facilitate urban restructuring and the redevelopment of Dharavi.

Despite the chorus of voices from the local elite and political leadership that had vowed to turn Mumbai into a node of global investment and a site of economic innovation, a pro-growth coalition never quite emerged. When the state endorsed the project and took up Bombay First's charge to "turn Mumbai into Shanghai," such a coalition appeared to be coming together and Mukesh Mehta would be able to direct its attention to Dharavi. Yet while Mehta's insider-outside status helped him sell the project to the government and to outside investors and developers, it proved detrimental to his efforts to direct this development coalition, or at least build support within it for the DRP. With few professional or political contacts when he returned to India in the mid-1990s, he proved unable to build the broader base of support required for Dharavi's redevelopment. He deliberately positioned himself outside of the political party structure, which gave him the freedom to work with whomever was necessary to garner government endorsement. But without political party support, politicians' commitment to him could prove just as fickle as his was to them. By maintaining the marginality of municipal officials, Mehta underestimated the authority they wielded and failed to situate himself within Dharavi's local political networks. Once opposition began to mount against him, he found himself isolated and with few allies beyond the chief minister. While the technical side of project planning proved that it can be "one-man-handled," the political side clearly requires a broader base of support.

However, while Mehta may have underestimated the importance of politics and civil society both within and outside of Dharavi, he recognized the entrenched power of Dharavi's residents and their embeddedness in (global) networks of housing activists. Early on in the project's planning process, Mehta discovered that he would have to contend with the numerous housing rights groups that had emerged in spaces like Dharavi in the 1970s and 1980s, premised on maintaining the rights of slum residents and pavement dwellers to "stay put." The next chapter details Mehta's efforts but ultimately demonstrates the deep entrenchment of these groups and their spaces in the city's social and political landscape.

CHAPTER FIVE

The Right to Stay Put

The postmonsoon humidity felt even stickier than normal from within the small courtyard in Kumbharwada, the potters' settlement in the southeast corner of Dharavi. The potters' ovens emitted heat and smoke, working overtime to bake enough small clay lamps for the upcoming Diwali festival season. On this morning in late September, several women were busy working, taking clay-stuffs from the ovens and laying lamps, bowls, and planting pots to cool in the warm, smoky air. The men milled about the small open space between the squat brick, aluminum-roofed homes and workshops of Kumbharwada, waiting for Mukesh Mehta to arrive and the meeting to begin. Standing out among the fifteen or so men, wearing not the button-down shirts and gray polyester pants typically worn by the Kumbhar men, but the neo-Gandhian activist uniform of a *khadi kurta* and pajama pants, was Ramesh Khandare. Although not himself a Kumbhar, Khandare was well known in the community and had been invited to speak on behalf of the Kumbhars at the morning's meeting. Khandare was one of the founding members of Dharavi Bachao Samiti (DBS), or the Save Dharavi Committee, a group formed two years earlier in opposition to the Dharavi Redevelopment Project (DRP). Also known for writing scathing critiques of the redevelopment scheme on the editorial pages of the community newspaper he had published from within Dharavi for the past several years, Khandare had become one of the DRP's most visible opponents. Waiting for Mehta to arrive, the men of Kumbharwada discussed their strategy for the meeting.

After some time Mehta rushed into the courtyard, apologizing for his tardiness. He wore a full gray suit and silk tie. Sweat dripped from his face as he was ushered to the front of the courtyard and instructed to take a seat next to Khandare. The other men sat in facing chairs and turned attentively to listen to what they imagined would be a heated debate about the impacts of the development project on the potters' community. Immediately Mehta launched into the description of the plan he had been repeating almost daily for the past three years. But rather than delivering the speech in Hindi or English as he usually did, he spoke in his native Gujarati, the vernacular language of the Kumbhars.[1] After outlining the basic features of the DRP, Mehta emphasized its particular benefits for Kumbharwada: "The situation is bad for you now because Dharavi is not developed. The roads are bad, and you have to transport your clay long distances. When Dharavi is developed, your work will be easier."[2]

Although Kumbharwada is one of the smallest communities in Dharavi, made up of roughly two thousand families, or less than 2 percent of Dharavi's total population, Mehta had been spending considerable time over the previous several months defending the impacts of the DRP on Kumbharwada and attempting to build support for the project among the Kumbhars.[3] Although Mehta and local government officials defensively claimed that the proposed redevelopment scheme would not disrupt the activities of the community and will ultimately improve the production and distribution of their pottery, in addition to improving their residential conditions and ensuring their housing tenure, critics of the project within and outside of Kumbharwada remained skeptical.

This skepticism was revealed once Mehta concluded his speech and invited questions from the meeting participants. A man in the audience stood up to express his concerns about the spatial layout of the housing proposed in the plan. When Mehta responded that the housing units will be a significant improvement over those constructed under the current slum scheme, another man retorted that the "current slum scheme" does not apply to them because Kumbharwada is not a slum. When he elaborated that the Kumbhars have a lease on their land dating back to the "Britishers' times," Mehta retorted that their lease expired in the 1970s and they are technically squatters on the municipally owned land. As Mehta debated housing tenure and the definition of a slum with meeting participants, Ramesh Khandare sat quietly.[4] After a half hour of debate with the audience, Mehta began to strike a more conciliatory tone and bring quick closure to the meeting. Conceding that ownership and tenure were still somewhat unclear, he asked the meeting participants to help conduct a survey of Kumbharwada, to clarify the number of households, unit size, residential occupancy, and tenure. As a now humbler Mehta asserted the Kumbhars' importance to Dharavi and to the project's planning process, the meeting participants mumbled agreement to help with the survey. Apparently satisfied, Mehta noted his busy schedule and made his way out of the courtyard.[5] Once Mehta was gone, the meeting attendees looked uneasy, concerned that they had agreed to more than they wanted. They also looked somewhat disappointingly at Khandare, whom Mehta had clearly outdebated.

Speaking later with Mehta about the meeting, I asked why he was expending effort to elicit the Kumbhars' support for the project if they had no legal claims on the land. Couldn't the government simply rehouse the Kumbhars according to the official policy for squatters? Mehta responded humbly, "I am nobody. I need to connect with the residents. We want to stay morally correct. That's our motivation for working with these groups." He explained the need to maintain a fair planning process. "We couldn't be perceived as having run roughshod. The perception mattered. The political leadership," he explained, "wanted [the project's planning process] to be done in a participatory manner."[6]

During my time in the field I observed Mehta and other government officials attend many meetings like the one in Kumbharwada. Although there were few democratic checks on development planning in Mumbai and no legal requirements for resident consent or participation at the time,[7] I observed significant energy being expended to garner the support of Dharavi's residential and laboring communities, as well as the leaders of the city's numerous housing rights organizations. While such efforts appeared merely rhetorical, initially more intent on creating the perception of participation than on securing meaningful inclusion, Mehta considered meetings like these to be vital to the success of the project. While he generally regarded municipal administrators and Dharavi's elected ward councilors as marginal to the DRP's planning process, Mehta actively worked to elicit the support of Dharavi's residents and activists. But beyond simply wanting it to be done in a participatory manner, these efforts revealed the importance he placed on the support, or at least the acceptance, of these groups. Acknowledging this history of failed development plans in Mumbai and elsewhere in India, Mehta recognized that—in contrast to MCGM ward councilors—these communities had power to derail the project.

The Right to Stay Put

Development planners and political leaders in Mumbai have had to recognize the political importance of informal residents and the activists agitating for their rights. Administrators first recognized the power of these groups in Dharavi while undertaking the planning for the Prime Minister's Grant Project (PMGP) in the late 1980s and were compelled to bring some activists, including SPARC, NSDF, and PROUD, on board with the project's planning process. While some project planners have had the foresight to elicit the support of these groups, relations between project planners and housing activists have typically been more antagonistic. But as resident mobilization has become a critical feature of spaces like Dharavi, contributing to these areas' durability in the face of periodic redevelopment projects and the grand designs of ambitious master planners, planners like Mehta have had to contend with these groups.

The history of residential informality in Mumbai demonstrates that while slum demolitions are a consistent presence in the lives of the urban poor, they rarely go unanswered. The clearance campaigns carried out across the city in the early and mid-1980s marked a turning point in this regard, with numerous housing rights groups—differentiated along the lines of ideology and strategy—forming in response to the violence. The field of housing activism is a densely populated terrain in which struggles around the "right to stay put" are an enduring feature of Mumbai's political landscape. These struggles, which are at times both confrontational and negotiational, employ a variety of strategies, including protests and direct actions, electoral politics, and the strategic use of the courts. In contrast to broader "right to the city" movements observed elsewhere, the main thrust of these claims is usually the simple demand to not be moved. While demands for improved housing quality and long-term security are frequently made by advocacy groups in other arenas, the immediate threats of periodic displacements often divert attention away from these longer term goals and keep the debate focused on issues like regularization, tolerance dates, and the definition of a slum.

The right to stay put was the focus of the activist response to the demolition drive carried out by the government of Maharashtra in late 2004 and early 2005. Within a month of the campaign's launch, numerous protests were held on the Azad Maidan, an open space in South Mumbai near the administrative offices of the state government. Thousands of people representing most of the city's political parties and dozens of housing and advocacy organizations gathered there. During one particular rally, more than a hundred evicted residents and activists stormed the Mantralaya, or state government headquarters, demanding an explanation for the evictions. Several more protests were held over the next four months, as a coalition of organizations came together under the name Zopadpatti Bachao Samyukta Kruti Samiti (Joint Action Committee to Save the Slum

Housing rights advocates protesting the Supreme Court decision allowing redevelopment of the textile mill lands, May 1, 2006. Photograph by the author.

Dwellers). Groups like these form on a fairly regular basis, as government
actions push perpetually mobilized groups to enact what has become a
familiar repertoire of action.[8]

Given the familiarity of this repertoire and its influence on the political life of settlements like Dharavi, Mehta and the planners for the DRP
recognized the need to work with these groups, particularly with the more
mobilized and symbolically important communities like Kumbharwada.
Although this recognition was not immediate and the solicitation of resident participation was initially more rhetorical than substantive, Mehta
soon came to recognize the importance of these groups and their claims
for the right to stay put. Particularly given his efforts to elicit the involvement of international developers and global real estate investors who may
be more risk averse and constrained by stricter time frames than domestic
builders, Mehta took steps to prevent an opposition that he recognized
could delay or obstruct the project. Yet despite these efforts, resident mobilizations are still threatening the DRP. When potential developers began
withdrawing from consideration on the project in October 2009, they

Annapurna Mahila Mandal (Annapurna Women's Council) protests Mumbai's land and housing policy, May 1, 2006. Photograph by the author.

cited not only administrative complexity but also political complications that diminished the attractiveness of investing in the entrenched settlement of Dharavi, despite the potential for profit.

Discursive Democracy

When the Maharashtra government made the decision to endorse the DRP and carry out Mehta's plan as a government initiative, officials asserted that the project's planning should be presented as fully consensual and participatory. Mehta attributes then housing secretary Suresh Joshi with helping him recognize the importance of local support in the project. In 2003, as the chief minister's cabinet debated endorsement of the project, Mehta and Joshi began reaching out to the city's housing advocacy organizations, most of which had expressed suspicion toward Mehta's plan. As Mehta recalls:

> It was Joshi's idea to call all of these groups together. He said that we
> should call together these groups and make a presentation and give
> them a chance to voice their concerns. Then they could never say that
> they were not notified.[9]

Another consultant in Mehta's office concurs that they had taken a systematic approach in the early years to build support, or at least notify potential opponents about the project:

> [Joshi] was very methodical. What he did initially, before the cabinet
> had passed it . . . was he took literally every type of stakeholder, starting
> with the NGOs, the slum dwellers, senior politicians, MLAs [Members
> of the Legislative Assembly], corporators [councilors], the ward officers.
> I mean literally every single stakeholder, and we made presentations to
> each one of them and had thorough discussions with them where they
> were allowed to raise—in fact, we told them in those meetings, we want
> you to ask the toughest, the nastiest questions possible, and we're not
> worth our salt if we can't answer your questions.[10]

According to Mehta, few criticisms of the plan were ever voiced in those meetings. Mehta maintained that these groups could not find anything wrong with the plan but chose to maintain their opposition purely for political reasons. Responding to this claim, Priya Shah, the head of a prominent housing organization, once explained her reticence to me. "Our visions are so different," she said. "There is no conversation to be had. We cannot arbitrate with him. We cannot enter into criticism with him. He wants us to talk about his grand plan, but there's nothing to talk about.

We would rather publish criticism of the plan than talk to him about it."[11] Shah claims to have recognized the disingenuous character of these meetings, seeing them as little more than public relations stunts. But it was also apparent that Mumbai's community of housing activists was somewhat unsettled by Mehta's and Joshi's openness. More familiar with protest politics and having to fight to have their voices heard, they did not know quite how to respond to this apparent willingness to include them in the planning process.

But even while many of these groups remained suspicious of Mehta's intentions and refused to engage in direct negotiations with the project administrators, these meetings provided Mehta a certain degree of legitimacy. The project, which had up to this point been designed and promoted by a single political entrepreneur with the support of only the housing secretary, could now be presented as a government-supported initiative with broad support and the involvement of local NGOs, politicians, and community members. When the chief minister announced his official backing of the DRP at a cabinet meeting in January 2004, the project was presented as a collaborative effort, developed in consultation with all of Dharavi's major stakeholders.

In addition to these meetings, Mehta had also set up an office in Dharavi in the late 1990s and spent time talking with Dharavi residents about iterations of the plan. While some local leaders in Dharavi dispute Mehta's claims that he was a visible presence in Dharavi in these early years, he maintains that he had become integrated in community institutions. Whenever the project is criticized as a top-down scheme, as it has been throughout the planning process, Mehta retorts that this time in Dharavi, speaking to residents, both informally and in meetings with the heads of more than "fifty cooperative housing societies," shaped the plan considerably (Menon 2004).

Sitting in his car years later, as I accompanied him to appointments with government officials and private-sector partners, Mehta recalled how those early meetings had forced him to compromise on his original vision. He drew a map for me of the plan he had originally wanted to pursue. The map showed a cluster of high-rise buildings along the perimeter of Dharavi, adjacent to the train tracks that form the southern and eastern edges of the settlement. The rehabilitated slum dwellers would be rehoused in twenty-story buildings along the perimeter and their homes would face out on a golf course. The market-rate buildings would be clustered on the other side of the golf course, along Dharavi's northern and western edges, adjacent to the Bandra-Kurla Complex (BKC). Looking longingly at the map, he said that it was a good plan that should have made everyone happy. The residents would have had access to transportation, the commercial occupants would be near the BKC, and the city would have a golf course and a park as a public amenity. "But," as he explained, "I had to give up this plan because of the iterative process that revealed that slum dwellers didn't want to move from the place in Dharavi where they are now. People objected to a golf course on principle. So I changed the plan and came up with the sectors."[12] He explained that this "iterative process" ultimately improved the plan, but as he looked down at his hand-drawn map, it was obvious that he felt his original vision was superior.

Despite these consultations, and a process Mehta claims was open to considerable public scrutiny, the project planning remained a private endeavor with limited democratic oversight. The project was directed almost solely by Mehta, and most of the activities associated with the physical designs, regulatory changes, and community relations were coordinated by his consulting firm. Although an Indian Administrative Service (IAS) officer at the Slum Rehabilitation Authority (SRA) was designated as the official head of the Dharavi Project, his activities were largely political as he acted as a liaison between Mehta and the chief minister. Although retroactively evaluating Mehta's claims of a transparent and open early planning process is difficult, particularly because his claims are disputed by certain community leaders in Dharavi, clearly no institutional mechanisms were created at the time to ensure public oversight.

Resident Consent and Opposition

Critics generally described the early Dharavi meetings as one-way interactions where Mehta simply explained the plan to audiences who had no opportunity to respond or critique it. According to some attendees, the plan he presented sounded like a fantasy. An attendee at one of these meetings quipped that Mehta had proclaimed that he would "make Dharavi like America" (Bunsha 2004). Even as Dharavi residents attended these meetings, most remained suspicious of Mehta's promises and assurances that a place would remain for them in a redeveloped Dharavi.

At one widely discussed meeting in mid-2004, the intentions of Mehta and the SRA were called directly into question.[13] The state had recently announced its endorsement of the scheme, and many residents were concerned about the security of their housing tenure and whether they would continue to have access to employment. Rumors had been circulating about the scheme for years, and many residents saw the meeting as an opportunity to clarify the actual elements of the project and voice their concerns. As the attendees entered the meeting, they were asked to sign what most believed was an attendance sheet but later learned was a statement of written consent for the project. When, after the meeting, it was learned that hundreds of Dharavi residents had unknowingly given their consent to a scheme that many of them actually opposed, vocal public opposition to Mehta and his scheme emerged.

Speaking about the incident more than a year later, Mehta angrily placed the blame on officials in the SRA who he claimed were attempting to sideline the project and deliberately mislead meeting attendees. He claimed that government bureaucrats, concerned about retaining their "turf," were intentionally trying to sabotage his credibility among Dharavi residents. Officials in the SRA referred to the incident as an "unfortunate miscommunication." Regardless of whether the attendees were deliberately misled and by whom, most observers, including Mehta, recognized that the incident undermined his credibility in Dharavi and had the potential to disrupt the project. This point was revealed when activists quickly mobilized to oppose the scheme in the aftermath of the incident. In response to the public outcry, the signatures were eventually discarded, and no further attempts were made to collectively acquire resident consent.

In addition to highlighting the contested nature of the project, this event was the first in a series of disputes about the "resident consent clause" of the Slum Rehabilitation Scheme (SRS) in the case of the DRP. These disputes culminated in November 2006 when the state of Maharashtra decided that it would no longer require consent in the case of DRP. At the time of the infamous meeting in mid-2004, the policy governing the project stipulated that the scheme would require the written consent of at least 60 percent of Dharavi's residents in order to proceed.[14] As officials in the SRA explained its rationale, the consent clause had been included in the scheme to prevent potentially unscrupulous builders from coercing residents to participate against their will. It is widely recognized, however, that the consent clause has done little to prevent such abuses, and residents now claim that they are coerced to give their official consent stipulated by the policy. But while the effectiveness of the consent requirement has been questioned, residents and housing advocates have viewed the clause as the only democratic check on the SRS. With considerable authority held by the builders and the SRA specifying the features of the buildings and housing units, the only input the residents have had over the scheme is the granting of their consent.

Consequently, after the meeting in which Dharavi's residents were publicly misled in an attempt to secure their consent, opposition to the DRP began to mount. Although the emergence of an opposition movement in mid-2004 can only partially be attributed to this incident, it is frequently cited by project opponents as evidence of Mehta's dubious character. Shekhar Varde, a Mumbai-based housing activist and former politician, once explained to me that the incident simply affirmed what many had understood about the scheme for years: that Mehta was attempting to trick Dharavi residents and steal the land out from under them.[15] The incident proved to be a political opportunity effectively seized by the project's most vocal opponents.

One of the groups that became most outspoken at the time was the People's Responsible Organisation for United Dharavi (PROUD). Generally shying away from contentious politics, PROUD has its roots in church-based community organizing, mobilizing residents to make demands for improved civic infrastructure and the protection of their housing security. At times, however, PROUD has taken a more confrontational stance, as in the early 1980s, when the group's leadership mobilized in response to the proposed eviction of roughly eighty Dharavi families and successfully prevented the demolition (Chatterji 2005). Seeking again to protect the housing security of Dharavi residents, the advocacy organization took a strong stance in mid-2004 in opposition to the DRP.

Among those working with PROUD at the time was Ramesh Khandare, the activist invited to speak on behalf of the Kumbhars in the meeting that opened this chapter. Khandare, a Dharavi resident and active member of the Communist Party of India, launched a community newspaper to begin disseminating information about the project. On July 4, 2004, Khandare and hundreds of critics of the scheme, including representatives from all of Maharashtra's major political parties, staged a protest march in Dharavi and formed Dharavi Bachao Samiti (DBS). Under Khandare's leadership, several more protests were held over the next several months. Speaking to a newspaper reporter at an event in August 2004, a prominent housing activist with NSDF explained that because Dharavi was built by its residents, they should be involved in its redevelopment. But he noted that Mehta had not involved them in the plan (Menon 2004).

These project opponents did not have a clear set of demands but simply opposed the way the project had been handled. All opponents were clear to assert that they too wanted Dharavi "to be developed." They wanted residents to have better-quality housing, access to sanitation facilities, and less dangerous work spaces, but they were skeptical that the DRP would bring these benefits to the area's current residents. A leader with DBS, whose family has lived in Dharavi for four generations, expressed the general concern held by most of the opponents. "In Dharavi, the poor people are suffering. But government doesn't want to solve that. . . . The actual motivation is to take the highly valuable land. They don't want to help the people."[16] Organized now as an opposition movement, the activists were better placed to ensure that the benefits of redevelopment remained in Dharavi.

Co-Opting the Opposition

When I arrived in Mumbai to begin fieldwork in September 2005, the opposition movement that had seemed strong a year before had all but disappeared. Khandare had stopped publishing his community newspaper, and the city's housing activists had moved on to other concerns. Over the next several months, I came to recognize that two factors explained the movement's dormancy: project delays and the relatively successful co-optation of project opponents. Because there had been no significant activity on the project since the state had endorsed it in January 2004, many residents and opponents had grown skeptical that it would ever be implemented. When I asked project critics about the now dormant movement, some responded by asking why they should actively oppose a scheme that may exist only on paper.[17] When developer interest was invited in June 2007 and it was clear the project was moving forward, the opposition movement was quickly revived. The movement's dormancy was also an outcome of a tactical change adopted by Mehta and the SRA. Recognizing that participatory rhetoric had been insufficient to secure community support and prevent a visible and politically harmful opposition movement from arising, the state began a series of more substantive negotiations with potential opponents. These negotiations, it is clear, cannot be interpreted as mere rhetoric, but constitute meaningful—although certainly imbalanced—engagement of Dharavi residents as citizens.

In late 2004 Mehta recognized the need to respond to the protestors and work to build support within Dharavi. He began meeting directly with representatives from PROUD and requested meetings with the scheme's most vocal opponents. Although Ramesh Khandare and Priya Shah refused to meet with him at the time, PROUD's leadership was more willing to discuss ways they could be involved in the planning process. The willingness of PROUD to negotiate with Mehta created a split in the opposition movement. A project opponent once explained to me that

"PROUD started out nicely; now they are not functioning properly." He noted that because PROUD became "good friends with Mukesh Mehta," he decided to join DBS instead and work with them to undermine the scheme.[18] Other vocal opponents disassociated themselves from PROUD, and many accused the organization of taking money from Mehta in exchange for its support.

Ashwin Paul, a community organizer who remained active with PROUD, adamantly refutes this charge, insisting that he and others simply recognized that Mehta's plan could be beneficial to Dharavi's residents. Furthermore, if they worked with Mehta, they could help ensure that current residents benefitted most directly from the scheme. As Paul explained to me, "This will be PROUD's role, to hold them to these promises. PROUD will have to keep people aware of the promises and keep demanding that the builders and SRA keeps them. PROUD can mobilize the people to pressurize [sic] them."[19] With Mehta apparently willing to invite PROUD into the planning process, Paul recognized that they could play this important role from the inside.

A small group of local community leaders in Dharavi. The mobilization of community groups in opposition to the Dharavi Redevelopment Project upset local power structures and existing networks of leadership. Photograph by the author.

These more convivial relations were revealed at a meeting I attended early on in my fieldwork.[20] At a town-hall-style meeting held in the upstairs auditorium of Dharavi's Saint Anthony's Church, I noticed Ashwin Paul sharing the lectern with Mehta, along with representatives from other Dharavi-based organizations. As Mehta presented his plan to the roughly seventy Dharavi residents gathered for the meeting, Paul and the other representatives sat quietly alongside him, offering their silent endorsement of the project. Even after the audience turned more antagonistic and began arguing with Mehta about his plans for implementation, his efforts seemed more legitimate because of this apparent community support. Other meetings like this were held over the coming months, following roughly the same format of Mehta making a PowerPoint presentation that detailed the plan's most attractive features and then opening the floor to questions. Mehta openly welcomed criticism in these meetings, requesting that his critics make their opposition public. With less vocal opposition and the legitimating presence of community groups, discussions about the DRP took on a more consensual tone.

In addition to these public displays, Mehta and SRA officials also began holding a series of private negotiations with the leaders of particular communities in Dharavi, such as the Kumbhars. Recognizing the need to establish firmer ties within Dharavi, the SRA had hired Roopa Shinde as chief community development officer for the project. Charged with managing community relations, Shinde had become a visible presence in Dharavi and was referred to affectionately by many of my informants as Mrs. Shinde. Speaking in her office at the SRA headquarters one day,[21] she explained the importance of what she referred to as Dharavi's "sensitive populations," communities like the Kumbhars that have special claims to housing or productive spaces in Dharavi. She explained the importance of addressing these groups' demands because of the symbolic recognition they carry in Dharavi and throughout the city.

One of the most sensitive populations Shinde identified was the Kolis. As Dharavi's original inhabitants and the only group calling Mumbai its native place, the Kolis have a politically important position in the city. Also, as longtime Dharavi residents with recognized leases on their land dating back to the late eighteenth century (Rajyashree 1986), the Kolis have made significant investments in Dharavi and have constructed some of the nicest homes in the area. The prospect that these homes could be demolished and replaced with 250-square-foot apartments invoked serious concern throughout Mumbai. Dharavi's Kolis are also a politically active group, frequently running for and holding office on Shiv Sena party

Workers recycle ballpoint pens in Dharavi's main industrial district in the
Thirteenth Compound. No salvageable piece of plastic goes to waste in Dharavi's
recycling industry. Photograph by Benji Holzman.

tickets.[22] This political presence has provided them a particular bargaining
position in the planning for the DRP, as Shinde explained. Mehta echoed
this sentiment, explaining to me that among all of Dharavi's communities,
"They are the most important and government recognizes it, because they
are the original 'sons of the soil.'"[23] Given this position, however, and
the robust legal claims on their land, they have been the most difficult
community with which to negotiate. While acknowledging the importance
of the Kolis, both Mehta and Shinde explained that they were putting off
substantive negotiations with this community until the other features of
the plan are settled.

Another group recognized as a critical constituency in this regard is
Dharavi's industrialists, whose engagement was actively elicited in the early
planning process. This group is ethnically and occupationally diverse, comprising Tamil leather workers and snack manufacturers, North Indian Muslim scrap dealers and soap makers, and Maharashtrian garment manufacturers. Many of these groups have lived in Dharavi for generations, working
in shops built by their fathers or grandfathers. These groups give Dharavi
its industrial character, and their productivity is publicly commended. Aside
from their symbolic position, Dharavi's industrialists are also politically

Dharavi welders in a manufacturing workshop in Dharavi's Thirteenth Compound. Photograph by Benji Holzman.

influential. As one of the settlement's wealthier groups, the industrialists, especially the scrap dealers, are recognized to be regular contributors to the election coffers of local politicians. As a result, these groups have been invited to play a significant role in drafting the DRP's industrial policy, including what manufacturing activities would be allowed to remain in Dharavi and how much space manufacturers would receive under the plan.

Sitting in a small air-conditioned office amid Dharavi's scrap piles and recycling machinery, Ahmed Khan, a wealthy scrap dealer and head of Dharavi's largest industrial cooperative, expressed his satisfaction with the DRP's planning process. Khan had been living in Dharavi for almost forty years, moving with his family in the early 1970s from the northern state of Uttar Pradesh after several bad agricultural seasons. With the support of relatives working in Mumbai's scrap business, he set up one of Dharavi's first plastic processing plants. Khan's business grew over time, and he now employs more than seventy-five workers, all of whom live in Dharavi. Given this history and his contributions to the area's productivity, he explained his importance to the redevelopment efforts:

> Dharavi is both a residential and a commercial space, and it must
> remain as both. Finding space for the residents is less of a problem
> than for us. They will build tall. Government will make a profit, and

this will be good for everyone. But we are Dharavi. We have seen this area when it was in bad condition. We want to see it when it is in good condition. . . . If they don't meet our demands, we won't support the project . . . and they need our support.[24]

In order to garner this support, Mehta and Shinde had been holding meetings with Khan and other industrialists to discuss the plan's industrial policy, and Khan seemed genuinely satisfied with the negotiations. With a satisfied tone, he explained that "the industrialists have had a say in the decisions about the plan" and were "consulted about the whole industrial policy."[25] While he recognized that compromsies would have to be reached, he expressed confidence that the industrialists would be well accommodated in a redeveloped Dharavi. While these efforts were being made to win over the industrialists, as well as the Khumbars and Kolis, Shinde and Mehta continued holding public forums and worked to elicit the support of the city's prominent housing activists. The SRA also printed pamphlets in the six major languages spoken in Dharavi and distributed details of the plan throughout the area. While the information dissemination, public forums, and private negotiations did not represent a major shift from the earlier, more rhetorical approach to democratic participation, what seemed to change most was the urgency with which Mehta and SRA officials undertook these activities.

Eliminating Consent, Preparing for PILs

Despite these efforts and the growing local support for the scheme, government officials remained concerned about their ability to secure the resident consent required by the SRS. Even with the consent requirement reduced to 60 percent, it was becoming apparent that the lowered level would be difficult to secure as well. Consequently, efforts were being made to eliminate the consent rule altogether in the case of the DRP. In the months leading up to its elimination, however, government officials denied that such efforts were actually being made. After mentioning some opposition to the scheme I had observed in Dharavi, a high-ranking official in the SRA contradicted me, explaining that there was almost universal resident support for the project. "Although 70 percent consent is required," he explained (even though the consent requirement had already been reduced to 60 percent by this time), "the SRA is attempting to secure resident support at 85 percent."[26] He explained that this higher consent standard would be easy to garner given the widespread community backing for the project and the efforts Mehta and Shinde were making to expand this support. But in November 2006 the state government adopted the draft housing policy that codified elements of the DRP. Included in the policy was a "clarification" that because the DRP, unlike other SRS projects, was an official "government" scheme, then it would not be necessary to secure resident consent. While this clarification was stated as a minor detail, its consequences for the planning process were significant, as it eliminated the consent requirement in the case of the DRP.

Sitting in a conference room at Mehta's office in the elite suburb of Bandra soon after the housing policy was adopted, I asked how the change would affect his efforts to secure local support. With consent no longer required, I asked, did he still need to engage the Kolis, the Kumbhars, and the industrialists in the planning process? He admitted the importance of eliminating the consent clause, acknowledging that it had been a barrier to implementation, but he mused that Dharavi residents still had power. "India is an anarchy, not a democracy. If people have vested interests, they can stop something."[27] When I pressed him to explain how exactly these groups could stop the project, he explained that they could create delays. But always an optimist, he explained that the energy he was expending at this point in the process, trying to bring these groups on board, would pay off down the road with a smoother implementation and a reduced likelihood of project delays.

Among the ways the groups could undermine it, Mehta cited the likelihood that disgruntled groups would bring legal action against the state in the form of public interest litigation (PIL):

> They will be filed, no doubt. But they should be cleared quickly. Both the High Court and the Supreme Court are in support of the scheme. . . . Ramesh Khandare, Shekhar Varde, Priya Shah could file them. Not Medha,[28] but maybe Shabana Azmi.[29] But it will be quick. Writs will be cleared away because they are costly for the courts.[30]

He felt confident that the efforts he had been making to draft the policy and elicit local support would protect against such a challenge. Others expressed skepticism. Vijay Kamble, a small-scale developer who had been building SRS buildings in Dharavi for almost a decade, speculated:

> They will probably take the issue to the courts. And they have sufficient support to do so. And the court will hear the case. The SRA cannot prevent a PIL or create a policy that will be able to withstand a PIL. About 50 percent of the people oppose the plan. People here are aware.[31]

Vijay Kamble was proved correct in mid-2006, when a coalition of housing activists challenged certain aspects of the scheme in a PIL. One of the opponents' principal charges was that the government had violated its own policy of regularization by excluding residents who had settled in Dharavi between 1995 and 2000. In November 2006 the Bombay High Court ruled against the activists and found that government had the right to exclude all Dharavi residents who settled after 1995. Responding to an appeal, however, the Indian Supreme Court ruled in April 2008 that eligibility should be extended to those who settled up to 2000. Although the ruling did not extend eligibility to those who have settled since 2000 or to those who could not document ownership of their hutments, activists hailed the ruling as a victory for the tens of thousands of Dharavi residents who would be able to maintain their right to stay put. Estimates place this number at more than thirty thousand households, increasing the number of units to be constructed under the scheme from fifty-seven thousand to ninety thousand (*Economic Times* 2008).

Globalizing the Project (and Its Opponents)

Throughout the planning process, Mehta and other state officials emphasized the importance of the DRP's global character. In addition to helping transform Mumbai into a world-class city by creating additional commercial space and constructing affordable housing, the project has actively sought the participation of international developers. Explaining the rationale for soliciting global investment, Mehta noted:

> International investors will bring funds; second, they will bring technology. They will bring international design levels, environmental-related issues, all of that. So that's one thing. Second, this is only a starting point. We are also showcasing to the international community that the government of India has in very many ways taken the most progressive step of doing the kind of project that has pioneered like this anywhere in the world. I mean, this kind of an integrated effort has not happened anywhere else in the world, ever before.[32]

The project's innovative, high-profile character, he speculated, would help generate interest, revealing Mumbai and India to be leaders in infrastructure construction and slum redevelopment.

Although some growth has taken place among Mumbai's producer services and globally reaching firms, foreign investors moved very hesitantly into Mumbai's property markets (Bhandare 2006). Even after restrictions on foreign investment in real estate were lifted in February 2005, only a handful of projects secured foreign investment, and no projects have been pursued outside of a consortium that includes local partners. This limited interest is usually attributed to the perception that land development in India, and in Mumbai in particular, is a messy affair. With a regulatory context perceived to be cumbersome, overly bureaucratic, and corrupt, international development firms have generally found it financially unviable to invest in Mumbai's land markets (Nijman 2000). Not only are the regulations and bureaucratic costs perceived to be high, but there is also a history of project delays and projects abandoned because of local opposition and direct agitation.[33] But as Mehta explained:

> This project will show that if it's done in a systematic manner, and the government is involved, they can hold your hand through the process. So if you want to buy an open tract of land and invest a hundred million dollars or you want to do it in clumps, both can be done without fear of the ten different issues that could possibly arise on a project.[34]

His efforts to build local support for the scheme and draft a policy able to withstand legal challenges represented efforts to dispel these perceptions and make Mumbai a more attractive site for investment.

Mehta's efforts to secure international interest in the DRP proved successful once the Expression of Interest (EOI) applications were invited from prospective developers in June 2007. Of the twenty-six developer consortia, comprised of seventy-eight firms, that had submitted applications by August 2007, almost all included at least one foreign investment or development firm, including firms from the United States, Dubai, the United Kingdom, China, and South Korea. In January 2008 the twenty-six consortia were whittled down to nineteen by a government committee evaluating the financial and technical viability of the consortia. Each of the nineteen remaining consortia comprised an international and a domestic partner.[35]

Even before the EOI documents were invited, local housing activists revitalized the opposition movement that had been dormant for more than two years. Enacting the familiar repertoire, mobilized groups launched a series of direct actions, filed PILs, and made appeals to transnational activists to help put a stop to the project. In late May 2007, DBS and other project opponents announced their plans to undertake acts of civil disobedience. A prominent housing activist explained to a newspaper reporter that if the global tender issued by the state government was found to be unacceptable, then the residents would take to the streets in protest, blocking roads and railway lines (*DNA* 2007). Although they did not create blockades when the tender was issued on June 1, thousands of protesters, including representatives of all of the state's major political parties (except the ruling Congress Party), came out two weeks later to protest the DRP. Some protesters shaved their heads, and most wore orange hats and T-shirts in solidarity (*The Hindu* 2008). Despite the strong stance taken by the protesters, project opponents continued to insist that they did not oppose the merits of the scheme but simply wanted to be included more directly in the planning process. Other demands were more specific, such as the demand that the size of housing units be increased (from 225 square feet per unit to 400 square feet per unit), that more Dharavi residents be deemed eligible for the scheme (from those who could prove residency in Dharavi since 1995 to those who could prove residency since 2000), and that a detailed survey of Dharavi residents be initiated before the scheme is implemented (Tare 2008).

In a letter emailed to friends and colleagues in India and abroad, Sheela Patel, the director of SPARC, articulated the position of many of the project's critics:

> Dharavi, we believe is symbolic of local struggles overcome by global investment in front of whom our governments bow down to deliver projects which are often at the cost of local concerns. We seriously feel concerned about the capacity of the present state institutions to arbitrate between the interests of the communities of the poor and international capital and local and national real estate businesses, who are in fact the new planners of cities.[36]

In response to Patel's email, a letter signed by prominent activists and scholars from outside of India—including Professors Arjun Appadurai, Partha Chatterjee, and Saskia Sassen; former undersecretary-general of the United Nations, Shashi Tharoor; and the former president of Ireland, Mary Robinson—addressed to the Indian prime minister and the chief minister of Maharashtra expressed a "profound sense of disquiet" and requested that the project be looked at afresh and the support of the larger community be secured before the government proceeds with the scheme (Tare 2008).

Over the next several months, the government of Maharashtra responded by addressing certain demands of the transnationally linked activists. In March 2008 the state commissioned a detailed census of Dharavi to be carried out by the Pune-based research firm Mashaal (*Indian Express* 2008). The chief minister announced the following month that the size of housing units to be constructed under the plan would be increased from the original 225 square feet to a compromise 269 square feet (Ghadyalpatil 2008). And in April 2008 the Supreme Court found in favor of the housing advocates' PIL and extended eligibility in the program from those living in Dharavi since before 1995 to those since before 2000 (Menon 2008). Although the mobilized housing rights groups continued to press for the unmet demands—including even larger housing units and the reinstatement of the consent clause—the Maharashtra Government exhibited an unprecedented willingness to accommodate the activists.

While these steps taken to ease the fears of risk-averse international (and some domestic) developers initially appeared to be yielding success, the future of the DRP was thrown further into doubt by ongoing political and institutional conflicts on the project—including the increasingly vocal opposition of the Committee of Experts—and the global economic crash of 2008. While nineteen developer consortia had been interested in bidding on the redevelopment of one of Dharavi's five sectors in January 2008, that number had been reduced to just eight a year-and-a-half later. While four of the consortia withdrew from consideration amid the financial crisis of 2008, including the consortium that had included the now-defunct financial firm Lehman Brothers, seven more withdrew their applications amid the public fights between the Committee of Experts, Mehta, the MP, and the chief minister in October 2009 (*Indian Express* 2008; Tembhekar 2009; Bharucha 2009c). Firms in this second set, meanwhile, also cited the problems in the global real estate market, but it was apparent that the local political context also contributed to their decision to withdraw (Bharucha 2009c). With the public withdrawal of these potential developers and an uncertain level of commitment among the remaining bidders, the government of Maharashtra put the project on hold in early 2010. Although the state has not actually canceled or withdrawn its endorsement of the project, the fate of the DRP remains unclear. While the project's uncertain future cannot be attributed exclusively to the direct agitations and demands of Dharavi's mobilized public, development planning and slum redevelopment in Mumbai and Dharavi cannot be understood without accounting for activist engagement around the right to stay put.

Engaging Political Society

Holding aside the question of whether these mobilizations successfully undermined the DRP, the involvement of Dharavi's residents and small-scale industrialists and the influence of housing activists on the planning process raises an important set of issues. Given most characterizations of the engagements between the Indian state and the urban poor, or what Chatterjee (2004) has called "political society," the DRP's early planning process seems to reveal a less antagonistic form of engagement more akin to the negotiations undertaken with civil society or middle-class "citizen groups." These engagements were, at least in part, the product of project administrators' desire to facilitate a smooth and relatively uncontested development process, particularly in light of their efforts to court international investment and undertake the type of developments believed to bolster Mumbai's standing as a world-class city. When earlier development schemes were launched in the 1970s and 1980s, they were financed by either government funds or World Bank loans, and their work was undertaken by government workers and civil servants, not the large domestic and foreign developers participating in the DRP. Project delays and negative publicity were anticipated on these projects and not as actively avoided. Given the volatility of real estate investment and the risks associated with global land speculation—revealed only too clearly in the global financial meltdown in the fall and winter of 2008—Mehta and Shinde worked to avoid delays and negative publicity and reduce some of these risks. In doing so, they engaged with Dharavi's political society to subdue opposition before it arose or immediately once it did. Amid the bourgeois revolution that Chatterjee and others have shown has diminished the state's interest to work with these groups, pressures for private and globally oriented development may also be creating the conditions for deeper or at least a different type of democratic engagement.

If we are to understand this engagement as a form of urban democracy, it is important to recognize the democratic consequences of Mehta's and Shinde's efforts to co-opt potential opponents within Dharavi. These efforts are strikingly similar to the process of co-optation first identified by Philip Selznick in the context of local planning efforts for projects under the Tennessee Valley Authority (TVA) in the 1940s. In both the TVA and the DRP, the efforts to bring the local community on board entailed a series of negotiations and compromises on both sides. While Selznick (1966 [1949]) found that through the process of co-optation, substantive power remained in the hands of the project planners, he also conceded that the involvement of the local community had significant influence on the scheme's outcomes. While we tend to think of co-optation as a one-sided interaction in which minority groups are bought off and assimilated into the majority, Selznick presents it as a two-way interaction akin to negotiation or mediation. This two-way dynamic must be emphasized if we are to think of co-optation as a form—albeit an imperfect form—of democratic engagement.[37]

The types of engagements that occurred in the DRP's early planning process may be familiar to students of the participatory turn in the field of professional planning, but they stand in contrast to most characterizations of urban development in the globalizing or neoliberal city. According to Brenner and Theodore (2002, 369), for example, development in this context typically entails "assaults on traditional relays of local democratic accountability," and efforts to replace them with "new institutional relays through which elite business interests can directly influence major local development decisions. While these shifts have been identified in a variety of sites in both the global north and south—and can certainly be discerned in Mumbai—the efforts to elicit resident and activist support in the DRP reveal important dynamics not fully shown in these accounts. The first dynamic is the political unfeasibility of displacing Dharavi residents to clear land for development. When Mehta first conceptualized the DRP, he envisioned the physical separation of Dharavi's market-rate properties from the housing for rehabilitated slum dwellers, but he never considered removing the slum dwellers from Dharavi altogether. The notion that illegal squatters have undisputed claims to land is remarkable in many contexts, but is understandable in Indian cities where, as Chatterjee explains, political society has traditionally held the balance of local power. Although demolition drives and clearance campaigns are unfortunately frequent occurrences, protective policies, including eligibility rules and cutoff dates, have been devised in response to the "moral assertion of popular demands" (Chatterjee 2004, 41). Because, by sheer demographic fact, local politicians depend on support from the urban poor, the local state cannot afford to dismantle vital constituencies like Dharavi and must acknowledge their right to stay put.

Another dynamic that sets the DRP's democratic engagements outside of typical accounts of the neoliberal city is the strength and vibrancy of Mumbai's field of housing activists, with many boasting influential transnational connections. If these groups had not been mobilized and actually in a position to undermine the project, then Mehta would not have had to engage them in the planning process. Because of earlier incidents in which mobilized oppositions were able to delay or entirely undermine development schemes in Mumbai and elsewhere in India,[38] the threats posed by project opponents carry weight. Even after the opposition to the DRP had been dormant for years, local activists were able to activate familiar repertoires once developer interest was invited for the project. The ability of these groups to elicit support from U.S.-based academics and international leaders is also noteworthy and has been recognized in other accounts of popular struggles in India (Khagram 2004). These dynamics have also been written about in the context of Mumbai, particularly in analyses of SPARC and other globally linked NGOs as purveyors of "grassroots globalization" (Appadurai 2000, 2001; McFarlane 2004, 2011). Yet while these studies have emphasized the transnational exchange of information and influence among transnationally linked NGOs, this case demonstrates the influence over development planning that these networks can enact.

Finally, the seemingly exceptional nature of this case must be attributed, at least in part, to Mehta's political entrepreneurship and his global acumen. While originally from Mumbai, Mehta is a U.S. citizen with more extensive experience in property development in the United States than in India. Consequently he has seen one of his main roles on the project as that of a translator, as someone who can help ease investors' fears about India's often cumbersome development context, while making government officials more aware of the concerns of international developers. While this role helped Mehta gain his unique position as a private consultant chiefly responsible for one of largest housing schemes pursued by the Maharashtra government, it has also helped him recognize the political payoffs of engaging with Dharavi's residents and activists.

Efforts to undertake globally oriented urban development may be altering the opportunities for the urban poor to influence the politics of urban development planning. While Mehta initially viewed democratic participation as little more than a rhetorical device, the opposition movement that emerged in mid-2004 made it clear that their rhetoric was insufficient and that potential project opponents should be more meaningfully engaged. As a consequence, Mehta and officials from the SRA undertook activities designed to garner more substantive support within Dharavi. Among these activities, they co-opted a respected Dharavi-based organization, held town-hall-style meetings in which they publicly confronted and debated project critics, negotiated directly with groups deemed influential and symbolically important, and disseminated propaganda to convince residents of the project's benefits. These activities did not prevent opposition from arising, however, and when the global tender was issued in June 2007, project administrators were faced with public protests, the filing of a PIL, and a letter from prominent international figures. The state responded quickly, addressing many of the activists' demands and working to quiet the mobilization.

With the increased participation of for-profit actors in the design and implementation of the DRP, representing what David Harvey and others have referred to as a neoliberal or entrepreneurial urban governance strategy, we may expect the project's planning to be wholly undemocratic, directed from above, and excluding the dissenting voices and demands of local residents. But as this chapter has detailed, certain of Dharavi's residential and laboring communities and Mumbai's housing activists, connected to globally networked activist groups, actually garnered significant influence in the project's design. Whether project opponents actually derailed the project remains unclear, but their inclusion in the political negotiations certainly altered the project's character and slowed its implementation. These activities, which can be understood as part of broader struggles around the right to stay put, are waged on a regular basis in the electoral, communal, and judicial arenas. These struggles have not always yielded their desired results or led to expanded tenure protections, but these institutions have been used by residents to maintain the durability of spaces like Dharavi. Yet even when the struggles around the right to stay put are successful, the victories won are not always so victorious, as the right to stay put often means the right to remain in dangerous, inadequate, and inhospitable conditions. As these efforts have made slum residents dependent on corrupt and extractive institutions and individuals, significant compromises are made in order to keep Dharavi in place.

Precarious Stability

Almost a decade after the Dharavi Redevelopment Project (DRP) was announced amid media fanfare and bold proclamations that Mumbai would soon be slum free, the promises have yet to be realized; the project seems poised to become another illustration of Mumbai's presumed planning pathologies. Caught between global development imperatives and local struggles over the right to stay put, the government has put the project on hold as it works to reconcile these competing objectives. But more than simply an illustration of popular insurgencies thwarting the state's modernist—and increasingly globalist—imaginings, the stalled DRP demonstrates the deep integration and ultimate inseparability of the slum and the city, even in an era of global real estate speculation and "world-class" aspirations. In contrast to most accounts in both the mainstream and academic press, which characterize places like Dharavi as vulnerable in the face of these powerful forces, this book has emphasized Dharavi's durability, pointing to its deep history, economic centrality, embedded politics, fragmented sovereignties, and popular mobilizations—some tapping into global activist networks. These conditions create and protect the megaslum and require that we make an analytic insertion into this category, rather than condemning these spaces as repositories of surplus humanity.

As I write this conclusion, the progress on the DRP has slowed to a halt. Although not completely abandoned, the project's future certainly looks bleaker than it did in June 2007 when the government of Maharashtra was issuing its global tender and inviting developer interest in the scheme. By the end of 2007, nineteen developer consortia, comprising some of the world's most prominent global and domestic developers, had submitted requests to bid on the project and had been deemed by a government committee to be financially and technically viable. While the consortia were preparing their bids and working with architects to draft designs for the sector layouts, a global recession hit. Given that the financial crisis was largely created by risky investments in housing, real estate, and development, several of the consortia were forced to withdraw from this potentially perilous venture. Receiving the most attention at the time was the departure of the consortium comprising Mumbai-based developer HDIL and the U.S. investment firm Lehman Brothers, after the latters firm's famous collapse in the late summer of 2008. Other consortia that withdrew at that time included Reliance Engineering Associates, L&T Limited, and the South Korean firm Hanhwa Engineering. The remaining fifteen consortia petitioned the government to reduce the scope of the project and loosen its expectation that they provide the bulk of the financing up front. Meanwhile, public fights between elected officials and civil society members, combined with continued pressure from Dharavi's residents and activists, were continuing to shake the confidence of these remaining bidders. In late 2009, more than half of them decided that the project was simply not worth the risk and withdrew from consideration. With few interested bidders remaining and support dwindling within the government, the chief minister officially put the DRP on hold. Although various proposals have been floated in the four years since, including the government of Maharashtra's seemingly viable plan to undertake the redevelopment of Sector 5 itself, continuing opposition and waning interest have kept these proposals from moving forward.

For many, these developments simply affirmed the suspicion they'd had when Mukesh Mehta began drafting the DRP's plans more than a dozen years ago: the project would never be implemented. For a time, their skepticism seemed unwarranted, and it looked like economic liberalization, deindustrialization, and the ascendancy of a new entrepreneurial urban agenda had produced a favorable context for development. Mehta, for his part, had been working tirelessly to build the requisite support within government, bring civil society on board with his vision, court international investors and developers, and co-opt project opponents. But these tenuously assembled threads began to unravel when the financial crisis hit. While Mehta and government officials publicly attribute the continued delays wholly to the volatile international real estate industry and temporary obstructions in the flow of global capital, the causes are clearly just as local. Viewed from within Mumbai's long history of attempted development plans and slum housing schemes, the project's failures and Dharavi's durability seem unsurprising. Although at odds with most visions of what

The Janata Housing Society, August 2006. More than eight years after construction began on the building, Janata remains uninhabitable above the fourth floor.
Photograph by the author.

a global or world-class city should look like, Dharavi continues to sit in the geographic, political, and symbolic center of Mumbai. This case offers an important corrective to the dominant narrative of the sweeping and totalizing effects of globalization and neoliberalization on poor communities. While these forces are often destructive—poor people around the world are certainly losing their homes and livelihoods in their wake—dispossession is not an inevitable outcome. Local political institutions and autonomous agents are also inhibiting, or at least mediating, these processes. The more abstract analyses of these structural transformations, while providing an important warning about the potential effects of global land grabs, are only able to capture a small sliver of this story. They tend to miss the messy and imperfect politics that keep at least some people in place. These politics—imperfect at best and exploitative and extractive at worst—have allowed Dharavi's seemingly disempowered residents to retain some of the most highly sought-after real estate in Mumbai.

Lost in Limbo

But Dharavi's durability is not altogether victorious. Most residents recognize that the DRP will likely soon be revived or replaced by an even grander scheme, and they are forced to make their homes and livelihoods under the shadow of perpetual uncertainty. A visual representation of this condition can be seen in an unfinished seven-story concrete structure that has stood just off Dharavi Cross Road for nearly fifteen years. The Janata Housing Society, habitable only in the lower four stories, sits in a suspended state of construction, itself a product of the institutional fragmentations, political conflicts, and popular mobilizations that have produced Dharavi's durability.

As with much of Dharavi, the precarious state of Janata dates back to the late 1990s, when land prices were soaring and developers all wanted their piece of the newly launched slum-housing scheme. One of these developers was Promod Sharma, a midsize builder who had been constructing residential buildings throughout the city since the early 1980s. In 1998 Sharma approached the roughly one hundred families living in the chawls where Janata now stands and offered them homes in a new mid-rise building. Although they now speak of him with disdain, the residents recall that he seemed trustworthy in those first few meetings. Sharma promised to build a *pucca* building with indoor plumbing, ample water supply, and other amenities, all in less than two years. Agreeing to his proposal and complying with SRS protocols, the residents organized themselves into a housing society and elected an eleven-person governing committee to oversee the arrangements. Sharma gathered required consent signatures from the residents and filed the requisite paperwork and permits with the SRA and MCGM. The residents were moved to temporary accommodations in a nearby transit camp, and construction began in early 1999.

Like many transit camps, the temporary accommodations for Janata's residents were bad. Residents now describe the camp as frightening and "full of goondas." Although the policy stipulates that the SRA is to certify the transit accommodations, Janata's residents were living in an unauthorized slum, and after two years there, the slumlord ordered them to leave. Although Sharma's firm had not yet completed construction on the building, he allowed them to move in, assuring them that work would soon be finished. The building was uninhabitable above the fourth floor, so Janata's families doubled up in apartments on its lower levels. The elevators had not yet been constructed and the plumbing system was still incomplete, but the residents tolerated the imperfect situation, believing it to be temporary.

Around the time the residents were moving in, officials in the SRA discovered that some of the requisite paperwork was missing and ordered a temporary stay on the construction. Although Sharma, the SRA, and the residents all have conflicting accounts of what happened to the missing paperwork, they agree that certain forms never reached their destination at the MCGM. They knew nothing of the situation at the time, but many Janata residents now blame party politics and intergovernmental conflicts between the state-level SRA and the municipal corporation. According to this account, Sharma was an active member of the Shiv Sena party, the political party in power at both the municipal and state levels at the time construction began. On good terms with municipal officials, most of whom were also Shiv Sainiks, Sharma was simply lax about filing the requisite paperwork with the MCGM. The same year that construction began, the Congress Party returned to power at the state level and a new administration took charge of the SRA. The change in power was far from smooth, and many of the builders who had been active with the Shiv Sena were now apparently facing closer scrutiny as retribution. Many projects overseen by Shiv Sena builders were ordered to halt construction. Sharma's missing paperwork, which just a few months earlier would have posed little problem, became grounds for suspending the entire project.

Soon after, this relatively small construction project became entangled in the much larger web of the DRP, which has kept it locked in this suspended state of construction ever since. In early 2004, when the state government announced its support for the DRP, it ordered a suspension of all SRS constructions then under way in Dharavi. Although some exceptions were granted, and some buildings nearing completion were allowed to be finished, Sharma was not given an exemption for Janata. Due to the vast amount of work still required on the building, along with the still unresolved problem of the missing paperwork, the SRA ordered that Janata remain incomplete until bids were selected and the entire sector was redeveloped as part of Dharavi's broader redevelopment.

Meanwhile, Janata's residents had made their lives in the incomplete building. Electrical connections were established, and a water tank was installed on the roof, providing the residents with water for drinking and cooking. The society's governing committee collected maintenance fees from the residents and organized the payment of the water and electricity bills. Sharma was complying with SRA regulations by providing most of the funds required to pay these bills. Most residents had no contact with Sharma and remained unaware of the building's administrative limbo, assuming, as they continued to be told, that construction would soon resume. In fact, the treasurer of the housing society acted as the exclusive point of contact between the residents and Sharma, carrying communications back and forth and ensuring that bills were paid. Although the treasurer had been on the governing committee since the housing society was first formed in the late 1990s, he had not lived in the chawl and even now did not stay in the incomplete building. Rather, he was a doctor who had owned a small medical clinic in the chawl and now operated his clinic from the building's ground-floor commercial space. Given his level of education and higher social status, the members of the governing committee chose the doctor to oversee the society's finances and communicate with the builder.

Despite the continuing delays and limited information, the doctor and the rest of the governing committee maintained their support for Sharma. Even as most residents were losing patience, the committee urged them to wait. The committee's support, however, seemed less rooted in trust and more in fear of the builder and his associates. As discussed briefly in chapter 3, Sharma reportedly had connections to local organized crime groups and so-called land mafias. Usually accompanied by a sizable entourage, Sharma was rarely seen without his associate, Babu, whom the residents regularly referred to as a goonda. The situation dragged on, and when the committee members sought meetings with Sharma, pressing him for updates on the building's progress, Babu would apparently order the men away. Meanwhile, the governing committee continued to assure the other residents that the situation would soon be resolved.

After several years, some of Janata's residents began to bypass the committee altogether. One of these residents was a middle-aged homemaker named Sitamani. Like most of her neighbors, Sitamani was originally from the Tirunelveli District of Tamil Nadu, coming to the city when she was married in the late 1970s. Although she recalls her disappointment with the area when she arrived as a young bride, she now speaks longingly about life in the chawl:

> The chawl was better than this building. There we had proper water
> supply and current. The chawl was our own place. Some people in the
> chawl had big rooms, and many people were getting rent from first-
> floor apartments. If this building had been good, we would prefer living
> here. But look at this! [She made a waving motion around the crowded
> room.] We wish we had stayed in the chawl.[1]

As the ones most severely impacted by the building's conditions, many of the women had grown tired of living two families per flat, carrying groceries and water upstairs on account of the unfinished elevator, and going downstairs to use the toilet. Sitamani pressed the men of the governing committee for an explanation. In early 2006, after living in the incomplete building for almost seven years, she brought the issue to her local women's group, or *mahila mandal*. Mahila mandals are generally not political organizations, usually providing basic supports to their members, such as rice and legumes when needed, and organizing computer and sewing classes in exchange for a small membership fee. But after Sitamani discussed Janata's situation at a meeting of the area-wide mahila mandal, the members decided to take up their plight.

The women of the mandal went to Sharma's office and requested information on the status of the building. When he refused to meet them, they went to the SRA, where they first learned of the missing paperwork and the suspension of construction activities seven years earlier. Upon the revelation of these details, Sitamani and the other women requested that the SRA demolish the building and resettle them until it could be rebuilt. As Sitamani explained:

> We trusted the committee members, and they lied to us. So now we
> will wait for government to build the sectors. If the government builds
> the building, it will be a proper building. Not like this one. If it takes
> ten years, it will be better than the conditions we're living in today. If
> MHADA doesn't destroy this building, the mahila mandal will tell them
> to, and they will listen.

Soon after the women met with the SRA, Sharma reportedly stopped paying the electricity bills as retribution. Babu came to Janata and ordered the residents to stop complaining, threatening that Sharma would evict them if they continued to "make trouble." This only emboldened Sitamani and the other women in the building. Meanwhile, the mahila mandal reached out to the nuns at the Dharavi-based St. Anthony Church, who put together a coalition that included the Committee for the Right to Housing (CRH) and other housing rights organizations to press for Janata's case. The coalition organized a series of direct actions with the objective of pressuring the SRA to demolish the building and resettle the residents. When the protest marches began to attract media attention, officials attempted to resolve the issue as quietly as possible. In the meantime, the residents filed a PIL, petitioning the Bombay High Court to order the building demolished. In July 2008 the court ruled on behalf of the women and declared the building inhabitable. Yet nearly five years later— fourteen years after construction on Janata began—the unfinished building still stands. Many of the original residents remain there, suspended in limbo, caught between the government's promises of a slum-free Mumbai and their own efforts to make homes and livelihoods. Struggles like these are under way across Dharavi, revealing the dark side of durability. The experience of Janata's residents demonstrates that disparities exist, living conditions can be deplorable, and many families get lost in limbo, possessing the opportunity for neither mobility nor security.

Inside the Megaslum

Embedded politics, institutional fragmentations, and popular mobilizations have erected barriers to a potentially destructive development scheme and kept residents stuck in a precarious state of stability. The stories of Janata and the DRP are familiar to those who know Mumbai's long history of state interventions in the slum. Plans like these routinely fail, and it is often a good thing that they do. If the grand visions of master planners—referred to by many in Mumbai as hallucinations—were realized, then the social dislocations they would bring about would be unimaginable. Holding aside the critical question of where they would all go, if the hundreds of thousands of "unauthorized," "unregularized," or "ineligible" Dharavi residents were evicted, the city would simply stop working. If the megaslum was to disappear, then Mumbai would lose so many of its drivers, domestic workers, garment manufacturers, garbage collectors, and office workers that India's commercial capital would simply cease to function. Sitamani and her neighbors, who make up the links in the chain of migrations that have settled in Dharavi from places like Tirunelveli, helped make the settlement, transforming it from a marshy garbage heap into a densely populated, economically productive, politically powerful city within a city. In doing so, they brought about Mumbai's industrial—and later postindustrial—transformation and made Mumbai into one of the most economically productive places in India.

The spatial arrangements, institutional configurations, and particular politics presented here are unique to Dharavi, but other historically entrenched yet powerfully dynamic settlements can be found in cities throughout the world. While the concept of the megaslum is usually reserved for iconic, sprawling townships like Dharavi, Orangi Town in Karachi, and Manila's Tondo district, the social, political, and spatial entrenchment discussed in this book can almost certainly be found in smaller, more mundane spaces as well. While long-standing interests and embedded political networks have produced these settlements and protected them and their residents for decades, a dangerous game of casino capitalism is now being played by global real estate speculators and liberal reformers in central planning offices, threatening the housing security of millions of informal urbanites around the world. And while Dharavi—at least for now—remains intact, many of these other slums are being dismantled. With distinct interests and particular political configurations battling to both preserve and eradicate these other settlements, further place-specific examinations are required to reveal the complex dynamics at work in each of these places. These analyses will lead us to further question our conventional wisdom and to remake our existing theories.

ACKNOWLEDGMENTS

I would first like to thank my dissertation committee, Richard Taub, William Mazzarella, Terry Clark, Diane Davis, and especially my dissertation chair and mentor, Saskia Sassen, who excitedly shouted "Bombay!" when I told her I was thinking of doing this research in India. Their feedback and support on this project and throughout graduate school were invaluable. A special thank-you goes to Diane Davis, who planted the seeds for this project (although neither of us knew it then) at the New School and has nurtured it all along the way. Deep gratitude goes to Philip Engblom, who gave me the language and the insights into Mumbai and Maharashtra that I needed to conduct the research.

My debts in Mumbai, while ultimately innumerable, include those who introduced me to their city, patiently answered my questions, and provided me with friendship. When I arrived in Mumbai, a vibrant conversation on the city was under way, and I was welcomed by the scholars, activists, and public intellectuals vigorously debating issues of access, land use, environmental degradation, historic preservation, and representation in its various forms. Chief among them was Sharit Bhowmik, who sent me on my first trip to Dharavi in the summer of 2004 and then helped me build my connections there when I returned. Other scholars generous with their time and insights include Marina Pinto, Sujata Patel, Swapna Banerjee-Guha, R. N. Sharma, Sudha Mohan, Dilip Nachane, Abhay Pethe, Sandeep Pendse, Anirudh Paul, and Varsha Ayyar. Deep appreciation goes to Navtej Nainan, whose understandings and critiques continually fed me with new ideas to explore. The many activists and public intellectuals whose insights shaped my thoughts on these issues include the folks at PUKAR, including Arjun Appadurai and the late Carol Breckenridge, Rahul Srivastava,

Anita Patil-Deshmukh, Aditya Pant, and Shilpa Phadke. They also include Darryl D'Monte, Kalpana Sharma, Shweta Damble, Arvind Adarkar, V. K. Phatak, Shirish Patel, and the committed folks at SPARC, including Sheela Patel, Sundar Burra, Aditi Thorat, and Devika Mahadevan. The many people who made my stay in Mumbai comfortable and fun include Milan Shinde, Bhavesh Shah, Pratap and Jaya Talreja, Devika Mahadevan and Kapil Gupta, Matt Daniels, and the Bombay Expats. Deep gratitude goes to Subramani Shankar and the entire Shankar family for their help, kindness, and a near constant supply of dosas.

Chicago dissertations are made in interdisciplinary workshops, and mine was a product of the Globalization Workshop and the Urban Workshop, as well as Theory and Practice in South Asia (TAPSA). Active participants who read and commented on unformed ideas and chapter drafts include Andy Abbott, Xuefei Ren, Rachel Harvey, Kathleen Fernicola, Eric Boria, Michal Pagis, Jennifer Buntin, Rachel Rinaldo, Robert Wyrod, Beth Tipton, Andrew Papachristos, Jolyon Ticer-Wurr, Beatrice Jauregui, Boria Majumdar, and Spencer Leonard. A very special thank you to the DSSers (Kathleen Fernicola, Rachel Harvey, Jennifer Buntin, Melissa Howe, and Jennifer Hanis-Martin) for the deadlines, invaluable feedback, friendship, and my sanity. And thank-you to John MacAloon and my fellow MAPSS preceptors, especially my officemate and writing partner, Avi Sharma, for providing me the institutional home, office space, pub nights, and Jimmy's outings that I needed to finish the dissertation.

Northeastern University proved the perfect place to transform the dissertation into the book, and I thank my colleagues and students here for the intellectual stimulation and help in this endeavor. Thank you especially to Steve Vallas for his fearless leadership and to Barry Bluestone and the Dukakis Center as well as to the Brudnick Center for research assistance. My supportive colleagues, including Linda Blum, Shelley Kimelberg, Alisa Lincoln, Jeff Juris, Chris Chambers, Silvia Dominguez, Doreen Lee, Nina Sylvanus, Mindelyn Bufford, and Tom Vicino, help make Northeastern a comfortable and stimulating home. My students and research assistants whose help is reflected here include Dechen Sherpa, Kate Acosta, Priya Murali, Autumn Mathias, and Rachael Gorab.

Countless others helped shape the ideas presented in this book with their inspiring ideas and critical feedback at conferences and less formal venues. They include Jonathan Anjaria, Navtej Nainan, Tarini Bedi, Solly Benjamin, Gavin Shatkin, Anush Kapadia, Sapana Doshi, Patrick Heller, Neil Brenner, Rahul Mehotra, Marygold Walsh-Dilley, Renu Desai, Romola Sanyal, Ryan Centner, Tara van Dijk, Nausheen Anwar, Gautam

Bhan, Xingming Chen, Smitha Radhakrishnan, Sam Cohn, Len Albright, Sheetal Chhabria, Mike Levien, Eduardo Moncada, Ashu Varshney, Marina Peterson, and Tony Roshan Samara. Thank you especially to Ananya Roy for reading the complete manuscript, twice, and giving me exactly the feedback I needed. Deep appreciation goes to the University of Minnesota Press and to Pieter Martin and Susan Clarke for their enthusiasm and for helping it all go so smoothly. Thank you to Benji Holzman and Jeff DeVries for use of your photographs and to John Myers for making my maps.

The material assistance and grants that supported this research came primarily from the Committee on Southern Asian Studies (COSAS) at the University of Chicago. Thank you to Elise Auerbach and to AIIS for their help with visas, and also to Madeline Hamblin, Brooke Noonan, and Richard Taub.

My family provided unending support (of the material, emotional, and intellectual kinds), and my deepest appreciation goes to them. I suppose dissertations on urban India are in my DNA, and I thank my parents, Jay and Marilyn Weinstein, for bringing me to India, to sociology, and to cities. Dinnertime conversations provided me the best training for this research. Thank you also to Bennett, Lisa, Eleanor, Lauren, Katie, Ron, and Betsy and John for your love and encouragement. My deepest gratitude is saved for the Myers boys: John, who was with me from the beginning and every step along the way, and Avi and Marcus, who joined us on this journey and made it all worthwhile. Thank you, finally, to my mother, Marilyn Weinstein, my greatest advocate. This book is dedicated to her memory.

NOTES

Preface

1. When referring to the city in its contemporary context, I use the current name of Mumbai, as opposed to its earlier name, Bombay. (When discussing the city prior to the change, I call it Bombay.) The city's name change in 1995, discussed in later chapters, reflects a politics of ethnic, linguistic, and religious chauvinism, and many social critics refused to use the new name for many years. However, now almost twenty years after the new name was given, resistance has softened and most now call the city "Mumbai," although nomenclature continues to vary by linguistic community and social class.

2. Maharashtra is the regional state within which Mumbai is located. As discussed in later chapters, urban policy and slum housing schemes generally fall under the authority of the state, rather than the municipal government.

Introduction

1. The term *pucca* literally translates to "cooked." Its antonym *kutcha*, or "raw," is often used to describe the partial or unfinished built structures typically found in slums.

2. See, for example, *National Geographic,* May 2007; *The Hindu Sunday Magazine*, November 2007; *Outlook Magazine*, March 2011; and several longer pieces on the *BBC* and *BBC.com* since 2007.

3. This approach is consistent with Solly Benjamin's (2008, 724) call to analyze "'slums'—and by extension 'slum policy' . . . in the context of changing institutional structure."

4. This debate parallels a similar one in U.S.-based urban sociology on the conceptual ambiguity and symbolic violence attributed to the term "ghetto." See the "symposium on the ghetto" in the December 2008 issue of *City and Community* 7(4) for the different sides of this debate.

5. Reflecting now, it is interesting how similar this line is to one offered by the character Salim in the movie *Slumdog Millionaire*. Looking down on the high-rise buildings being built atop of the slum in which he grew up, Salim muses, "India is the center of the world, and I am at the center of the center." Aneesh Shankar made this statement to me about Dharavi more than two years before the film's release.

6. These dynamics also most accurately describe the experience of structural adjustment in Latin America. A problem arises in Davis's argument, in my opinion, when he applies these dynamics to explain processes under way in nearly all other regions. See Ong 2011 for a useful discussion of the Asian experience of neoliberalization.

7. India's experience with structural adjustment and liberalization are discussed in more depth in chapter 3.

8. See, for example, Desai 2012; Ghertner 2011; Anjaria 2009; Baud and Nainan 2008; Zérah 2007; Nijman 2006; Harriss 2005; Fernandes 2004; Chatterjee 2004; Baviskar 2003; Benjamin 2000.

9. See also Desai (2012), who identifies the emergence of "flexible governing" strategies whereby state authorities use negotiation and cooptation to create a process of slum resettlement that may appear inclusive but ultimately facilitates the gentrification of Ahmadabad's riverfront.

10. A similar argument is made by Gavin Shatkin and Sanjeev Vidyarthi (2013), who discuss the reluctance of many theorists of urban India to embrace political economic approaches, and particularly "global city theory," to analyze processes of urban change, working instead within postcolonial or subaltern political frameworks. While this effort to "decolonize" urban theory or at least tread lightly while "transnational trespassing" (Roy 2004b) has resulted in a more careful and measured consideration of the impacts of globalization on Indian cities, it has also made it more difficult to engage in comparative reflection or reveal the field's contributions to scholarly inquiries on other regions. There are, of course, important exceptions, as some influential writings on the region have engaged with these more abstract frameworks (see, for example, Goldman 2011; Dupont 2011; Benjamin 2008; Roy 2004a; Appadurai 2001).

11. See Polanyi 2001 (1944),136. The discussion of these two developments as comprising a "double movement" is consistent with the characterization of contemporary processes of globalization as a second "great transformation," to use Polanyi's term. See, for example, Burawoy 2000, 2010; Hettne 1999; and Howard-Hassmann 2010.

12. The question of why this frame has taken hold more in some regions and national contexts than others is an interesting one. Centner (2011) has recently noted that Lefebvre's work was translated from French to Spanish before English-language translations appeared, and the timing of its Spanish-language appearance coincided with the emergence of antistate movements in Latin America.

13. Here I am using Lefebvre's framework as a stand-in for a broader argument about the revolutionary power of urban social movements. Another, closely related perspective on this was offered by Castells (1983) in his classic and highly influential *The City and the Grassroots*. Despite his earlier characterization of Lefebvre as "a left wing exponent of mainstream urban sociology" (Kipfer, Goonewardena, Schmid, and Milgrom 2008, 6), Castells's 1983 work highlighted numerous "urban-orientated mobilizations that influence structural social change and transform the urban meanings" (quoted in Mayer 2006, 202). Like Lefebvre, Castells is frequently employed in the broader urban studies literature on political mobilization but receives more limited treatment in the writings on urban India.

14. See also Lisa Bjorkman's recent (2012) writings on "vote bank politics," which suggest "neither a heroic narrative of subaltern resistance to bourgeois capitalism, nor a dystopic scenario of mass exploitation in which forces of 'marketization' empty the act of voting of meaning."

15. See, for example, Bjorkman 2013; Doshi 2012; Anand 2011; Anjaria 2011; Anand and Rademacher 2011; and Anwar 2011. Saskia Sassen, meanwhile, has located these politics—or, rather, the possibility of politics—in the strategic site of the global city. She writes that in the context of a strategic space such as a global city, the types of disadvantaged people described here are not simply marginal; they acquire presence in a broader political process that escapes the boundaries of the formal polity. Their presence signals the possibility of a politics. What this politics will be will depend on the specific projects and practices of various communities (Sassen 2006, 319).

16. See, for example, Ramanath and Ebrahim 2010; Nijman 2008; Chatterji 2005; Burra 2005; Ramanath 2005; McFarlane 2004; and Madon and Sahay 2002.

17. Another, and perhaps even more important, advantage of this framing over Lefebvre's and Castells's is the more general focus on space. As opposed to the "right to the city" or "urban social movements" framings, the "right to stay put" can also include rural struggles against forced evictions. This is particularly relevant in the Indian case, where movements frequently transcend spatial boundaries, as represented, for example, by the National Alliance of People's Movements (NAPM), which has taken up both struggles against rural river dam projects and those against urban slum demolitions. It is also relevant to struggles against displacement under way on the periurban fringe that defy dichotomous distinctions between urban and rural (see Roy 2003).

18. According to this rather patronizing narrative, voters are easily bribed and ultimately manipulated by cunning politicians. Although politicians are understood to "pander" for votes in this context, their actions are understood more nobly as representative democracy when they represent the interests of civil society.

19. Meanwhile, the populist promises made during election times are often translated into protective measures that exist on paper alone. Examples include

the litany of development restrictions on the books in Mumbai—such as rent control, the Urban Land Ceiling Act, and various environmental protections. Rather than creating more equitable distributions of land and housing, these laws have produced healthy markets of exemptions and backdoor modes of development, frequently managed through the practice of *goondagiri* (i.e., corrupt practices overseen by *goondas,* or thugs).

20. The perspective I employ is similar to the "political economy of housing and urban change" that Roy (2004b) associates with photographer Edward Popko's work on a Cali squatter settlement, in which he focuses "on the ways in which rural-urban migrants negotiate and create access to shelter, services, and community" (Roy 2004b, 291).

1. Becoming Asia's Largest Slum

1. Government of Bombay 1978 [1909]. Sheetal Chhabria (2012) has an interesting analysis of the figure of the Koli in mythmaking about Bombay's early history and contemporary politics.

2. Author's field notes, June 27, 2006.

3. See Perlman's classic *Myth of Marginality* (1976). In a more recent essay, however, Perlman (2004) demonstrates that marginality may have become a reality for Rio's favela residents in recent years, due to the impacts of drug trafficking, violence, and economic changes under way in Brazil.

4. While this argument never quite disappeared, it has recently been revived by Mike Davis (2006) in the form of his "urbanization without industrialization" thesis.

5. The term "vote bank"—first used by sociologist M. N. Srinivas (1955) in the context of village-level politics in the South Indian state of Mysore—suggests that politicians and local leaders have a reserve (or bank) of votes that they can mobilize and deliver during elections.

6. Chandravarkar (1994) estimates that the trust demolished the homes of sixty-four thousand working-class Bombay residents by 1918, but it only constructed housing for fourteen thousand of them. Hazareesingh (2001) estimates that, by 1909, the trust had rendered fifty thousand people homeless through slum demolitions and had constructed 2,844 rooms in chawls.

7. The whereabouts and terms of the lease are currently in dispute, and the Kumbhars' current claims to Kumbharwada are highly contested. These disputes are discussed in chapter 5.

8. The area's name refers to Riwa Fort, whose remnants can still be found in the northern end of Dharavi. Riwa Fort was built as a fortification by the East India Trading Company in the early 1700s (Ranganathan 2009).

9. There was considerable international circulation of town planners and architects during the postwar period of new town construction and development

in the major cities and capitals of newly independent nations, including the involvement of French urbanists in its North African colonies and in Latin American cities (See Jenkins, Smith, and Wang 2006). In the Indian context, the solicitation of non-Indian planners and consultants was driven by an embrace of the modern and a search for international recognition, as well as by a shortage of homegrown planners and urban designers (Kalia 1990).

10. Albert Mayer's name was proposed among the members of the BMC in the mid-1940s when the discussions of the plan first came up (Albert Mayer Papers, Box 17, Folder 19). He had, by this time, achieved prominence for town planning in North India and would go on to work on several more high-profile projects in India in the 1950s and 1960s, including a town plan for Delhi and the original design of Chandigarh. See Vidyarthi 2010 for more discussion of Mayer's role in the introduction of planning principles, such as the neighborhood unit, into India.

11. Mayer was paid eight thousand dollars, plus three round-trips between Bombay and New York, to aid in the preparation of the plan (Albert Mayer Papers, Box 17, Folder 19). He later invited William Cox, a highway and transportation expert from Connecticut, to assist him on the transportation aspects of the plan (Albert Mayer Papers, Box 17, Folder 20).

12. Mayer, in particular, felt that "the Dharavi layout" should be among the highest priorities for implementation. The urgency he felt about the Dharavi layout is revealed in letters exchanged between Mayer and Modak in February 1948 (Albert Mayer Papers, Box 17, Folder 25).

13. This was another aspect of the plan that Albert Mayer determined to be of the highest importance. In the months following the plan's publication, he initiated a campaign to raise awareness of the physical and social benefits of green space, sending letters and pamphlets to the city's civic leadership (Albert Mayer Papers, Box 17, Folder 19).

14. Although the sea-wall park was not built at the time, this area along Dharavi's northeastern edge was eventually developed by the Metropolitan Mumbai Development Authority and the World Wildlife Fund–India as the Mahim (and then later Maharashtra) Nature Park in the late 1970s. This area is among the only green space inside or adjacent to Dharavi, although the entrance gate is heavily guarded and Dharavi residents are barred access unless they visit with a preregistered group. When I once tried to enter the park with a Dharavi resident, I was told by the guard that they don't let people from Dharavi inside because "they steal things and make the place dirty" (Author's field notes, July 18, 2006).

15. Albert Mayer Papers, Box 17, Folder 25.

16. Ibid.

17. Ibid.

18. Ibid.

19. Author's field notes, June 19, 2006.

20. Vardhabhai is also the subject of several Godfather-like Hindi- and Tamil-language films and has attained mythical status in the Tamil community.

21. Author's field notes, July 20, 2006.

22. Author's field notes, August 1, 2006.

23. PROUD has been influential in Dharavi since the late 1970s. The role the group has played in the planning for the Dharavi Redevelopment Project (DRP) is discussed in chapter 5.

24. Author's field notes, August 1, 2006.

25. Ibid.

26. The first printed record I can find of this moniker is in Vandana Desai's 1988 article in *Habitat International*, entitled, "Dharavi: The Largest Slum in Asia: The Development of Low-Income Urban Housing in India." It was used as the subtitle to Kalpana Sharma's widely read 2000 book, *Rediscovering Dharavi: Stories from Asia's Largest Slum*.

27. In fact, when a comparison of slum settlements was included in the UN Development report of 2009, the report identified Karachi's Orangi slum as larger than Dharavi: "Karachi Is Asia's Largest Slum, Not Dharavi: UNDP," *Times of India*, September 6, 2009.

2. State Interventions and Fragmented Sovereignties

1. I acknowledge that my use of the term "failure" here is problematic and requires some qualification. I am using "failure" only in a narrow sense, to describe the discrepancies between the stated goals and accomplishments of the PMGP and later programmatic interventions. Yet as I have demonstrated in the preceding chapter and elsewhere, these programmatic failures are part of a complex landscape of state-society relations that enable residents to make homes and livelihoods under conditions of extreme inequality. Jonathan Shapiro Anjaria (2011, 58) makes a similar point in the context of corruption, noting that while bribes to low-level government officials are often characterized as failures, "They are better understood as ordinary spaces of negotiation that significantly shape the practices of citizenship and politics in the city."

2. The policy also did not apply to renters in slum settlements: those who did not possess the ownership documents but paid a monthly rent to the slumlord.

3. Maharashtra Slum Areas (Improvement, Clearance, and Redevelopment) Act of 1971.

4. Another of the more significant stipulations outlined in the act was the authority it granted to the state government to appropriate slum lands for the purpose of undertaking slum improvement and redevelopment projects (Bapat 1990). This stipulation has facilitated the land acquisition and cross-subsidization schemes that have underlaid most of the city's housing programs since the early 1990s, including the ongoing Dharavi Redevelopment Project.

5. Chapter 1, section 2(j).

6. Initially the policy identified 1976 as the cutoff date for eligibility for these protections. Periodically, the regularization cutoff date has been moved forward to 1980, 1985, 1990, and 1995. According to the current policy, the cutoff date is January 1, 1995, but project-specific exceptions have been made and extended eligibility in these cases to those who have documentation proving residence since January 1, 2000. It is no longer the case that slum dwellers must be in possession of photo passes but can use alternative forms of identification to prove length of residential tenure.

7. A related but distinct practice distinguishes between "notified" and "non-notified" slum areas, or between "declared" and "undeclared" slums. Notified or declared slums are those that the municipal corporation or another empowered local body (such as the Slum Improvement Board or Slum Rehabilitation Authority) has formally recognized by notification in the *Official Gazette*. Residents of notified slums are more likely to have access to basic services provided by the municipality. As Sundar Burra (2005, 68) notes, "Those living in informal communities may lobby hard for these to be officially designated as 'slums,' because this can bring particular advantages with regard to their relationship with the local authorities and to the possibilities of obtaining basic infrastructure and services." Despite these advantages, however, notification does not confer regularization, and unregularized residents may be living in notified or declared slum areas.

8. One of the most vivid depictions of this period in Bombay can be found in the Rohiton Mistry's 2001 novel, *A Fine Balance*.

9. Tenants in these top-floor rental units are among the most vulnerable populations in slums, as typically new migrants with tenuous local social networks. Regardless of their length of tenure, these tenants are generally ineligible for resettlement under the city's housing programs or slum clearance schemes (Pimple and John 2002).

10. Overall, the World Bank deemed ALIS a moderate success, citing the favorable outcomes of the LISP, or sites-and-services component of the program, which met its target of providing eighty-eight thousand households with serviced plots.

11. See Ramanath 2005 for a very useful history of many of these organizations, including SPARC, YUVA, and NHSS, and their relationship to the 1985 Supreme Court ruling.

12. Chatterji (2005, 206) also cites the shift from individual regularization (as under the SIP) to the granting of collective protections to housing societies (as under SUP and later programs) for the increased importance of representative housing rights organizations like PROUD and SPARC. She argues that these groups have come to play the increasingly important role of mobilizing housing societies to act as a collective unit.

13. It has been suggested that the BMC, now controlled by the Shiv Sena party, was bypassed for political reasons (Mukhija 2003), but it is unlikely that the municipality would have played a central role in the absence of interparty conflict, as the BMC had consistently been marginalized in development planning.

14. In her account of the PMGP planning process, Sharma (2000) notes that the Correa Committee recommended that forty-three thousand families could be accommodated in the redeveloped Dharavi, rather than the thirty-five thousand families noted by Mukhija (2003). Chatterji (2005), meanwhile, cites Sharma's figure of forty-three thousand. I was unable to locate an official source and could not confirm which, if either, of these figures is correct.

15. The term "governmentality" was coined by French political theorist Michel Foucault (1991 [1978], 102) to describe "the ensemble formed by the institutions, procedures, reflections, the calculations and tactics that allow the exercise of this complex form of power." This form of power, which he describes as "the art of government," is rooted in government's possession of proprietary knowledge about its territory and subjects in order to maintain the legitimacy of its authority. Meanwhile, Appadurai (2001, 34) has characterized the process of self-surveying and the information-gathering activities by groups like SPARC as "governmentality from below . . . animated by the social relations of shared poverty, by the excitement of active participation in the politics of knowledge, and by its own openness to correction through other forms of intimate knowledge and spontaneous everyday politics."

16. Chatterjee later became vice president of MHADA and in July 2008 was named the CEO of the Dharavi Redevelopment Authority, the agency given the charge of carrying out the Dharavi Redevelopment Project (DRP) discussed in subsequent chapters.

3. From Labor to Land

1. From this chapter onward I refer to the city's name as Mumbai. As discussed in this chapter, the name was changed in 1995, once the Shiv Sena–BJP–led coalition took control of the state government.

2. These figures account only for employment in the formal economy. In this period, there was an overall decline of formal-sector employment and the growth of the informal economy (Harris 1995, 49).

3. In addition to pressure from the IMF, political economists also attribute the 1991 adoption of the reforms to the growing pressure from business elites, particularly younger business leaders in new growth sectors (Pedersen 2000; Varshney 2007).

4. In 2001, when the Congress Party returned to office, the government restarted the process of industrial land conversions and amended DCR 58 to encourage more redevelopment than the policy originally allowed. According

to the amendment, the two-thirds of the land that was designated for public purposes would now only apply to the vacant sections rather than to all of the defunct industrial lands, which meant that the vast majority of the six-hundred-acre area could now be sold and redeveloped for private projects. In 2005 the Bombay Environmental Action Group, with support from the Girni Kamgar Sangharsh Samiti (the Mill Workers Struggle Committee), filed a petition with the Bombay High Court to compel the government of Maharashtra to return to its original one-third formula under the 1991 DCR 58, which set aside almost four hundred acres of converted industrial lands for the construction of affordable housing, civic amenities, and open space, and allowed just two hundred acres for private development. In mid-2006 the Indian Supreme Court ruled that the Maharashtra government had the right to amend DCR 58 and allow private development on 94 percent of the six hundred acres of defunct industrial lands.

5. The current Congress incarnation, Congress (I) is the successor to the Indian National Congress (INC). The main Congress splinter party in Maharashtra is the National Congress Party (NCP), formed by Sharad Pawar in 1999.

6. The influence of politically dominant caste groups in the modern democratic system was first identified by M. N. Srinivas in the mid-1950s. It was elaborated upon by Rudolph and Rudolph (1976) and has featured prominently in political analysis of the Indian subcontinent since. This thesis has been employed to analyze state-level politics in Maharashtra, most notably by Lele (1981).

7. One notable exception is Rajendra Vora's (1996) postelection analysis published in *Economic and Political Weekly* within months of the election. Thomas Blom Hansen (2001, 205) has also noted the Shiv Sena's "Mumbai-centrism," but has not extensively discussed the implications of this focus for statewide politics and urban investments.

8. "Saffronization" describes the political "Hindu-ization" or the rise of Hindu imagery and religious chauvinism in electoral politics. The term is a reference to the saffron-colored robes worn by Hindu clerics.

9. "Rehabilitation" refers to the on-site resettlement of slum dwellers in tenement buildings as specified by the SRS. The SRS is outlined in a 1995 amendment to the Slum Areas Act of 1971.

10. As discussed below, often the builder, rather than the slum dwellers, proposes forming a housing society and initiates the rehabilitation process.

11. Author's field notes, July 3, 2006.

12. Author's field notes, June 19, 2006.

13. Author's field notes, November 14, 2006.

14. Author's field notes, June 19, 2006.

15. Author's field notes, November 14, 2006.

16. Author's field notes, November 18, 2005.

17. Despite the manner in which his plan linked slum clearance with develop-

ment, none of these new infrastructure projects were specifically slated for sites of cleared hutments.

18. For example, at a January 2006 meeting of nonresident Indians (NRIs) held in Hyderabad, the head of the state's task force, Sanjay Ubale, solicited NRI interest and investment in the two projects concurrently (Lokhande 2006).

19. Eligibility is determined by both length of tenure and possession of documents proving ownership of the dwelling. With respect to tenure, the current policy on the DRP states that residents residing in their current residence since January 1, 2000, are eligible to participate. Third-party renters—even if they have been renting for more than a decade—are not eligible, however. Most of the features described here have been a source of significant conflict. See chapter 5 for a discussion of the negotiations surrounding each of these project features.

4. Political Entrepreneurship and Enduring Fragmentations

1. I heard this exact statement on several occasions, but one particular instance came when speaking to another Dharavi ward councilor on August 8, 2006.

2. Author's field notes, August 4, 2006.

3. Was formerly the Bombay Municipal Corporation or BMC.

4. The primary governance reform undertaken in Mumbai was the creation of twenty-four ward committees, which bring together municipal administrators, elected officials, and representatives of local NGOs to redress citizens' grievances, make budget recommendations to the MCGM regarding expenditures in the ward, and grant administrative approval and financial sanctions for municipal works projects to be undertaken in the ward (Pinto and Pinto 2005, 30).

5. Some observers also believe that the municipality has not shown any interest in assuming responsibility from the state. V. K. Phatak, the former chief planner of the MMRDA and a current adviser to World Bank on their Mumbai programs, conceded that "some of the blame rests with the city. Mumbai's city government does not have any long-term strategy or innovative ideas for governance here. So it's not just a matter of the state failing to implement legal devolution," he explained to me; the municipality should be inserting itself in the process (Author's field notes, November 28, 2005).

6. Author's field notes, August 18, 2006.

7. Ibid.

8. Author's field notes, June 19, 2006.

9. Author's field notes, August 18, 2006.

10. Ibid.

11. Ibid. Conversations with Chahal confirmed his support for the project, but he did not describe it to me as the most important one in his career.

12. Author's field notes, June 19, 2006.

13. Author's field notes, August 18, 2006.

14. Author's field notes, November 14, 2006.

15. Municipal elections were held in 2007, and two of Dharavi's Congress-held seats were lost, one to the Shiv Sena and one to the Bahujan Samaj Party.

16. Author's field notes, August 4, 2006.

17. Author's field notes, September 11, 2006.

18. G-North is the administrative ward in which Dharavi is located. It also includes the neighborhood of Mahim and the western sections of Dadar.

19. Author's field notes, September 18, 2006.

20. Author's field notes, September 8, 2006.

21. Author's field notes, August 8, 2006.

22. Interview with Karmayog director Vinay Somani (Author's field notes, October 26, 2005).

23. Author's field notes, December 21, 2005.

24. http://www.mcgm.gov.in/irj/portal/anonymous/qlmayoffice, accessed April 25, 2009.

25. Author's field notes, November 18, 2005.

26. Author's field notes, November 20, 2005.

27. Public letter to Hon Shri Ashok Chavan from Committee of Experts, dated July 7, 2009.

5. The Right to Stay Put

1. I was later told that the meeting participants appreciated being addressed in their native language, although the more cynical attendees quipped that was just a cheap ploy to build support.

2. Author's field notes, September 20, 2006.

3. The Kumbhars also have a certain symbolic power that distinguishes them from many of Dharavi's other communities. As one of the oldest settlements in Dharavi with roots in the area dating back to the early 1930s, Kumbharwada, in many people's minds, is Dharavi. Furthermore, because the Kumbhars were living in Dharavi before the area came to be regarded as a slum, they neither consider themselves slum dwellers nor are they considered such by most Mumbai residents, but are generally thought of as members of a traditional Hindu laboring caste.

4. Meeting participants later expressed disappointment that Khandare remained so quiet, speaking up only once during the entire meeting. It is likely, however, that Khandare, a Maharashtrian and non-Gujarati speaker, was linguistically locked out of the discussion. This only occurred to me later, and I never asked Khandare about communication challenges he faced during the discussion. At the time, I interpreted his silence—as many meeting participants did—as intimidation in front of Mehta.

5. I saw Mehta employ this particular negotiational strategy frequently. He practically never left a meeting without getting the meeting participants to agree to something. Whether the Khumbars ever helped with the survey seemed irrelevant; it only seemed to matter that they pledged their cooperation, and I never heard mention of this Kumbharwada survey again.

6. Author's field notes, November 14, 2006.

7. As I discuss later in the chapter, resident consent had been a requirement for the project before November 2006 when it was announced that the consent requirement of Slum Rehabilitation Scheme (SRS) would not apply in the case of the DRP. The "consent clause" of the SRS is outlined in The Maharashtra Slum Areas (Improvement, Clearance, and Redevelopment) Act, 1971, chapter I-A, 4–19.

8. Similar strategies have been employed by activists and workers seeking redress in the case of the textile mill lands conversions. As discussed in chapter 3, environmental groups and mill workers' organizations engaged in direct agitations and the filing of PILs in the early 2000s. The objectives of these actions were to pressure the government to slow the process of industrial land conversion and high-end development in *Girangaon*, as well as ensure that the few displaced mill workers still residing in the area could retain their right to stay put in this increasingly exclusive area.

9. Author's field notes, November 14, 2006.

10. Author's field notes, June 19, 2006.

11. Author's field notes, November 14, 2006.

12. Author's field notes, August 18, 2006.

13. This meeting occurred before I began my fieldwork and I was not present for it. It was described to me, however, by several informants throughout my research period. Some of the accounts I was given have conflicting details, and I have not been able to corroborate their accounts. Consequently, my description of the meeting remains vague.

14. The consent clause is discussed in the Development Control Rules of Greater Mumbai, DCR 33(10), the policy governing all projects entailing the rehabilitation (or rehousing) of slum dwellers in mid-rise buildings. Although the policy requires resident consent at the 70 percent level, the SRA quietly reduced the consent requirement to 60 percent for the DRP in 2004. Few activists or housing advocates and practically no Dharavi residents were aware of the rule change until years later. Public officials with whom I spoke in 2005 and 2006 were cagey about the consent clause, sometimes explicitly citing the seventy percent figure, although it had been reduced to 60 percent months earlier.

15. Author's field notes, January 16, 2006.

16. Author's field notes, September 20, 2006.

17. The same explanation was invoked by Herbert Gans in 1962 to account for the limited opposition he found to the redevelopment of Boston's West End

in the late 1950s. "Over the years, they began to realize that the redevelopment plans were in earnest, but they were—and remained—skeptical that the plans would even be implemented. On the day of the taking, the person just quoted told me: 'I don't believe it; I won't believe it till it happens. I'll wait till I get my notice. . . . You'll see, they'll start at the lower end, but they'll never come up here" (Gans 1962, 322).

18. Author's field notes, September 20, 2006.

19. Author's field notes, June 27, 2006.

20. Author's field notes, May 8, 2006.

21. Author's field notes, October 17, 2006.

22. Koliwada's political importance is partially due to the Kolis' support for the Shiv Sena, while the remaining districts in Dharavi are considered Congress strongholds.

23. Author's field notes, November 14, 2006.This phrase, and particularly its Marathi term *bhumiputra,* carries significance in Mumbai and has been a major organizing trope of the Shiv Sena party and its assertion of "nativist" claims to Mumbai.

24. Author's field notes, September 7, 2006.

25. Ibid.

26. Author's field notes, February 14, 2006.

27. Author's field notes, November 14, 2006.

28. Medha Patkar, founder of the National Alliance of People's Movements, is a prominent social activist in housing rights issues in Mumbai. She has also been involved in other high-profile struggles, including protests in response to the World Bank's Narmada River Dam project and the Dhabol Power Plant built by Enron.

29. A Bollywood actress who, as leader of Nivara Hakk (Right to Shelter), has been active fighting for the rights of Mumbai's slum dwellers.

30. Author's field notes, November 14, 2006.

31. Author's field notes, September 12, 2006.

32. Author's field notes, June 19, 2006.

33. In a high-profile example, the scandalized energy firm Enron had attempted to construct a power plant eighty miles south of Mumbai, but was met with considerable protests in the mid-1990s. Although these mobilizations were not the only political problem facing the project, they provided the state justification to stall on implementation. The power plant was still not completed in 2001 when Enron collapsed under the weight of scandal (Mehta 2000).

34. Author's field notes, June 19, 2006.

35. Despite considerable efforts I was unable to compile a complete list of the domestic and internal firms that submitted EOI documents on the project. The following list represents this effort but is incomplete and may be inaccurate:

International Firms

1. The Africa Israel Investment Ltd. (Israel)
2. Emaar MGF (Dubai)
3. Limitless/Dubai World (Dubai)
4. Hawnha Group (South Korea)
5. Banaldin Group (Saudi Arabia)
6. Neptune Investments (UK)
7. MRMGF (Dubai + India–Bangalore)
8. Lehman Brothers (US)
9. Hines Development (US/UK)
10. Shimao (China)

Domestic Firms

1. Oberoi Construction (India–Mumbai)
2. Housing Development and Infrastructure Ltd. (India–Mumbai)
3. Akruti Developers (India–Mumbai)
4. Reliance Engineering Associates Pvt Ltd. (India–Mumbai)
5. DLF Building (India–Delhi)
6. Magarpatta Township Development & Construction Company (India–Pune)
7. Sindhu Resettlment Corporation (India–Gujarat)
8. Larsen and Toubro Ltd. (L&T) (India–Mumbai)
9. Nagarjuna Construction Company (India–Hyderabad)
10. Lanco Infratech Ltd. (India–Hyderabad)
11. Videocon Realty & Infrastructures (India–Aurangabad)
12. Lodha Group (India–Mumbai)
13. Godrej Properties (India–Mumbai)
14. Kingston Properties Private Limited (India–Mumbai)
15. Runwal Developers (India–Mumbai)
16. Conwood Sales Company (India–Mumbai)
17. Kalpataru Properties Ltd. (India–Mumbai)
18. Indiabulls (India–Mumbai)

36. Personal email dated May 30, 2007.

37. This conception of cooptation is congruent with Ananya Roy's (2009) discussion of the populist mediations that comprise "civic governmentality." Our understandings of the democratic implications of these politics, however, differ somewhat.

38. Including the incidents of Enron's Dhabol power plant, the Narmada River Dam project, and opposition to the redevelopment of former textile mill lands in Mumbai led by labor unions.

Conclusion

1. Author's field notes, July 8, 2006.

BIBLIOGRAPHY

Albert Mayer Papers. 1934–1975. Box 17. Archives: University of Chicago Library.

AlSayyad, N. 2004. "Urban Informality as a New Way of Life." In A. Roy and N. AlSayyad, eds., *Urban Informality: Transnational Perspectives from the Middle East, Latin America, and South Asia*. Lanham, Md.: Lexington Books, 7–30.

Anand, N., and A. Rademacher. 2011. "Housing in the Urban Age: Inequality and Aspiration in Mumbai." *Antipode* 43(5): 1748–72.

Angotti, T. 2006. "Apocalyptic Anti-Urbanism: Mike Davis and His Planet of Slums." *International Journal of Urban and Regional Research* 30(4): 961–67.

Anjaria, J. S. 2006. "Urban Calamities: A View from Mumbai." *Space and Culture* 9(1): 80–82.

———. 2009. "Guardians of the Bourgeois City." *City and Community* 8(4): 391–406.

———. 2011. "Ordinary States: Everyday Corruption and the Politics of Space in Mumbai." *American Ethnologist* 38(1): 58–72.

Anwar, N. H. 2011. "State Power, Civic Participation, and the Urban Frontier: The Politics of the Commons in Karachi." *Antipode* 44(3): 601–20.

Appadurai, A. 2000. "Grassroots Globalization and the Research Imagination." *Public Culture* 12(1): 1–19.

———. 2001. "Deep Democracy: Urban Governmentality and the Horizon of Politics." *Environment and Urbanization* 13(2): 23–43.

Arabindoo, P. 2011. "Beyond the Return of the 'Slum.'" *Analysis of Urban Trends, Culture, Theory, Policy, Action* 15(6): 631–35.

Arora, S. K. 1956. "The Reorganization of the Indian States." *Far Eastern Survey* 25(2): 27–30.

Associated Press. 1985. "Slum Dwellers Face Eviction, Hut Demolition in Controversy over Poor." October 31.

Baken, R. J. 2003. *Plotting, Squatting, Public Purpose, and Politics: Land Market Development, Low Income Housing, and Public Intervention in India.* Burlington, Vt.: Ashgate Publishing.

Banerjee, S. 2000. *Warriors in Politics: Hindu Nationalism, Violence, and the Shiv Sena in India.* Boulder, Colo.: Westview Press.

Banerjee-Guha, S. 1995. "Urban Development Process in Bombay: Planning for Whom?" In S. Patel and A. Thorner, eds., *Bombay: Metaphor for Modern India.* New Delhi: Oxford University Press, 100–120.

Bapat, M. 1990. "Allocation of Urban Space: Rhetoric and Reality—Evidence from Recent Jurisprudence." *Economic and Political Weekly* 25(28): 1502–7.

Bardhan, P. 1996. "Decentralized Development." *Indian Economic Review* 31(2): 139–56.

Baud, I., and N. Nainan. 2008. "'Negotiated Spaces' for Representation in Mumbai: Ward Committees, Advanced Locality Management, and the Politics of Middle-Class Activism." *Environment and Urbanization* 20(2): 483–99.

Baviskar, A. 2003. "Between Violence and Desire: Space, Power, and Identity in the Making of Metropolitan Delhi." *International Social Science Journal* 55(175): 89–98.

Bayat, A. 1997. *Street Politics: Poor People's Movements in Iran.* New York: Columbia University Press.

———. 2004. "Globalization and the Politics of Informals in the Global South." In A. Roy and N. AlSayyad, eds., *Urban Informality: Transnational Perspectives from the Middle East, Latin America, and South Asia.* Lanham, Md.: Lexington Books, 79–102.

———. 2009. *Life as Politics: How Ordinary People Change the Middle East.* Palo Alto, Calif.: Stanford University Press.

Bedi, T. 2008. "Piety, Violence, and the Politics of Performance: Shiv Sena Women and the Feminine Subject in Maharashtra, India." Doctoral dissertation submitted to the faculty of the University of Illinois at Chicago.

Benjamin, S. 2000. "Governance, Economic Settings, and Poverty in Bangalore." *Environment and Urbanization* 12(1): 35–56.

———. 2005. "Touts, Pirates, and Ghosts." *Sarai Reader: Bare Acts.* New Delhi: Sarai Centre for the Study of Culture.

———. 2007. "Occupancy Urbanism: Ten Theses." *Sarai Reader 07: Frontiers.* Delhi: Sarai Programme, CSDS, 538–63.

———. 2008. "Occupancy Urbanism: Radicalizing Politics and Economy beyond Policy and Programs." *International Journal of Urban and Regional Research* 32(3): 719–29.

Bhagwati, J., and A. Panagariya. 2012. *Reform and Economic Transformation in India*. New York: Oxford University Press.

Bhandare, S. 2006. "Maintaining Mumbai's Premier Financial Service Center Status." In R. Swaminathan and J. Goyal, eds., *Mumbai Vision 2015: Agenda for Urban Renewal*. New Delhi: Macmillan India, 169–78.

Bharucha, N. 2009a. "Dharavi Makeover Hits Bump." *Times of India*, June 9.

———. 2009b. "Dharavi Remake Plan a Land Grab, Says Panel." *Times of India*, July 8.

———. 2009c. "7 Builders Left in Fray for 5 Dharavi Sectors." *Times of India*, October 30.

Bhowmik, S., and N. More. 2001. "Coping with Urban Poverty: Ex-Textile Mill Workers in Central Mumbai." *Economic and Political Weekly* 36(52): 4822–27.

Bjorkman, L. 2012. "You Can't Buy a Vote: Cash and the Discourse of Corruption in a Mumbai Election." Conference paper presented at the Centre for Modern Indian Studies (CeMIS) at the University of Göttingen, December 5–7.

———. 2014. "Becoming a Slum: From Municipal Colony to Illegal Settlement in Liberalization Era Mumbai." *International Journal of Urban and Regional Research* 38(1): 36–59.

Bombay First. 2003. *Bombay First: Adding Value to Mumbai*. Mumbai: Bombay First.

Bose, N. K. 1965. "Calcutta: A Premature Metropolis." *Scientific American* 213(3): 81–102.

Brenner, N. 2004. *New State Spaces, Urban Governance, and the Rescaling of Statehood*. New York: Oxford University Press.

———. 2011. "Urban Locational Policies and the Geographies of Post-Keynesian Statehood in Western Europe." In S. Patel and A. Thorner, eds., *Cities and Sovereignty: Identity Politics in Urban Spaces*. Bloomington: Indiana University Press, 152–75.

Brenner, N., and N. Theodore. 2002. "Cities and the Geographies of 'Actually Existing Neoliberalism.'" *Antipode* 34(3): 356–86.

Bunsha, D. 2004. "Developing Doubts." *Frontline Magazine* 21(12), January 5–18.

Burawoy, M. 2000. "A Sociology for the Second Great Transformation?" *Annual Review of Sociology* 26: 693–95.

———. 2010. "From Polanyi to Pollyanna: The False Optimism of Global Labor Studies." *Global Labour Journal* 1(2): 301–13.

Burra, S. 2005. "Towards a Pro-Poor Framework for Slum Upgrading in Mumbai, India." *Environment and Urbanization* 17(1): 67–88.

Business Standard. 2007. "Bandra-Kurla Land Deal Struck at Record Price." *Business Standard*, November 27.

Castells, M. 1983. *The City and the Grassroots: A Cross-Cultural Theory of Urban Social Movements*. Berkeley: University of California Press.

Centner, R. 2011. "Recombinant Geographies of Citizenship: Differentiations of the 'Right to the City' in São Paulo, Caracas, and Buenos Aires." Paper presented at the ASA Annual Meeting , Las Vegas, Nevada.

Chakrabarty, D. 1992. "Of Garbage, Modernity, and the Citizen's Gaze." *Economic and Political Weekly* 27(10/11): 541–47.

Chandavarkar, R. 1994. *The Origins of Industrial Capitalism in India: Business Strategies and the Working Classes in Bombay, 1900–1940*. Oxford: Oxford University Press.

Chatterjee, P. 2004. *Politics of the Governed*. New Delhi: Permanent Black.

Chatterji, R. 2005. "Plans, Habitation, and Slum Redevelopment: The Production of Community in Dharavi, Mumbai." *Contributions to Indian Sociology* 39(2): 197–218.

Chatterji, R., and D. Mehta. 2007. *Living with Violence: An Anthropology of Events and Everyday Life*. London: Routledge.

Chhabria, S. M. 2012. "Making the Modern Slum: Housing, Mobility, and Poverty in Bombay and Its Peripheries." Doctoral dissertation submitted to the faculty of Columbia University.

Chibber, V. 2003. *Locked in Place: State-Building and Late Industrialization in India*. Princeton, N.J.: Princeton University Press.

Clothey, F. 2006. *Ritualizing on the Boundaries: Continuity and Innovation in the Tamil Diaspora*. Columbia: University of South Carolina Press.

Committee for the Right to Housing (CRH). 2006. *Demolitions: Driving Urban Poor to the Edge—Impact Assessment Study of Demolitions in Mumbai*. Mumbai: Committee for the Right to Housing.

Corbridge, S., and J. Harriss. 2000. *Reinventing India: Liberalization, Hindu Nationalism, and Popular Democracy*. Malden, Mass.: Polity Press.

Dandekar, H. C. 1986. *Men to Bombay, Women at Home: Urban Influence on Sugao Village, Deccan Maharashtra, India, 1942–1982*. Ann Arbor: Center for South and Southeast Asian Studies, University of Michigan.

Das, P. K. 2003. "Slums: The Continuing Struggle for Housing." In S. Patel and J. Masselos, eds., *Bombay and Mumbai: The City in Transition*. New Delhi: Oxford University Press, 207–34.

Davis, D. E. 2011. "Theoretical and Empirical Reflections on Cities, Sovereignty, Identity, and Conflict." In D. E. Davis and N. Libertun de Duren, eds., *Cities and Sovereignty: Identity Politics in Urban Spaces*. Bloomington: Indiana University Press, 226–56.

Davis, K., and H. H. Golden. 1954. "Urbanization and the Development of Pre-Industrial Areas." *Economic Development and Cultural Change* 3(1): 6–26.

Davis, M. 2006. *Planet of Slums*. London: Verso.

Denoon, D. B. H. 1998. "Cycles in Indian Economic Liberalization, 1966–1996." *Comparative Politics* 31(1): 43–60.

Desai, A. R., and S. D. Pillai. 1972. *A Profile of an Indian Slum*. Bombay: Popular Prakashan.

Desai, R. 2012. "Governing the Urban Poor: Riverfront Development, Slum Resettlement, and the Politics of Inclusion in Ahmedabad." *Economic and Political Weekly* 47(2): 49–56.

Deshmukh, S. 2007. "78 Firms in Race for Dharavi Makeover." *DNA*. August 31.

Dhareshwar, V., and R. Srivatsan. 1996. "'Rowdy-Sheeters': An Essay on Subalternity and Politics." In S. Amin and D. Chakrabarty, eds., *Subaltern Studies IX*. New Delhi: Oxford University Press.

D'Monte, Darryl. 2002. *Ripping the Fabric: The Decline of Mumbai and Its Mills*. New Delhi: Oxford University Press.

DNA (*Daily News and Analysis*). 2007. "Dharavi Slumdwellers Threaten Agitation." May 29.

———. 2008. "Panel for Redevelopment of Dharavi Slum." August 13.

Doshi, S. 2012. "The Politics of the Evicted: Redevelopment, Subjectivity, and Difference in Mumbai's Slum Frontier." *Antipode* 45(4): 844–65.

Dossal, M. 1991. *Imperial Designs and Indian Realities: The Planning of Bombay City, 1845–1875*. Bombay: Oxford University Press.

Drèze, J., and A. Sen. 1995. *India: Economic Development and Social Opportunity*. Delhi: Oxford University Press.

Dua, A. 1989. "Towards Shelter for All: The Bombay Experiments." In National Institute of Urban Affairs, ed. *Urban Management in Asia: Issues and Opportunities*. New Delhi: National Institute of Urban Affairs, 161–73.

Dupont, V. 2011. "The Dream of Delhi as a Global City." *International Journal of Urban and Regional Research* 35(3): 533–54.

Dwivedi, S., and R. Mehotra. 2001. *Bombay: The Cities Within*. Mumbai: Eminence Designs.

Economic Times. 2008. "90,000 Dharavi Slum-Dwellers to Be Rehabilitated: NGO." May 6.

Fernandes, L. 2004. "The Politics of Forgetting: Class Politics, State Power, and the Restructuring of Urban Space in India." *Urban Studies* 41(12): 2415–30.

Foucault, M. 1991 (1978). "Governmentality." In G. Burchell, C. Gordon, and P. Miller, eds., *The Foucault Effect: Studies in Governmentality*. Chicago: University of Chicago Press, 87–104.

Frankel, P. 1980. "The Politics of Poverty: Political Competition in Soweto." *Canadian Journal of African Studies* 14(2): 201–20.

Frontline Magazine. 1998. "Editorial: Article 356, Bommai and Fair Play." July 4–17.

Gans, H. 1962. *The Urban Villagers: Group and Class in the Life of Italian-Americans.* Glencoe, Ill.: Free Press of Glencoe.

Ghadyalpatil, A. 2008. "Govt's Bid to Hike Flat Size Halts Dharavi Makeover." *Economic Times.* May 1.

Ghertner, D. A. 2011. "Gentrifying the State, Gentrifying Participation: Elite Governance Programs in Delhi." *International Journal of Urban and Regional Research* 35(3): 504–32.

Gilbert, A. 2004. "Love in the Time of Advanced Capital Flows: Reflections on the Links between Liberalization and Informality." In A. Roy and N. AlSayyad, eds., *Urban Informality: Transnational Perspectives from the Middle East, Latin America, and South Asia.* Lanham, Md.: Lexington Books.

———.2007. "The Return of the Slum: Does Language Matter?" *International Journal of Urban and Regional Research* 31(4): 697–713.

Goldman, M. 2011. "Speculative Urbanism and the Making of the Next World City." *International Journal of Urban and Regional Research* 35(3): 555–81.

Government of Bombay. 1882. *Gazetteer of the Bombay Presidency.* Volume 14: *Thana, Places of Interest.* Bombay: Government Central Press.

———.1946. *Preliminary Report of the Development of Suburbs and Town Planning Panel.* Bombay: Post-War Development Committee.

———. 1978 (1909). *The Gazetteer of Bombay City and Island, Volume 2.* Pune: Government Photozinco Press.

Government of India. 1992. *The Constitution (Seventy-fourth Amendment) Act,* http://india.gov.in/govt/documents/amendment/amend74.htm.

Gurumukhi, K. T. 2000. "Slum Related Policies and Programmes." *Shelter* 3(2).

Handelman, H. 1975. "The Political Mobilization of Urban Squatter Settlements: Santiago's Recent Experience and Its Implications for Urban Research." *Latin American Research Review* 10(2): 35–72.

Hansen, T. B. 2001. *Wages of Violence: Naming and Identity in Postcolonial Bombay.* Princeton, N.J.: Princeton University Press.

Hansen, T. B., and F. Stepputat. 2005. "Introduction." In T. B. Hansen and F. Stepputat, eds., *Sovereign Bodies: Citizens, Migrants, and States in the Postcolonial World.* Princeton, N.J.: Princeton University Press, 1–36.

Harris, N. 1995. "Bombay in the Global Economy." In S. Patel and A. Thorner, eds., *Bombay: Metaphor for Modern India.* New Delhi: Oxford University Press.

Harriss, J. 2005. "Middle-Class Activism and Poor People's Politics: An Exploration of Civil Society in Chennai." *London School of Economics Development Studies Institute Working Paper Series,* N. 05–72.

———. 2007. "Antinomies of Empowerment: Observations on Civil Society, Politics, and Urban Governance in India." *Economic and Political Weekly* 4(26): 2716–24.

Hartman, C. 1974. *Yerba Buena: Land Grab and Community Resistance in San Francisco.* Glide Publications.

———. 1984. "The Right to Stay Put." In C. Geisler and F. Popper, eds., *Land Reform, American Style.* Totowa, N.J,: Rowman & Allanheld, 302–18.

Harvey, D. 1989. "From Managerialism to Entrepreneurialism: The Transformation of Urban Governance in Late Capitalism." *Geografiska Annaler: Series B, Human Geography* 71(1): 3–17.

———. 1990. *The Condition of Post Modernity.* Cambridge, Mass.: Blackwell Publishers.

———. 2003. *The New Imperialism.* Oxford: Oxford University Press.

———. 2008. "The Right to the City." *New Left Review* 53 (September–October 2008): 23–40.

Hazareesingh, S. 2001. "Colonial Modernism and the Flawed Paradigms of Renewal: The Uneven Development of Bombay City, 1900–1925." *Urban History* 28(2): 235–55.

Hettne, B. 1999. "Globalization and the New Regionalism: The Second Great Transformation." *Globalism and the New Regionalism* 1: 1–24.

The Hindu. 2008. "Residents of Dharavi Oppose Redevelopment Plan." June 19.

Howard-Hassman, R. E. 2010. *Can Globalization Promote Human Rights?* University Park: Pennsylvania State University Press.

Huezé, G. 1995. "Cultural Populism: The Appeal of the Shiv Sena." In S. Patel and A. Thorner, eds., *Bombay: Metaphor for Modern India.* New Delhi: Oxford University Press.

Indian Express. 2005. "Crores to Be Spent to Turn Mumbai into Shanghai." February 8.

———. 2008. "Dharavi Makeover: 19 Consortia in the Running." January 10.

Jenkins, P., H. Smith, and Y. P. Wang. 2006. *Planning and Housing in the Rapidly Urbanising World.* London: Routledge.

Jessop, B. 2002. "Liberalism, Neoliberalism, and Urban Governance: A State-Theoretical Perspective." *Antipode* 34(3): 452–72.

Kalia, Ravi. 1990. *Chandigarh: The Making of an Indian City.* New Delhi: Oxford University Press.

Kamat, A. R. 1980. "Politico-Economic Developments in Maharashtra: A Review of the Post-Independence Period." *Economic and Political Weekly* 15(40): 1669–71,1673, 1675, 1677–78.

Kamath, N. 2010a. "Is Dharavi Consultant Being Paid Out-of-Turn?" *Hindustan Times*, Mumbai edition, March 4.

———. 2010b. "State Still Spending Crores for Stalled Dharavi Makeover." *Hindustan Times*, Mumbai edition, August 28.

Katzenstein, M. F. 1979. *Ethnicity and Equality: The Shiv Sena Party and Preferential Policies in Bombay.* Ithaca, N.Y.: Cornell University Press.

Katzenstein, M. F., U. Mehta, and U. Thakkar. 1997. "The Rebirth of Shiv Sena: The Symbiosis of Discursive and Organizational Power." *Journal of Asian Studies* 56(2): 371–90.

Kaviraj, S. 1997. "Filth and the Public Sphere: Concepts and Practices about Space in Calcutta." *Public Culture* 10(1): 83–113.

Khagram, S. 2004. *Dams and Development: Transnational Struggles for Water and Power.* Ithaca, N.Y.: Cornell University Press.

Kipfer, S., K. Goonewardena, C. Schmid, and R. Milgrom. 2008. "On the Production of Henri Lefebvre." In K. Goonewardena et al., eds., *Space, Difference, and Everyday Life: Reading Henri Lefebvre.* New York: Routledge.

Kosambi, M. 1986. *Bombay in Transition: The Growth and Social Ecology of a Colonial City: 1880–1980.* Stockholm: Almqvist & Wiksell International.

Lefebvre, H. 1996 (1998). "The Right to the City." In E. Kofman and E. Lebas, eds., *Writings on Cities.* Malden, Mass.: Blackwell.

Lele, J. 1981. *Elite Pluralism and Class Rule: Political Development in Maharashtra, India.* Toronto: University of Toronto Press.

———. 1995. "Saffronization of the Shiv Sena." In S. Patel and A. Thorner, eds., *Bombay: Metaphor for Modern India.* New Delhi: Oxford University Press

Lemarchand, R., and K. Legg. 1972. "Political Clientelism and Development: A Preliminary Analysis." *Comparative Politics* 4(2): 149–78.

Lokhande, D. 2006. "NRIs Eye Dharavi after BKC Auction." *Midday.* January 10.

Lynch, O. 1974. "Political Mobilization and Ethnicity among Adi-Dravidas in a Bombay Slum." *Economic and Political Weekly* 9(39): 1657–792.

———. 1979. "Potters, Plotters, and Prodders: Marx and Meaning or Meaning versus Marx." *Urban Anthropology* 8(1): 1–27.

McCartney, M. 2010. *Political Economy, Growth, and Liberalization in India, 1991–2008.* New York: Routledge.

Madon, S., and S. Sahay. 2002. "An Information-Based Model of NGO Mediation for the Empowerment of Slum Dwellers in Bangalore." *Information Society: An International Journal* 18(1): 13–19.

Mahadevia, D. 1998. "State-Supported Segmentation of Mumbai: Policy Options in the Global Economy." *Review of Development and Change* 3(1): 12–41.

Mahadevia, D., and H. Narayanan. 2008. "Shanghaing Mumbai: Politics of Evictions and Resistance in Slum Settlements." In D. Mahadevia, ed., *Inside the Transforming Urban Asia: Processes, Policies and Public Actions.* New Delhi: Concept Publishing, 549–89.

Mangin, W. 1967. "Latin American Squatter Settlements: A Problem and a Solution." *Latin American Research Review* 2(3): 65–98.

Manor, J. 1978. "Where Congress Survived: Five States in the Indian General Election of 1977." *Asian Survey* 18(8): 785–803.

Marpakwar, P. 2006. "McKinsey Shows Makeover Way." *Times of India.* November 2.

Marx, K., and F. Engels. 1978. "The Communist Manifesto." In Robert Tucker, ed., *The Marx-Engels Reader.* New York: W. W. Norton.

Mazumdar, R. 2007. *Bombay Cinema: An Archive of the City.* Minneapolis: University of Minnesota Press.

Mbembe, A. 2001. *On the Postcolony.* Berkeley: University of California Press.

McFarlane, C. 2004. "Geographical Imaginations and Spaces of Political Engagement: Examples from the Indian Alliance." *Antipode* 36(5): 890–916.

———. 2008. "Sanitation in Mumbai's Informal Settlements: State, 'Slum,' and Infrastructure." *Environment and Planning A* 40(1): 88–107.

———. 2011. *Learning the City: Knowledge and Translocal Assemblage.* London: John Wiley and Sons.

Mehta, A. 2000. *Power Play: A Study of the Enron Project.* Mumbai: Orient Longman.

Mehta, R. 2009a. "Dharavi Redevelopment Plan Is Caught in the Crossfire." *DNA: Daily News and Analysis.* November 2.

———. 2009b. "Dharavi Panel in the Firing Line." *DNA: Daily News and Analysis.* November 3.

Mehta, S. 2005. *Maximum City: Bombay Lost and Found.* New York: Knopf.

Menon, M. 2004. "Dharavi Residents Wary of New Project." *The Hindu.* August 8.

———. 2008. "Supreme Court Order Cheers Dharavi Residents." *The Hindu.* April 6.

Menon, M., and N. Adarkar. 2004. *One Hundred Years, One Hundred Voices: Mill Workers of Girangoan: An Oral History.* Calcutta: Seagull Books.

Mitra, S. K. 2001. "Making Local Government Work: Local Elites, Panchayat Raj, and Governance in India." In A. Kohli, ed., *The Success of India's Democracy.* New Delhi: Cambridge University Press.

Modak, N,. and A. Mayer. 1948. *An Outline for the Master Plan for Greater Bombay.* Bombay: Bombay Municipal Printing Press.

Mukhija, V. 2001a. "Enabling Slum Redevelopment in Mumbai: Policy Paradox in Practice." *Housing Studies* 16(6): 791–806.

———. 2001b. "Upgrading Housing Settlements in Developing Countries: The Impact of Existing Physical Conditions." *Cities* 18(4): 213–22.

———. 2003. *Squatters as Developers: Slum Redevelopment in Mumbai.* Burlington, Vt.: Ashgate.

Naidu, R. 2006. "Dilapidation and Slum Formation." In S. Patel and K. Deb, eds., *Urban Studies.* New Delhi: Oxford University Press.

Nainan, N. 2006. "Parallel Universes: Quasilegal Networks in Mumbai Governance." Presented at *Urban Governance in an International Perspective Seminar,* Amsterdam, January 7.

National Slum Dwellers Federation (NSDF). 1986. *Dharavi Survey,* http://wwwNAPMdharavi.org/.

Nayar, B. R. 2001. *Globalization and Nationalism: The Changing Balance of India's Economic Policy.* Thousand Oaks, Calif.: Sage.

———. 2006. *India's Globalization: Evaluating the Economic Consequences.* Washington, D.C.: Policy Studies 2, East-West Center.

Newman, K., and E. Wyly. 2006. "The Right to Stay Put, Revisited: Gentrification and Resistance to Displacement in New York City." *Urban Studies* 43(1): 23–57.

Nijman, J. 2000. "Mumbai's Real Estate Market in the 1990s: De-Regulation, Global Money, and Casino Capitalism." *Economic and Political Weekly* 35: 575–82.

———. 2006. "Mumbai's Mysterious Middle Class." *International Journal of Urban and Regional Research* 30(4): 758–75.

———. 2008. "Against the Odds: Slum Rehabilitation in Neoliberal Mumbai." *Cities* 25(2): 73–85.

O'Hare, G., D. Abbott, and M. Barke. 1998. "A Review of Slum Housing Policies in Mumbai." *Cities* 15: 269–83.

Ong, A. 2011. "Introduction: Worlding Cities, or the Art of Being Global." In A. Roy and A. Ong, eds., *Worlding Cities: Asian Experiments and the Art of Being Global.* Malden, Mass.: Wiley Blackwell, 1–26.

Palmer, N. D. 1976. "India in 1975: Democracy in Eclipse." *Asian Survey* 16(2) (A Survey of Asia in 1975, part 2): 95–110.

———. 1977. "India in 1976: Politics of Depolticization. *Asian Survey* 17(2) (A Survey of Asia in 1976, part 2): 160–80.

Panwalkar, P. 1995. "Upgradation of Slums: A World Bank Programme." In S. Patel and A. Thorner , eds., *Bombay: Metaphor for Modern India.* New Delhi: Oxford University Press.

Patel, S., and D. Mitlin. 2002. "Sharing Experiences and Changing Lives." *Community Development Journal* 37(2): 125–36.

Patel, S. B. 1996. "Slum Rehabilitation in Mumbai: Possible If Done Differently." *Economic and Political Weekly* 31(18): 1047–50.

Patel, S., C. d'Cruz, and S. Burra. 2002. "Beyond Evictions in a Global City: People-Managed Resettlement in Mumbai." *Environment and Urbanization* 14 (1): 159–72.

Pedersen, J. D. 2000. "Explaining Economic Liberalization in India: State and Society Perspectives." *World Development* 28(2): 265–82.

Pendharkar, S. P. 2003. *Population and Employment Profile of the Metropolitan Mumbai Region.* Mumbai: Metropolitan Mumbai Regional Development Authority.

Perlman, J. 1976. *The Myth of Marginality.* Berkeley: University of California Press.

———. 2004. "Marginality: From Myth to Reality in the Favelas of Rio de Janeiro, 1969–2002." In A. Roy and N. AlSayyad, eds., *Urban Informality: Transnational Perspectives from the Middle East, Latin America, and South Asia.* Lanham, Md.: Lexington Books.

Pimple, M., and L. John. 2002. "Security of Tenure: Mumbai's Experience." In A. Durand-Lassarve and L. Royston, eds., *Holding Their Ground: Secure Land Tenure for the Urban Poor in Developing Countries.* Sterling, Va.: Earthscan Publications, 75–85.

Pinto, D. A., and M. Pinto. 2005. *Municipal Corporation of Greater Mumbai and Ward Administration.* Seattle, Wash.: Konark Publishers.

Pinto, M. 2000. *Metropolitan City Governance in India.* Thousand Oaks, Calif.: Sage.

———. 2008. "Urban Governance in India—Spotlight on Mumbai." In I. Baud and J. de Wit, eds., *New Forms of Urban Governance in India: Shifts, Models, Networks and Governance.* New Delhi: Sage.

Polanyi, K. 2001 (1944). *The Great Transformation: The Political and Economic Origins of Our Time.* Boston: Beacon Press.

Pugh, C. 1989. "The World Bank and Urban Shelter in Bombay." *Habitat International* 13(3): 23–49.

Raffin, A. 2011. "Imperial Nationhood and Its Impact on Colonial Cities: Issues of Inter-Group Peace and Conflict in Pondicherry and Vietnam." In D. E. Davis and N. Libertun de Duren, eds., *Cities and Sovereignty: Identity Politics in Urban Spaces.* Bloomington: Indiana University Press, 28–58.

Rajyashree, K. S. 1986. *An Ethnolinguistic Survey of Dharavi.* Mysore: Central Institute of Indian Languages.

Ramachandran, S. 2003. "'Operation Pushback': Sangh Parivar, State, Slums, and Surreptitious Bangladeshis in New Delhi." *Economic and Political Weekly* 38(7): 637–47.

Ramanath, R. 2005. "From Conflict to Collaboration: Nongovernmental Organizations and Their Negotiations for Local Control of Slum and Squatter Housing in Mumbai, India." Doctoral dissertation submitted to the faculty of the Virginia Polytechnic Institute and State University.

Ramanath, R., and A. Ebrahim. 2010. "Strategies and Tactics in NGO-Government Relations: Insights from Slum Housing in Mumbai." *Nonprofit Management and Leadership* 21(1): 21–42.

Ramanathan, U. 2005. "Demolition Drive." *Economic and Political Weekly,* July 2.

Ramesh, R. 2005. "Poor Squeezed Out by Mumbai's Dream Plan." *The Guardian.* March 1.

Ranganathan, M. 2009. *Govind Narayan's Mumbai: An Urban Biography from 1863.* New York: Anthem Press.

Rao, V. 2006. "Slum as Theory: The South/Asian City and Globalization." *International Journal of Urban and Regional Research* 30(1): 225–32.

Rao, K. R., and M. S. A. Rao. 1991. "Cities, Slums and Urban Development: A Case Study of a Slum in Vijayawada." In M. S. A. Rao, C. Bhat, and L. N. Kadekar, eds., *A Reader in Urban Sociology*. Hyderagad: Orient Longman, 314–34.

Raval, S. 2000. "Mills and Boom." *India Today*. May 8.

Risbud, N. 2003. "The Case of Mumbai, India." In *Understanding Slums: Case Studies for the Global Report on Human Settlements*. Nairobi: UN-Habitat. www.ucl.ac.uk/dpu-projects/Global_Report/home.htm.

Roy, A. 2003. *City Requiem, Calcutta: Gender and the Politics of Poverty*. Minneapolis: University of Minnesota Press.

———. 2004a. "The Gentlemen's City: Urban Informality in Calcutta." In A. Roy and N. AlSayyad, eds., *Urban Informality: Transnational Perspectives from the Middle East, Latin America, and South Asia*. Lanham, Md.: Lexington Books, 147–70.

———. 2004b. "Transnational Trespassings: The Geopolitics of Urban Informality." In A. Roy and N. AlSayyad, eds., *Urban Informality: Transnational Perspectives from the Middle East, Latin America, and South Asia*. Lanham, Md.: Lexington Books, 289–317.

———. 2009a. "Why India Cannot Plan Its Cities: Informality, Insurgency, and the Idiom of Urbanization." *Planning Theory* 8(1): 76–87.

———. 2009b. "Civic Governmentality: The Politics of Inclusion in Beruit and Mumbai." *Antipode* 41: 159–79.

Roy, A., and N. AlSayyad, eds., 2004. *Urban Informality: Transnational Perspectives from the Middle East, Latin America, and South Asia*. Lanham, Md.: Lexington Books.

Rudolph, L., and S. H. Rudolph. 1976. *The Modernity of Tradition: Political Development in India*. Chicago: University of Chicago Press.

———. 1987. *In Pursuit of Lakshmi: The Political Economy of the Indian State*. Chicago: University of Chicago Press.

Sassen, S. 2006. *Territory, Authority, Rights: From Medieval to Global Assemblages*. Princeton, N.J.: Princeton University Press.

Scott, J. C. 1972. "Patron-Client Politics and Political Change in Southeast Asia." *American Political Science Review* 66(1): 91–113.

———. 1976. *The Moral Economy of the Peasant: Rebellion and Subsistence in Southeast Asia*. New Haven, Conn.: Yale University Press.

Searle, L. G. 2010. "Making Space for Capital: The Production of Global Landscapes in Contemporary India." Doctoral dissertation submitted to the faculty of the University of Pennsylvania.

Sebastian, P. A. 1981. "Operation Eviction." *Economic and Political Weekly* 16(38): 1526.

Selznick, P. 1966 (1949). *TVA and the Grassroots: A Study in the Sociology of Formal Organization*. New York: Harper Torch Books.

Sharma, K. 1995. "Chronicle of a Riot Foretold." In S. Patel and A. Thorner, eds., *Bombay: Metaphor for Modern India*. New Delhi: Oxford University Press, 268–86.

———. 2000. *Rediscovering Dharavi: Stories from Asia's Largest Slum*. New Delhi: Penguin Books.

Sharma, R. N. 2004. "Housing Market in Metropolitan Mumbai and Its Irrelevance to Average Citizens." Unpublished white paper.

Shatkin, G., and S. Vidyarthi. 2014. "Contesting Space: Power, Politics, and Claims to the City." In G. Shatkin, ed., *Global Visions and Politics of the Local*. Malden, Mass.: Blackwell, 1–38.

Shaw, A. 1996. "Urban Policy in Post-Independence India." *Economic and Political Weekly* 31(4): 224–28.

———. 2004. *The Making of Navi Mumbai*. Hyderabad: Orient Longman.

Sheng, Y. K. 1989. "Some Low-Income Housing Delivery Subsystems in Bangkok, Thailand." *Environment and Urbanization* 1(2): 27–37.

Singh, G. 1986. "Bombay Slums Face Operation Demolition." *Economic and Political Weekly* 21(16): 684–87.

Singh G., and P. K. Das. 1995. "Building Castles in Air: Housing Scheme for Bombay's Slum-Dwellers." *Economic and Political Weekly* 30(40): 2477–81.

Smith, N. 2002. "New Globalism, New Urbanism: Gentrification as Global Urban Strategy." *Antipode* 34(3): 427–50.

Sovani, N. V. 1969. "The Analysis of 'Over-Urbanization.'" In G. W. Breese, ed., *The City in Newly Developing Countries: Readings on Urbanism and Urbanization*. Englewood Cliffs, N.J,: Prentice-Hall, 322–30.

SPARC. 1998. *Enumeration as a Tool for Mobilization: The Community Census of Structures in Dharavi*. Mumbai: Society for the Preservation of Area Resources.

Spodek, H. 1983. "Squatter Settlements in Urban India: Self-help and Government Policies." *Economic and Political Weekly* 18(36/37): 1575–77 and 1579–86.

Srinivas, M. N. 1955. "The Social System of a Mysore Village." In M. Marriott, ed., *Village India*. Chicago: University of Chicago Press, 1–35.

Srinivasan, S. 2005. "Tsunami-Like Devastation Hits Mumbai Slum Dwellers." *Inter Press Service*. January 30.

Srivastava, S. 2005. "Mumbai Struggles to Catch Up with Shanghai." *Asian Times*. March 16.

State of Maharashtra. 1971. *Maharashtra Slum Areas (Improvement, Clearance and Redevelopment Act), 1971*. Mumbai: Department of Urban Development.

———. 2004. *Transforming Mumbai into a World-Class City*. Mumbai: Chief Minister's Taskforce.

———. 2007. *Global Expression of Interest for Dharavi Redevelopment Project*. Mumbai: Slum Rehabilitation Authority. (Advertisement run in several newspapers, including *Times of India*. June 1.)

Stepan, A. 1999. "Federalism and Democracy: Beyond the U.S. Model." *Journal of Democracy* 10(4): 19–34.

Supreme Court of India. 1985. *Olga Tellis & Ors v Bombay Municipal Council [1985] 2 Supp SCR 51.* http://www.escr-net.org/docs/i/401006.

Swanstrom, T., and R. Kerstein. 1989. "Job and Housing Displacement: A Review of Competing Policy Perspectives." In M. P. Smith, ed., *Pacific Rim Cities in the World Economy: Comparative Urban and Community Research.* New Brunswick, N.J.: Transaction Publishers, 254–96.

Tare, K. 2008. "Parties Tally behind Sena on Dharavi." *Daily News Analysis: DNA.* March 13.

Tarlo, E. 2003. *Unsettling Memories: Narratives of the Emergency in Delhi.* Berkeley: University of California Press.

Taub, R. P. 1969. *Bureaucrats under Stress: Administrators and Administration in an Indian State.* Berkeley: University of California Press.

Tembhekar, C. 2009. "4 Firms Drop Out of Dharavi Plan." *Times of India.* March 3.

Times of India. 1985. "'Rasta Roko' Stir to Be Resumed." *Times of India.* June 18

———. 2008. "Give Right to Choose Developer: Dharavi Slumdwellers." August 14.

Tummala, K. K. 1992. "India's Federalism under Stress." *Asian Survey* 32(6): 538–53.

Turner, J. F. C. 1969. "Uncontrolled Urban Settlement: Problems and Policies." In G. W. Breese, ed., *The City in Newly Developing Countries: Readings on Urbanism and Urbanization.* Englewood Cliffs, N.J.: Prentice-Hall, 507–34.

———. 1976. *Housing by People: Towards Autonomy in Building Environments.* London: Marion Boyars.

Van Wersch, H. 1995. "Flying a Kite, Losing the String: Communication during the Bombay Textile Strike." In S. Patel and A. Thorner, eds., *Bombay: Metaphor for Modern India.* New Delhi: Oxford University Press, 64–85.

Varshney, A. 2007. "Mass Politics or Elite Politics? Understanding the Politics of India's Economic Reforms." In R. Mukherji, ed., *India's Economic Transition: The Politics of Reforms.* New Delhi: Oxford University Press, 146–69.

Verney, D. V. 1995. "Federalism, Federative Systems, and Federations: The United States, Canada, and India." *Publius* 25(2): 81–97.

Vidyarthi, Sanjeev. 2010. "Reimagining the American Neighborhood Unit for India." In P. Healy and R. Upton, eds., *Crossing Borders:International Exchange and Planning Practices.* London: Routledge, 73–94.

Vora, R. 1996. "Shift of Power from Rural to Urban Sector." *Economic and Political Weekly* 31(2–3): 171–73.

Wapner, P. 1995. "Politics beyond the State: Environmental Activism and World Civic Politics." *World Politics* 47(3): 311–40.

Ward, P. M. 1976. "The Squatter Settlements as Slum or Housing Solution: Evidence from Mexico City." *Land Economics* 2(3): 330–46.

Weber, M. 1946 (1921). "Politics as a Vocation." In Gerth and Mills, eds., *From Max Weber: Essays in Sociology*. New York: Oxford University Press, 77–128.

Weiner, M. 1977. "The 1977 Parliamentary Elections in India." *Asian Survey* 17(7): 619–26.

Weintraub, R. M. 1988. "Burgeoning City Slums Change Face of India; Millions Leave Villages in Countryside to Find Work, Resources in Urban Areas." *Washington Post*. October 15.

Weisman, S. R. 1988. "Bombay Journal; A City Where Stark Contrast Is King." *New York Times*. July 23.

Werlin, H. 1999. "The Slum Upgrading Myth." *Urban Studies* 36(9): 1523–34.

Wiebe, P. D. 1975. *Social Life in an Indian Slum*. Durham, N.C.: Carolina Academic Press.

World Bank. 1997. *Implementation Completion Report: India: Bombay Urban Development Project*. wds.worldbank.org/.

World Bank and UN-Habitat. 1999. *Cities Alliance for Cities without Slums: Action Plan for Moving Slum Upgrading to Scale*. Washington D.C.: The World Bank.

Youth for Unity and Voluntary Action (YUVA). 1999. "Our Home Is a Slum: An Exploration of a Community and Local Government Collaboration in a Tenants' Struggle to Establish Legal Residency." Unpublished Discussion Paper no. 107. August.

Zérah, M.-H. 2007. "Middle Class Neighbourhood Associations as Political Players in Mumbai." *Economic and Political Weekly* 42(47): 61–68.

INDEX

abattoir, 32
accumulation by dispossession, 14, 16, 21, 87, 114
Adi Dravida, 2, 37, 38, 50,
Adi Dravida Mahajan Sangh, 2
Affordable Low Income Shelter (ALIS) program, 63, 69–71, 77, 78, 187
Ambedkar, B. R., 59
Anand, Nikhil, 17, 71, 183
Anjaria, Jonathan Shapiro, 65, 132, 182, 183, 186
Antulay, A. R., 72
Appadurai, Arjun, xii, 18, 79, 123, 161, 165

Babri Masjid demolition, 96
Back Bay reclamation project, 33, 36
Bandra Kurla Complex (BKC), x, xi, xiv, 6, 108, 109, 148, 149
Banerjee–Guha, Swapna, 45
Bangalore, 103, 105–7, 194
Bardhan, Pranab, 119
Baviskar, Amita, 15, 182
Bayat, Asef, 16, 17, 29
Benjamin, Solomon, 16, 19, 29, 30
Bhagwati, Jagdish, 12–13
Bharatiya Janata Party (BJP), 94–96, 98, 100, 101, 105–6, 131, 188
Bharucha, Nauzer, 136, 137, 162

Bhowmik, Sharit, x, 90, 91
Bombay. *See* Mumbai
Bombay Chamber of Commerce and Industry (BCCI), 98, 105, 106
Bombay Development Department (BDD), 35–36
Bombay First, 105, 106, 108, 117, 133, 139
Bombay Improvement Trust (BIT), 35, 36, 184
Bombay Port Trust, 63, 117
Bombay Urban Development Project (BUDP), 69
Bose, N. K., 28–30
Brenner, Neil, 21, 88, 164
Brihanmumbai Municipal Corporation (BMC; also referred to as Bombay Municipal Corporation), 39, 42, 49, 51, 58, 60–64, 66, 68, 71–76, 81, 95, 98, 101, 107, 115, 117–19, 127–33, 143, 171, 185, 190
British Raj, 58, 142
Burawoy, Michael, 87, 182
bureaucracy. *See* Indian Administrative Service

caste: as a basis of identity, 28; main caste groups in Dharavi, 2, 25, 32,

211

215

Olga Tellis v. Bombay Municipal Corporation, 72, 73, 76
Operation Demolition, 71, 74, 75, 78
Operation Eviction, 71, 72
Operation Slum–Wreck. *See* Operation Demolition
Orangi Town (Karachi), 11, 175, 186
overurbanization thesis, 28

parastatal planning agencies, 65, 100, 119, 126
partition (of India and Pakistan), 48
Patel, Sheela, 79, 161
Patel, Shirish, 67
Patkar, Medha, 193
patronage politics, 29, 30, 50–51, 64
Pawar, Sharad, 74, 189
People's Responsible Organization for United Dharavi (PROUD), xii, 51, 56, 75, 78, 79, 144, 151–53, 186, 187
People's Union for Civil Liberties, 72
Persons of Indian Origin (PIO), ix
Pinto, Marina, 34, 35, 58, 66, 80, 118, 119, 121, 132
planning and land use, 13, 21, 23, 27, 32–34, 39, 42, 44–46, 52, 53, 58, 60, 63, 70, 76, 78, 91, 103, 109, 110, 112, 115–28, 132–39, 142–44, 147–49, 164, 167, 177, 185
Polanyi, Karl, 87, 182
political society, 17, 30, 52, 162–63
Post–War Development Committee, 39, 44, 47, 60
premature metropolis thesis, 28–30, 38
Prime Minister's Grant Project (PMGP), 55–57, 71, 76–83, 99, 100, 109, 111, 144, 186, 188
Project Management Consultant. *See* Mehta, Mukesh

Public Interest Litigation (PIL), 19, 29, 158, 160, 161, 165, 174
PUKAR, xii

Rajiv Gandhi Nagar, 4, 6
real estate, ix, x, 5, 13–15, 23, 34, 85, 86, 88, 89, 91, 92, 99, 100, 102–3, 111–12, 114, 135, 145, 146, 159–63, 167, 168, 170, 175
Rent Control Act, 70, 184
rescaling theory, 138
resident consent, 143, 149–51, 157, 158, 162, 171, 192
right to stay put, 18, 19, 21, 23, 56, 83, 144, 145, 159, 162, 164, 166, 183, 192
right to the city, 15–19, 144, 183
Roy, Ananya, 16, 18, 29, 121
Rudolph, Lloyd, 90, 118, 125, 189
Rudolph, Suzanne, 90, 118, 125, 189

Samyukta Maharashtra movement, 62–63
Sassen, Saskia, 161, 183
Selznick, Philip, 163
Seventy-Fourth Amendment, 119, 120, 128, 132, 138
Sharma, Kalpana, 32, 36–38, 48, 56, 64, 65, 76–82, 95, 97,
Shatkin, Gavin, 88, 182
Shiv Sena party, 72, 74, 76, 81, 93, 95–97, 99, 100, 101, 105, 110, 112, 131, 154, 171, 188, 189, 191, 193
Singh, Gurbir, 60, 71, 73–75
Singh, Manmohan, 107
Sion, 6, 33, 35, 37
slum: clearance (*see* evictions); contested terminology, 2, 3, 8–11; definition, 9, 64; demolitions (*see* evictions)
Slum Areas (Improvement and Clearance) Act (1956), 60–61, 63

(continued from page ii)

Liza Weinstein is assistant professor of sociology at Northeastern University.